New Primary Leaders

Also available from Continuum

Developing a Self-Evaluating School, Paul K. Ainsworth
Learn to Transform, Graham Corbyn and David Crossley

New Primary Leaders

International Perspectives

Edited by

Michael Cowie

continuum

Continuum International Publishing Group
The Tower Building   80 Maiden Lane
11 York Road   Suite 704
London SE1 7NX   New York NY 10038

www.continuumbooks.com

British Library Cataloguing-in-Publication Data
A catalogue record for this book is available from the British Library.

ISBN: 978-1-4411-0307-9 (paperback)
       978-1-4411-0687-2 (hardcover)

Library of Congress Cataloging-in-Publication Data
A catalog record for this book is available from the British Library.

New primary leaders: international perspectives/[edited by]
Michael Cowie.
    p. cm.
Includes index.
ISBN 978-1-4411-0307-9 — ISBN 978-1-4411-0687-2 — ISBN
978-1-4411-7143-6 — ISBN 978-1-4411-7065-1 1. Elementary school
principals—Cross-cultural studies. 2. Elementary school
administration—Cross-cultural studies. I. Cowie, Michael. II. Title.

LB2831.9.N49 2011
372.12'012—dc22   2011000389

Typeset by Newgen Imaging Systems Pvt Ltd, Chennai, India
Printed and bound in India

Contents

Acknowledgements

Very grateful acknowledgements are made to each of the school principals who agreed to participate in this book.

Editor's Note

In this collection of narratives from 12 diverse contexts, the authors have different preferences for particular terms, spellings and the use of the hyphen. These have been retained.

Contributors

Israel Aguilar is earning a Ph.D. in school improvement at Texas State University, San Marcos. His research agenda involves principal preparation and educational leadership for social justice. He has participated in an international research team studying the effectiveness of principal preparation programmes in transnational contexts, a project studying the effects of national student protest for educational equity in Chile, and has theorized possibilities for transforming principal preparation to enhance social justice leadership in schools and communities. Israel brings to his research 5 years of professional experience as a K–12 educator at the secondary and middle school levels in Texas.

Professor Simon Clarke is currently deputy dean of the Graduate School of Education at The University of Western Australia where he researches, supervises and teaches in the substantive area of educational leadership. He has been widely published and is the co-author of the recent Routledge book, Leading Learning. Simon is a member of the International Study of Principal Preparation.

Dr Michael Cowie is an Honorary Fellow of the College of Humanities and Social Science at the University of Edinburgh. A former headteacher and local authority officer, Michael was previously co-director of the master's programme in educational leadership and management at the University of Edinburgh and director of the North of Scotland Head Teacher Preparation Consortium, a partnership involving the universities of Aberdeen and Dundee and nine education authorities. His development work, research interests and publications centre on headteacher preparation and development and school governance. Michael is a member of the International Study of Principal Preparation.

Dr Megan Crawford is reader in education at Oxford Brookes University. She previously worked at the Institute of Education, London; Warwick University and the Open University. Her background is in primary schools, where she was a deputy headteacher. She is currently chair of the British Educational Leadership, Management and Administration Society. Megan is very involved in governing schools, and was the Teaching Awards Governor of the Year, East of England, in 2009–10. She has been a governor of five schools, and is chair of governors at Oakgrove School, Milton Keynes. Her research encompasses principal preparation and emotion and leadership. Her book Getting to the Heart of Leadership was published by Sage in 2009. Megan is a member of the International Study of Principal Preparation.

Professor Carmen Cretu is based at the University of Iasi, Alexandru Ioan Cuza, in the Faculty of Psychology and Educational Sciences. She provides courses on educational policies and management, curriculum theory and methodology and on differentiated and personalized curriculum for highly able and gifted people. She is a national expert involved in major programmes of educational reform and innovation and has led several national and European research projects in the fields of educational policies and giftedness. She also works as an independent researcher in the field of education for the European Commission in Brussels. Carmen is a member of several professional and scientific associations, including the International Association for the Advancement of Curriculum Studies, the World Council for Gifted and Talented Children and the European Council for High Ability.

Dr Jose-Maria Garcia Garduno is a former elementary school teacher. He gained a BA in clinical psychology and a master's in education at Universidad Iberoamericana. He also obtained a master's in educational administration at New York State University, Albany. He earned his Ph.D. in educational administration at the University of Ohio. He is a professor at Universidad Autonoma de la Ciudad de Mexico. His research interests are related to educational leadership and curriculum theory. His recent publications focus on educational leadership, management and administration in Mexico. Jose Maria is a member of the International Study of Principal Preparation.

Dr Ovidiu Gavrilovici is an associate professor at the University of Iasi, Alexandru Ioan Cuza, in the Faculty of Psychology and Educational Sciences. He is a graduate of Case Western Reserve University, Cleveland, Ohio, USA. Ovidiu teaches psychological counseling, narrative therapy and trans-generational therapy in undergraduate and post-graduate clinical programmes in psychology and psychotherapy. He also is involved in master's programmes in human resources at the university's School of Business. Ovidiu participated in the Transformation of Educational Management Project in 1999–2001, a Dutch Educational Management Institute-led initiative, and set up the Romanian Institute for Educational Management in Iasi, which he has directed since 2001. Ovidiu is a board member of and consultant to numerous non-profit regional and national organizations of social services in Romania.

Dr Xiao Liang is director of the Canadian Research Centre, Hunan province, Changsha, People's Republic of China. Being an associate professor, she teaches English public speech, comparative education and a series of other English or education-related courses. She has also established international educational cooperative programmes between China and countries around the world. Xiao graduated from the University of Calgary, Canada, with a Ph.D. degree in comparative and international education in 2003. Following a 3-year spell as a vice dean of International College, Hunan Agricultural University, Xiao Ling set up a high school in Shaanxi province in northwest China. Her current post is with Hunan Business College. Xiao Ling also serves as a member of various academic and international associations and is a judge in nation-wide English competitions.

Professor Gema López-Gorosave is based at Universidad Autónoma de Baja California, México. She previously served as professor at Escuela Normal Estatal in Ensenada, B.C., México and Universidad Pedagógica Nacional, and was dean at Escuela Normal Estatal. Her major research interest is the educational leadership of public basic schools in Mexico. Gema has published several articles and book chapters about the early years of school principals. She is a member of the International Study of Principal Preparation and of the Latinamerican Red de Convivencia Escolar.

Professor Reynold Macpherson has taught and led educators in many countries, held chairs in educational and strategic leadership in three universities, provided a number of ministerial commissions and led a polytechnic and a university. He has researched and published in many areas related to educative forms of leadership. In recent years he has delivered a number of international consultancies, most recently evaluating school-based health centres.

Dr Susana Martínez Martínez gained her Ph.D. in education at the University of Tijuana in 2010. Her current responsibilities include co-ordination of the bachelor of primary education programme and the Institutional Assessment Department at the Meritorious State Normal School 'Professor Jesus Prado Luna'. Susana has organized national and international conferences on school leadership and management and is a member of the Ibero-American Network for Research on Change and School Effectiveness and an international Support Network for Educational Management. Her research focus is on schools building a context for learning and democratic coexistence.

Professor Kobus Mentz is a professor in educational management and leadership and director of the School of Education at the Potchefstroom campus of the North-West University, South Africa. He started his career as a secondary school mathematics teacher before joining the (then) Potchefstroom University in 1985. In his research he focuses on diversity in leadership and the experiences of beginning principals. His most recent publications deal with a comparative study of the experiences of beginning principals in Canada and South Africa and with the leadership aspirations of female teachers in South Africa. Kobus is a member of the International Study of Principal Preparation.

Dr Sarah W. Nelson earned her Ph.D. in public school executive leadership from the University of Texas at Austin. Currently she is a member of the graduate faculty at Texas State University-San Marcos in the education and community leadership and education PhD programmes. Sarah teaches courses in principal preparation, research, school law, educational policy and educational environments. Her research interests are on national and international policies and practices related to educational equity. Before joining the faculty at Texas State University, Sarah served as the principal and instructional leader of a large urban school. She continues to work in the field with educators to develop culturally responsive teaching and learning environments and to create community-based leadership practices. Sarah is a member of the International Study of Principal Preparation.

Brown Onguko is a lecturer at the Aga Khan University, Institute for Educational Development-Eastern Africa. He teaches information communications technology in education and educational leadership programmes at the university. Brown is currently a full-time doctoral student at the University of Calgary. His research interests are in the use of information communication technology in education and specifically blended and mobile learning and in educational leadership preparation. Brown previously worked as a teacher trainer at Asumbi Teachers' College in Kenya, as an education management trainer at the Kenya Education Staff Institute and as assistant director of education at the Ministry of Education headquarters in Nairobi, Kenya, where he also served as the national co-ordinator of the Education for All Initiative.

Dr Diane Purvey is an associate professor of education in the Faculty of Human, Social and Educational Development at Thompson Rivers University in Kamloops, B.C., where she teaches in both the undergraduate and graduate programmes. She also serves as co-coordinator to the master's of education programme. Research interests include the history of deathscapes and memorial-building by adolescents in high schools, restorative justice practices in elementary schools and the history of deinstitutionalization of mental health clients in B.C. She is the co-author of *Private Grief, Public Mourning: The Rise of the Roadside Shrine in British Columbia* (Anvil Press, 2009) and the co-editor of *Child and Family Welfare in British Columbia: A History* (Detselig Press, 2005). Currently, she is working on a history of Vancouver from 1930 to 1960, entitled *Vancouver Noir*, which explores representations in the photographic record of crime, criminality and justice.

Professor Charles L. Slater is professor of educational administration at California State University, Long Beach. He previously served as professor at Texas State University, San Marcos, and was superintendent of schools in Texas and Massachusetts. His major research interest is educational leadership in the United States and Mexico. Charlie teaches in doctoral programmes in Mexico and is fluent in Spanish and French. His work has been widely published in a range of international journals. He is a member of the International Study of Principal Preparation.

Professor Charles F. Webber is dean of the Faculty of Human, Social and Educational Development at Thompson Rivers University. His current research focuses on the influence of school leaders on student achievement and on cross-cultural leadership development, including technology-mediated leadership development. During his career as an educator he has served as a classroom teacher, curriculum consultant, principal, professor, associate dean and dean. His work appears in national and international journals, and he has served as an invited presenter in conferences, seminars and workshops in North America, Europe, Asia, Africa, the Middle East, New Zealand and Australia. Charlie is a member of the International Study of Principal Preparation.

Professor Helen Wildy is Winthrop Professor and dean of the Faculty of Education at The University of Western Australia. Her background as a student of a very small, rural primary school in Western Australia underpins her commitment to education, particularly the leadership of small schools.

She currently conducts research and supervises doctoral and master's students in a range of leadership and school improvement topics. She is the director of Performance Indicators for Primary Schools (PIPS) Australia, a literacy and numeracy assessment programme for students entering school, used by over 800 schools in all Australian states and territories. She frequently uses narrative as a research approach in her work in the field of school leadership, especially the principal of small rural schools in Australia. Helen is a member of the International Study of Principal Preparation.

New Principals: Context, Culture, Preparation, Induction and Practice

Michael Cowie

Introduction

Leading a primary or elementary school in any context is not for the faint hearted. The school principal position is complex and challenging, and carries huge responsibilities and public accountabilities. All over the world, the responsibilities of school principals are changing as the role of school principal becomes even more complex under the influence of global population shifts, information and communication technology, pluralism and multiculturalism. The complexity of school leadership has been well documented in books and professional journals, but while it's relatively easy to talk and write about school leadership and what principals should or should not do, former and serving principals know that it is much more difficult to lead and manage a school responsibly and well, even within a stable, relatively homogeneous community. Perhaps no one can be truly aware of what is involved in leading and managing a school without having experienced the reality of whole school responsibility.

Nevertheless, this collection of narratives by novice primary (elementary) school principals leading and managing schools in very different cultural continents across five continents is an attempt to give a true picture of what it feels like to become and be a new school principal. The book therefore goes beyond thinking of educational leadership purely as a theoretical concept. Each individual was selected and invited to contribute by a colleague interested or engaged in preparing principals for the demands of the post, and there is no suggestion that the principals are typical or representative of principals in each context. The only selection criterion that contributors were given was that the principal had to be new or relatively new. Otherwise, the selection of each principal was a matter of personal judgement.

Given the complexity of school leadership and the demands placed on school principals it is worth exploring why individuals want to become school principals and what it feels like to be a new school principal. Most aspiring principals will have worked closely with their own school principals and are aware of the complexities and challenges involved in leading and managing a school, and so the decision to take on the role of principal is one that is not taken lightly. However, new principals often find that the 'bumpy ride of reality' (Draper and McMichael, 1998, p. 207) can be difficult when they assume whole-school responsibility, relinquish and de-identify with their former role and identity and assume a new one. The interest of all who contributed to this book is in what this process feels like and how well new principals cope with the transition.

All of the chapters provide a vignette, nourished by a different culture and context, in which a relatively new principal tells his or her story. Each story provides an impression that gives a particular insight into the character of the principal, the nature of the setting and the challenges encountered. The narratives are necessarily succinct and do not tell the full story. Twelve individual volumes would be needed to do justice to the complexities of the experience in each individual case.

Through the accounts of 12 novice principals in 12 very different social, geographical and cultural contexts, the reader gains access to the reasoning and feelings of novice principals as they construct their new professional identities and respond to the challenges that they face. The 12 principals relate when or at what stages in their careers they decided that they wanted to become a principal and talk about what or who influenced their career ambition. They also talk about how and when they began to prepare themselves for the role of principal and its responsibilities, the expectations they had when first appointed, their early experience in the post, the extent to which their expectations have been fulfilled and their hopes and fears for the future. What they have to say may be of benefit to aspiring and beginning principals in different contexts; to those who help prepare teachers for the responsibilities of leadership and to those responsible for their recruitment, induction and professional development.

The bond between all the contributing authors is our shared interest or engagement in principal preparation and our fascination for what it feels like to become and be a school principal, perhaps particularly in situations where the contextual challenges are exceptionally challenging. Each principal who agreed to be interviewed was advised that we wanted to know what it feels like to live and breathe the role, to work in a new role in a new school with teachers, parents and others in a new community, all of whom have a stake in how well the principal performs. We wanted a complete, intimate and above all, honest account of their early experience. In semi-structured interviews based on a common schedule, the novice principals were encouraged to talk about their levels of confidence and where and when they felt vulnerable. We also wanted to know about any reservations they had and how sure they were that they had taken the right decision. We explored their anxieties and concerns and how they coped with their worries; discussed their professional development and how they learn and develop; and talked about what made them the individuals that they are, the kind of principals they would like to be and their hopes and fears for the future. Taken together, their personal narratives provide a unique insight into the experience and development of beginning principals across a range of diverse contexts, jurisdictions and cultural settings.

Studying principal preparation in different contexts

The cross-cultural collaboration required to generate the 12 narratives was nurtured by participation in the International Study of Principal Preparation (ISPP), an international collaboration of scholars spanning a wide range of countries. The study was developed in response to our perceived need for a better cross-cultural understanding of principal preparation and how it might be developed.

Our starting point was a shared belief that schools are special places, that school leadership has special purposes (Begley, 2008) and that schools therefore need to be led and managed by good people. By 'good people' we meant well-meaning individuals equipped with the values, knowledge, understanding and personal abilities that schools and the children in them need and deserve. We also shared the view that principal preparation is an important aspect of school development as well as personal and professional development, and that programmes of preparation should have positive outcomes for schools as well as for the individuals who undertake them.

Educational leadership studies have sometimes been criticized for their focus on westernized responses to educational choices (Dimmock and Walker, 2000; Hallinger and Leithwood, 1996; Heck, 1996, 1998; Leithwood and Duke, 1998), but the ISPP design was intentionally international in scope. As colleagues in the ISPP project have pointed out elsewhere, although this has made sense insofar as education is locally governed and influenced by local political policy context and culture, education is a universal human endeavour and we thought that there may be benefits to be gained from 'the same broad approach that has characterized other disciplines' (Slater et al., 2005, p. 4).

The project has had four assumptions from the beginning – that good leadership and management can be taught and nurtured; the primary purpose of headship is to facilitate effective teaching and learning; principals' learning needs vary as they progress through their career and cross-cultural perspectives can inform theory and practice. These assumptions also underpin this book.

In one phase of the ISPP, case studies were conducted in each country to describe the early career experience and perceptions of small groups of primary or elementary school principals. The aim was to research the experiences of principals in their first year of appointment in different systems to identify the challenges they had faced and therefore how their preparation might have been improved.

In much of the literature, school leadership and management are portrayed as 'sanitised' concepts, but an important perspective on the ISPP came from the principals themselves. In each of our contexts, we wanted to know who our new principals were, why they wanted to become principals, how they became principals, what drove them and how they handled their new duties and responsibilities. Because of its focus on the relational and the 'reality producing' nature of the interview (Roberts, 2002, p. 15), the research was undertaken with a narrative approach in mind. This seemed appropriate in an investigation into the early years of headship, because of its emphasis on 'the "lived experience" of individuals, the importance of multiple perspectives, the existence of context-bound, constructed social realities and the impact of the researcher on the research process' (Muller, 1999, p. 223).

Encouraged by the insights gained in ISPP, we decided to use an amended version of the semi-structured interview to encourage new principals in 12 different countries to talk about themselves, their backgrounds, the context in which they operate, their experience to date, their future plans for their schools and themselves and what it feels like to be a novice school principal in the early part of the twenty-first century in each of their particular contexts. A core group of researchers has been involved in the ISPP since its inception, while others have become involved in different ways over time, and with one exception, all of the contributions to this book are from researchers with some involvement in the ISPP. Through narrative, they bring us into contact with new principals from different international contexts. These are people engaged in the process of interpreting themselves, and the testimonies they elicit provide verbal evidence of their experience and beliefs over a critical period of their lives and professional careers.

The backdrop to the 12 testimonies provided in this publication is the changing nature of the job and the unrelenting pressure on schools and school principals to strive for improvement in what they do. Principals may be required to develop their schools as 'learning organisations', develop staff capability and ensure a distributed approach to leadership, engage teachers in collegial or consultative decision-making, become adept at crisis management, develop entrepreneurial skills, manage budgets prudently, engage with the wider community, work collaboratively with other agencies, resolve conflict, ensure fairness and equity in responding to the needs and demands of families from very different ethnic, cultural or socioeconomic backgrounds and make sure that all the children that they are responsible for succeed. In addition, anxieties regarding school performance in a competitive global economic environment bring considerable political pressure to raise educational standards, parents are ever more demanding and in the past two decades or more school principals have had to come to terms with increased expectations and increasing public accountabilities.

As a result of such pressure and accountability, the role of school principal demands more time, energy and expertise than ever before and fewer people seem to be interested in becoming a school principal because school systems are finding it difficult to recruit school principals with appropriate knowledge, skills and experience (Gronn, 2003). This should not surprise anyone, because with multiple (and often conflicting) accountabilities, increased demands and heightened expectations, the nature of the job has changed substantially and this has given rise to a set of expectations and working conditions that many capable people may find unattractive. What teachers see are hard-pressed principals working long hours with little financial reward and they may be forgiven for assuming that the kind of people required to fill vacant positions are 'miracle workers' (Evans, 1995) able to balance competing accountabilities, manage changing government policies and priorities, plan strategically in a turbulent educational environment, process mountains of paperwork, satisfy parental demands and improve educational standards with diminishing resources and little genuine autonomy.

In our ISPP writings we noted that in principal preparation at least two imperatives overlap (Cowie and Crawford, 2007). One has to do with the needs of the system to consider succession planning and ensure the quality and development of schools. From this perspective, there seems to be a supply problem in many countries because large numbers of vacancies are anticipated over the next few years. Across the nations reflected in the ISPP we found failure to plan for principal succession in countries with well-established educational infrastructures such as Scotland (Cowie and Crawford, 2007) as well in developing countries such as Mexico (Slater et al., 2007) and Kenya (Onguko, Abdalla and Webber, 2008), where unclear processes mar the credibility of new principals.

The second important issue relates to a recurrent theme across both the work of colleagues in the ISPP and the stories of the novice principals in this book. That is the need to address the needs of individuals and allow teachers to develop confidence in their leadership and management capabilities and acquire appropriate knowledge, understanding and skills. The personal and often intimate narratives in this book get to grips with what the novice principals think, why they think the way that they do and what makes them tick, and while it is clear that the job is challenging and requires commitment, it is also a job that is 'doable'. Most of the accounts presented here provide an encouraging and positive perspective on principalship and high levels of commitment and enthusiasm are evident, even in sometimes challenging circumstances. The accounts also suggest that being a school principal can be a fulfilling and immensely satisfying experience, but the new principals faced a range of challenges, many of which were dependent on the cultural context, the policy context and the school context in which they found themselves, and how they reacted to them was dependent on their own developed abilities, values, knowledge, understanding and dispositions.

But the narratives also suggest that teachers who wish to become school principals do need to be supported in the early stage of their careers and equipped with the tools to do the job well. The experiences of novice principals in the 12 diverse contexts in this book confirm that the transition from being a teacher, or even a deputy principal, to being a school principal requires support and the development of fairly complex, practical and interactive processes and higher order skills, as well as a deep understanding of school contexts and cultures. Opportunities for aspiring and potential school principals to acquire appropriate knowledge and understanding and the skills that they require are therefore needed, but leadership development is incidental or absent in many countries (Wildy and Clarke, 2008), and where leadership development does exist, it is often in the form of an apprenticeship model that reinforces traditional conceptualizations of leadership and the status quo (Onguko, Abdalla and Webber, 2010).

The researchers and teachers involved in the ISPP agree that new principals need to be prepared for the demands of the post before they are appointed, but one model of preparation will not fit all circumstances and different school jurisdictions and contexts require models that are specific to their own particular circumstances. But although different models are likely to be more appropriate in different cultural, social and political contexts, we also agree that school principals need to develop frames of reference to guide their behaviour and decision-making (Bush, 1998, 1999), and that the knowledge and understanding that these reference frames require, and the qualities, attributes and skills needed by principals, can be learned and developed.

The new principals' narratives

Australasia

The first account from Australasia is provided by 'John Anderson,'[1] principal of a small aboriginal community school in a remote, arid area over 460 km from the Indian Ocean and 1,000 km from Perth, the capital city of Western

Australia. When Helen Wildy and Simon Clarke met with John he had been in post just over 3 years, which makes him the longest-serving principal featured in this book. As well as John, the school has four teachers, four teacher's assistants, a registrar and a gardener. The school roll fluctuates because many families move around and some children just do not attend school. The school is well resourced but the community has a chronic food shortage. In this chapter John talks about the challenge of coping with geographical and professional isolation, working with new and inexperienced teachers, keeping on top of endless tasks, dealing with competing pressures, accountability demands and the demands of dealing with issues in a dysfunctional community. John describes two critical incidents: the death of a much-loved teacher and the problems created by a destructive teacher. Both are reminders of the emotional demands of the role. After 3 years in post, John thinks that he now knows how to run a school but that he still has to learn how to be an educational leader.

In Chapter 3, Keita McIndoe, principal of a 57-pupil, 3-teacher, co-ed, rural state primary school in the centre of the North Island of New Zealand/Aotearoa, talks with Reynold McPherson about her development as a school principal. Having taught for 7 years, served for a year as principal of a single-teacher school, a term as a senior teacher and two terms as an acting principal, Keita is now responsible for three teachers, a secretary/teacher aide and a part-time cleaner. Large numbers of principals have reached retiral age in Keita's context, and accelerated career advancement without preparatory training is common. Accepting increasing responsibility as a teacher made her realize that she wanted to become a school leader, but she did not receive preparatory training prior to any of her four leadership roles. Keita talks about how her 'on the job' leadership development was supported by short training courses after appointment, with some mentoring and networking. She also talks about her reflective approach towards her own professional development, an early problem of acceptance, the importance of trust, improving communication with parents, the legacy of the previous principal and her focus on changing the culture of the school and improving the quality of teaching.

The Americas

Three accounts are provided from the Americas. The first is situated in Karl-Kate, an economically poor community in the state of Texas in the United States. Texas was once part of Mexico, which is just 15 miles away, and most of Karl-Kate's 3,000 inhabitants have Mexican ancestry. Over half the population lives below the poverty line. Unlike the other chapters in this book Chapter 4 is written in the third person. Here Sarah Nelson and Israel Aquilar construct the story of Xavier Rios, principal of Trevino[2] Junior High School. Xavier knows the area and understands the social conditions well, having been born and brought up in the Mexican-American side of Karl-Kate. He was appointed principal on short notice having previously served as an assistant principal for several years. In addition to social conditions associated with poverty, the community's proximity to the border means that illegal immigration and drug trafficking have contributed to an unsettled social climate in which the Border Patrol is a constant visible presence, young children are recruited as drug runners and homes are raided by the Drug Enforcement Agency. Trevino is the only school Xavier has worked in, and his commitment to the school and the community it serves is evident when talking about realizing his long-held ambition to become a principal, his transition from peer to principal, having to 'hit the ground running', his attempts to create a climate of collaboration and the debt he owes to others. Students and families depend on the school for more than schooling, and Xavier's account demonstrates his awareness of his responsibilities and the school's role in helping the community to develop.

The next account is provided by Rosa Eaton Guerrero, director of Estado de México Elementary School in the port of Ensenada, the oldest city in the Mexican border state of Baja California. The school has 163 students, most of whom suffer from educational deficits and social problems associated with poverty. Rosa accepted the role of director at the invitation of a school inspector following the illness of the previous director. Her passion and commitment are evident in Chapter 5 as she talks about the problems that she encountered in changing roles within the same school and dealing with the social, emotional and health problems of students as well as their academic progression. Rosa also talks about changing the attitude and perspective of teachers, helping them to recognize and work on developing their own weaknesses instead of attributing student deficiencies to the students themselves and their families. Once she had assumed responsibility for the school Rosa developed her leadership capability de facto by attending appropriate workshops, reflecting on circumstances and noting the difference between directors who are academic leaders and those who go through the motions. Rosa sees the role as an opportunity to put her ideas into practice and improve the life chances of her students. At times she is tired and frustrated, and she tells us that it's not easy to 'spin like a top all day, attending to a thousand things'. But she enjoys being the school principal.

In the third contribution from the Americas, Diane Purvey and Charles Webber meet with a novice First Nation school principal in British Columbia, Canada. Tsutsweye[3] is a First Nation leader who has not yet been in the post for 2 years. As a principal of a reserve school she has had to contend with the complex mix of social, emotional, financial and educational issues that go along with leading and managing a First Nation reserve school in a rural community in British Columbia. She is quite unique in that there are not many female First Nation principals in Canada. Tsutsweye has long-established roots in the First Nation community in which the school is located, and her commitment to the school and the community that it is part of is evident throughout her narrative. But she has also experienced success as a teacher outside of the aboriginal community, and in Chapter 6 she talks about how she feels that the experience of working elsewhere helped her configure her personal and professional identity and led to her being a stronger and wiser leader, capable of navigating the tensions between preserving and respecting First Nation knowledge and culture while working within the expectations of mainstream western societal ways.

Asia

Two accounts are provided from Asia. In Chapter 7, Sr Paulino de Carralho, the director of the primary school in the remote village of Aikua Rinkua in East Timor and Sr Paulino de Jesus Araujo, the chairman of its Parent and Teachers' Association talk with Reynold McPherson about their joy and pride in their village school. In marked contrast to countries with long-established education systems, Timor Leste is a new country, having gained full independence as recently as May 2002. School directors here work within an education system that is poor in terms of teacher capability, resources and classroom facilities. There are high rates of absenteeism among teachers and students, and high teacher–student ratios. School directors must also contend with language challenges and the legacy of occupation and therefore they must be verbally fluent and culturally aware with regard to local ethnicity. In this chapter, the chair of the Parent and Teachers' Association provides a history of Aikua Rinkua primary school. The school director, Paulino de Carralho, then describes how he committed himself to education as his personal contribution to national independence. His account of becoming and being the school director is therefore embedded in a context of post-conflict reconstruction and emphasizes how primary school leadership can give expression to national aspirations such as reconciliation and independence.

In the second contribution from Asia, Fan Huali, principal of Zhatang Elementary School in Changsha, Hunan province, in central southern China, talks with Xiao Liang about her first year as a principal in an urbanizing rural district. Scholars have gathered here since ancient times but Hunan province is now referred to as China's 'silicon valley'. Zhatang is a small school with 7 teachers and 77 students. Huali was appointed to Zhatang as a result of a meritocratic policy in which suitable applicants with a proven record in a previous position are temporarily appointed to a lower-level school in order to further develop their careers. She was told which school she was to be appointed to a day before taking up the post. With no formal preparation for principalship, Huali talks about how she prepared for school leadership by imitating how other principals spoke, modelling their attitudes and behaviour and reading appropriate literature. She also talks about how Zhatang lagged behind schools in other districts, the suspicions and expectations of an older staff and their reluctance to change, her efforts to improve staff capability and her determination not to settle for an easy existence but to work towards improving the school in the interests of students and the community. Despite her frustrations, Huali has been prudent, and she took care not to pursue dramatic change in her first year, but by personal example and adopting a collegial approach and working with staff to improve their capability, she appears to have made significant progress.

Africa

There are two narratives from principals in Africa. In the first, Cedric Matroos, principal of Frank Joubert School in Schauderville, a suburb of Port-Elizabeth in the Eastern Cape province of South Africa, talks about the language, political and cultural challenges that he has to address. Following apartheid, the suburbs of the cities in South Africa continue to be inhabited by racial groupings. Schauderville is no exception, having been established in the former regime as a suburb for so-called coloured people. Although English is the language of instruction in the school, Afrikaans is the mother tongue of most of the students. However, the parents of Xhosha-speaking black children from other suburbs are now enrolling their children in Frank Joubert because they hope that this will enable them to then attend English medium high schools at a later stage. This influx has provided a further challenge for the school and the local community. For Cedric, leading and managing the school well involves being clear about what is right and what is wrong, but in Chapter 6, his frustrations surface as he talks about the significance of the language of instruction; his difficulties in communicating with the education department and what he regards as incompetent governance; the role of the school governing bodies, the attractions of alternative educational models and his hopes and fears for the future.

The second African account is from Mandizini School, situated in a remote and rural area in Tanzania. One hundred and twenty-six students are enrolled and there are three teachers, including the headteacher, Tupa Lugendo. In Chapter 10, Tupa talks with Brown Onguko and Musa Mohammed about how he leads and manages the school in difficult circumstances. The school is poorly equipped and there are problems with the teachers: when one is in school the other is often absent. The former head was demoted and continues to teach in the school. The school has seven grades but only one classroom. Most teaching takes place in the open.

Tupa did not apply for the post, nor did he seek or want to become a headteacher. He was appointed without specific preparation, received no formal induction and has had no in-service training following his appointment. He assumed duty with no firsthand knowledge of the culture of the area. Nevertheless, Tupa accepted the responsibilities involved and for the past year he has committed to the role and relied on experiential learning to carry out his leadership tasks. Faced with huge challenges Tupa adopted a pragmatic, philosophical and participatory approach. In this chapter, he talks about his vision for the school and the steps he has taken towards achieving it by working closely with the chairperson of the school committee, the chairperson of the village, the village elder and others.

Europe

Three accounts are provided from Europe. Falkland Primary School in Scotland is the only school in a small, historic village. It is located in a relatively affluent area within commuting distance of Edinburgh, and parental expectations are high. Gillian Knox has been the headteacher for about 3 years. In Chapter 11, Gillian recalls that her first few weeks in the post were quite daunting. What surprised her most was that staff expected her to know how to run the school and how the school was run. It did not take her long to realize that there was much that she did not know. While Gillian wanted a collaborative and collegiate approach and develop shared responsibility, the staff seemed happy to be told what to do. Gillian notes that considerable progress has been made over the past 2 years, but argues that good is not good enough. Her priority is to stay focused on making things better but confesses that she is finding it difficult to engage teachers in self-refection and to persuade them to talk to each other about learning and teaching. At times Gillian finds the volume of work overwhelming and her work/life balance has been adversely affected, but she loves the job and cannot envisage doing anything else.

Ion Creanga School, named after a well-known writer of children's literature and fairy tales in Romania, is located in the small city of Targu Frumos, in the northeast of the country. In Chapter 12, the school director, Ana Maria Doleanu, talks with Ovidiu Gavrilovici and Carmen Cretu about her experience during the first 3 years of being the school director. Ana talks about being a new director each year because she holds an acting position; having been initially appointed for a couple of months, she has been reconfirmed in the post at the beginning of the school year for the past 3 years. Although she holds an interim position and could be replaced, Ana accepts the responsibility, gets on with the job and has demonstrated a clear commitment to working with others and shown determination in developing Ion Creanga as an inclusive community school. Here she talks about her lack of experience, knowledge and understanding on appointment; how she developed a theoretical frame of reference through further study and how she values the support of colleagues she met while studying school leadership and management. But with a more developed and nuanced understanding of the responsibilities and complexities of leading and managing a school, after 3 years in the post, Ana now finds the job more stressful than she did in her first year. Although she takes pride in what has been achieved, Ana also talks about the emotional aspects of the job and having to make decisions that have an impact on others and about how the incessant workload, accountability and the all-consuming nature of the job have affected her personal and family life.

In Chapter 13, Melody,[4] a new headteacher in southern England, talks with Megan Crawford about challenges of a different kind during what she describes as the worst year of her life. Surprises often await new principals (Draper and McMichael, 1998) but in this particular situation the school turned out to be very different from the school that had been depicted when she applied for the post, so much so that her first year as a headteacher was a period of deep emotional stress. It did not take the Melody long to discover that the values and culture of the school conflicted with her personal and professional values, and it also soon became clear that her style of leadership and management was very different from the way in which the previous head operated. Her core beliefs were challenged and she lacked internal support, but in her first year of headship she had the strength to instigate disciplinary procedures in relation to some school staff members, and this led to the suspension of some teachers. In this chapter, Melody talks candidly about her frustrations and how she found the first year of headship to be a bewildering and challenging experience. She also talks about the effect that these challenges have had on her health, the pressures that made her feel inadequate and how she had to draw on her inner reserves for support. Preparation for headship may be important, but Melody says that nothing could have prepared her for the experience that she went through.

Summary

The narratives provide an insight into why the new principals became principals. They tell us how they have struggled, with different degrees of success and sometimes at great personal cost, to deal with the challenges that they've encountered. Despite these challenges, and with few exceptions, they are motivated to continue to learn and remain committed and determined to improve the life chances of the children and work with others to develop the communities that they serve.

What the narratives do not do is tell aspiring principals how to prepare themselves for the responsibilities of leadership or how to lead and manage a school. Those responsible for programmes that prepare principals will not find out what the content of those programmes should be or how they should be structured, and those responsible for inducting new principals will not be offered guidance. The narratives suggest that becoming and being a school principal involves a wide range of elements, and to some extent these depend on chance and individual circumstances. Following their appointment, individuals will react to being a principal in ways that cannot be predicted, but what this collection does is provide an insight into 12 experiences of becoming and being a school principal in 12 diverse cultural contexts.

The narratives are reviewed in the final chapter. A thematic review of the 12 narratives outlining the personal experience of selected novice principals in very diverse contexts is not a strong basis for recommending improvements to the preparation of aspiring principals or to generalize across education systems. But although generalization is not warranted, in the final chapter Megan Crawford and I, without reaching too far beyond what is said in the narratives, reflect on the principals' accounts in relation to some of the research literature in the field of school leadership development.

We hope that these vignettes will help aspiring principals to prepare for and supplement their experience. For serving principals, and those involved in preparing and supporting principals, the personal narratives also provide an opportunity to reflect on their own experience and to better understand the experience of others.

Notes

1　John is not his real name, as the principal preferred to remain anonymous.

2　Both Xavier and Trevino are fictitious names.

3　Tsutsweye is a pseudonym.

4　Melody is a pseudonym.

References

Begley, P. T. (2008), 'The nature and specialized purposes of educational leadership', in J. Lumby, G. Crow and P. Pashiardis (eds), *International Handbook on the Preparation and Development of School Leaders*. London: Routledge.

Bush, T. (1998), 'The national qualification for headship: the key to effective school leadership?', *School Leadership and Management*, 18, (3), 321–33.

—(1999), 'Crisis or crossroads? The discipline of educational management in the late 1990s', *Educational Management, Administration and Leadership*, 27, (3), 239–40.

Cowie, M. and Crawford, M. (2007), 'Principal preparation – still an act of faith?', *School Leadership and Management*, 27, (2), 129–46.

Dimmock, C. and Walker, A. (2000), 'Developing comparative and international educational leadership and management: a cross-cultural model', *School Leadership and Management*, 20, (2), 143–60.

Draper, J. and McMichael, P. (1998), 'Making sense of primary headship: the surprises awaiting new heads', *School Leadership and Management*, 18, (2), 197–211.

Evans, R. (1995), 'Getting real about headship', *Education Week*, 14, 29–36.

Gronn, P. (2003), *The New Work of New Educational Leaders: Changing Leadership Practice in an Era of School Reform*. Paul Chapman: London.

Hallinger, P. and Leithwood, K. (1996), 'Culture and educational administration: a case of finding out what you don't know you don't know', *Journal of Educational Administration*, 34, (5), 98–116.

Heck, R. H. (1996), 'Leadership and culture: conceptual and methodological issues in comparing models across cultural settings', *Journal of Educational Administration*, 34, (5), 4–97.

—(1998), 'Conceptual and methodological issues in comparing models across cultures', *Peabody Journal of Education*, 73, (2), 51–80.

Leithwood, K. and Duke, D. L. (1998), 'Mapping the conceptual terrain of leadership: a critical point of departure for cross-cultural studies', *Peabody Journal of Education*, 73, (2), 31–50.

Muller, J. H. (1999), 'Narrative approaches to qualitative research in primary care', in B. F. Crabtree and W. L. Miller (eds), *Doing Qualitative Research*. London: Sage.

Onguko, B., Abdalla, M. and Webber, C. F. (2008), 'Mapping principal preparation in Kenya and Tanzania', *Journal of Educational Administration*, 46, (6), 715–26.

Roberts, B. (2002), *Biographical Research*. Buckingham: Open University Press.

Slater, C. L., Boone, M., Alvarez, I., Topete, C., Iturbe, E., Munoz, L., Base, M., Romer-Grimaldo, L., Korth, L., Andrews, J. and Bustamante, A. (2005), 'School leadership preparation in Mexico: metacultural considerations', *Journal of School Leadership*, 15, (2), 196–214.

Slater, C. L., Boone, M., Nelson, S., De La Colina, M., Garcia, E., Grimaldo, L., Rico, G., Rodríguez, S., Sirios, D., Womack, D., Garcia, J. M. and Arriaga, R. (2007), '*El Escalafón y el Doble Turno*: an international perspective on school director preparation', *Journal for Educational Research and Policy Studies*, 6, (2), 60–90.

Wildy, H. and Clarke, S. (2008), 'Principals on L-plates: rear view mirror reflections', *Journal of Educational Administration*, 46, (6), 727–38.

Part 1
Australasia

At the Edge of the Silent Centre: An Australian Principal's Reflections on Leading an Isolated School

A novice principal reflects on his experience with Helen Wildy and Simon Clarke

Context

Apart from Mt Augustus and a couple of smaller ranges, there is little to break the landscape stretching flat in all directions for hundreds of kilometres. The dark red soil is dotted with spindly stunted shrubs bearing sparse, small, silver-grey foliage and the occasional windmill against the horizon. This is cattle country. Kangaroos, feral goats, some sheep, black crows and wide-winged eagles live and die here. Sunsets are spectacular, but driving at sunrise or sunset is dangerous: carcasses of kangaroos, goats and cars litter the roadsides. The main road is the highway to the minefields further north. Road trains carrying dongas (portable houses), dump trucks, graders and refrigeration units hurtle along at 110 km per hour. This is not a trip for novices.

We are 1,100 km north of Perth, the capital city of Western Australia, and 460 km inland from the Indian Ocean. The quickest way to get here is to take a regular though infrequent flight from Perth to one of three airports within 700 km of the community. From there you can charter a small plane. The drawbacks are that the charters are very costly and also inflexible because they fly in and back on the same day. Alternatively, you can hire a four-wheel-drive vehicle from one of the three locations. The drawbacks to this option are that the vehicles, though pre-booked, are not always available when you arrive, and the roads are unsealed and some are quite dangerous. The most flexible and reliable, though time-consuming, travel option is to do as we did and hire a vehicle in Perth and drive the 1,100 km yourself. The trip takes one and a half days. All you need is a robust vehicle, a long-range fuel tank, a good driver and plenty of patience.

The community is situated 40 km from Australia's largest monolith, Mt Augustus. But this rock does not have the iconic status of the next largest monolith, Uluru (Ayres Rock) in the 'dead centre of Australia', which attracts millions of tourists each year. The only tourists here are occasional travellers lost on their way to Mt Augustus, hoping to buy food and fuel. Neither is available.

There is uranium here, but political pressures prevent the deposit from being mined. The land was previously a privately owned cattle station. After the Native Title Act of 1993, the property was released to its traditional owners, the Wadjarri tribe, whose families continue to roam this part of the state. As well as the school, there is a shop, a swimming pool, a health centre, an administration house, a telecentre, an oval and 50 residences. Up to 15 people may live in a house at a time, so the population varies between 20 and 300 people. Apart from the administrator, shopkeeper, pool manager, the telecentre manager and a few men who collect the rubbish and tidy the grounds, the only people in paid employment are the school staff and office staff.

Expanses of grass surround the school buildings. There's too much uranium in the bore water for it to be drinkable but it is fine for the lawn, which explains the grassed oval in front of the school and the expanses of lawn around the school buildings. John Anderson, the school principal, buys drinking water for his family from the shop in the nearest town, 303 km away on an unsealed road. Having to ration drinking water is only one of the challenges facing John and his family living in this remote Aboriginal community on the edge of the silent centre of Australia.

There are four classroom teachers, four Aboriginal and Islander Education officers (AIEOs, teacher assistants), the principal, the registrar and a gardener/ cleaner. There are 61 students on the roll, but the record attendance is 53 students. Twenty students on any day is considered good attendance. Today there are 15 students.

This is John's first principal appointment. He is halfway through his third year as principal, having taught for 13 years. John is married with two primary school-aged daughters. It is a sunny winter's day, and John is wearing shorts with a cotton, short-sleeved, checked shirt. He is relaxed and unhurried as we sit on a couch with our backs to the single security-screened window in his office. He swings around from his computer to face us and chat, and then takes us for a stroll around the school grounds. During these conversations and later over coffee in the staff room, he tells his story.

John's story

I trained as a secondary teacher with a bachelor's of education in environmental education. I did not set out to be a teacher, but by the time I had finished the programme I thought: Well it looks like teaching is what I have been trained for. I taught at a technical high school in Victoria for 7 years. I taught science, mathematics, home economics, outdoor education and society and environment. I remember clearly my first weeks as a teacher. I sat at my desk in the staff room and thought: 'I have no idea what to do. My last 4 years has not prepared me in the least for being in the classroom'. I always felt I wanted to extend myself beyond the classroom as a professional educator. During those years I was a year coordinator and a member of the principal's advisory committee. The school provided vocational training, and at recess and lunch times I hung out with the manual arts and tech guys, most of whom had careers as carpenters and plumbers and so on before becoming teachers. They used to rib me: 'You haven't had a life. You went to school then you went to college and now you are back at school. What do you know of life?' At the time I laughed this off, not taking it seriously. Over time, though, I must have reflected on what they were telling me and started to look beyond the classroom, beyond teaching and even beyond my life in the Victorian country town.

Before long I met J, who later became my wife. She must have related to the restless side of me. I have always considered that we are here for a good time, not a long time, especially as I notice how sedentary and cautious are the lives of my siblings and J's too. She said to me one day: 'What about going overseas?' I had been to New Zealand and Malaysia as a tourist previously but never worked overseas. We signed up for what is now called Australian

Volunteers International and we were offered Botswana. We had the time of our lives: it was a time of sadness and happiness; of both confronting and joyous experiences. We were adventurous, driving around Africa and camping in the bush, waking to the sounds of lions and hyenas. The curriculum was prescriptive and involved a great deal of assessment. Even as the only ex-pat teacher, I must have felt confident in myself because, unlike the other teachers, I was comfortable talking to the principal and offering ideas for teaching, particularly for integrating Internet Technology (IT), a role that probably led to my becoming the head of science at the secondary school in north Botswana at the age of 31.

When my contract ended I couldn't return to teach in Victoria. I had taken a redundancy package offered by the government to reduce the number of teachers in the public sector and was not allowed to teach in that state for at least 3 years. J and I had a new baby by the time we returned home to Victoria. Because we had always been attracted to the west of Australia, we decided to get in our old Land Cruiser and head west. I was offered a temporary science teaching position in the north of the state, at a town called P. 'Where is that?' I asked. After that I was offered another science-teaching job at M, still in the remote inland of Western Australia, where I taught for 2 years. When the deputy principal retired my wife encouraged me to apply for it in an acting capacity. I remembered that the deputy principal in Botswana had said to me: 'You'd make a good deputy'. I had that position for 2 years. When a substantive position in a rural town 1,500 km away in the lower southeast of the state was advertised, I was again encouraged by my wife, and also by the principal of M High School, to put in my application. I won that job and stayed the mandatory minimum 2 years. I did not like the job. It was a shared position between teaching and being a deputy. I felt I was doing neither well.

I had a phone call from the principal at M High School telling me of vacancies for both principal and registrar at nearby B Remote Community School. By then we had two children and my wife was an experienced registrar. It seemed as though those jobs were made for us. We applied for and won the positions. So back up to the northwest we moved, and this was the start of my time as a principal. There was no training or induction for the principalship. On offer, though, was a remote teaching service induction programme for all those starting in the outback. I went to this, but it was not very useful. I had already taught in some pretty outback places.

However, my first principalship was like being dropped onto a busy highway and I was running along behind trying to catch up. My predecessor had left the school in good shape. Although teacher turn-over in schools like this is very high, when I arrived all the teachers had been there the previous year. Teachers were well used to the context, and the school had established routines, functioning processes and harmonious relationships with the community. I was lucky.

The job turned out to be what I expected to some extent. I knew I would have to learn a great deal, not only about being a principal but also about the school community. I did not appreciate how much I would have to learn about being the head of a school that catered for students from kindergarten (aged 4 years) right through to the end of secondary school (aged 17 years). I thought I would be well prepared from my years as a secondary teacher. In reality, the students performed at around low primary level, even the secondary students. I desperately needed to learn about the primary curriculum, early-years teaching strategies and working closely with teachers on curriculum and pedagogy. All this was new to me.

Despite these challenges I did not for 1 minute doubt that I could do the job. I am easy going and get on well with people. I might be stressed at times but I never show this. I might be quiet at home or snappy at my wife, but generally I have good coping skills. Looking back over the time as a principal I see that I had to do some things that do not come easily to me. One of these is to tackle issues up front. I don't like creating waves. I prefer to let things slide, believing that they will work themselves out in the end. Perhaps I am too laid back! But this attribute led me to have a very difficult time last year.

Some parents don't worry too much about school. Families move around a fair bit. The students might be on our roll but come to school here only a couple of weeks in a year. They might go to another school, but mostly they don't bother. The central office might track them down; our registrar phones other schools to try to find them. I go round regularly and talk to the parents. However, many children simply don't go to school. I think that it is the responsibility of families to get an education for their children. We offer it to them, but we can't make them come to school. We can ensure our programmes are engaging, stimulating and relevant. There are many other reasons for nonattendance. The most powerful is the funeral ritual. Later this week two funerals are scheduled at towns in the area. Of course, all families here are related in this part of the state. It is customary for all relatives to attend funerals, even when this entails a couple of days driving each way. By the end of this week I expect the only students at school will be the children of the teachers. Even our AIEOs will attend the funerals.

This year all our teachers are new and inexperienced. They are not, how-ever, young. Each brings a former career and many rich life experiences. For example, our one male teacher, though recently graduated, was formerly an opera singer and he brings a background of art, music and drama to his specialist teaching responsibilities in these fields. The early-years teacher, an indigenous women, and unofficially the deputy principal, grew up in this part of the state and spent some years as an AIEO before undertaking studies to qualify her to teach. The middle primary teacher has Years 3 to 6 classes. Prior to training as a teacher, she worked as a theatre nurse and travelled the world. She is here this year, in her first year of teaching, with her 13-year-old daughter who had previously attended a prestigious and competitive academic school in the city. This young girl is now beginning her secondary schooling at our school, as one of a dozen or so secondary students, ranging up to 17 years of age. This group has one teacher, another new graduate, who teaches all subject areas through literacy and numeracy. That this teacher is trained as a primary teacher is not a drawback: in fact, she is perfectly suited to the students she has, as they perform at a low-to-middle primary level. Our challenge, though, is to cater for the teacher's 13-year-old daughter. I wonder how we can provide her with a rich curriculum of learning areas and experiences that will prepare her for tertiary entrance in the future.

Like all Aboriginal community schools in this state and elsewhere in Australia, our school is richly resourced. Our classrooms are packed with teaching materials and we struggle to spend all the funds we are allocated in a year. For example, ten new computers have recently arrived. They are sitting in boxes in the staff room. One day we will set them up in the computer room, which is already fully equipped and little used. In the recent federal government stimulus package we have been allocated funds for a new library. When this is built we will have another spare room and we can use one for a large storeroom. Most teachers probably don't know what we have stored already. Cleaning out the storeroom is useful: we will all see what is there.

While the community is rich in material goods, it is chronically short of food. I don't know what the community folk eat. We go to town, 303 km away, and buy $1,000 worth of groceries for our family and for the school. We provide apples and oranges for the students at morning recess. When the community people go to town they buy only what they can afford and that doesn't last long. Adults receive government living allowances but often this is used for alcohol. The local shop no longer operates because it ran into deep debt. When it did operate, the owners would go to town and bring back pies, soft drinks and chips to sell. These didn't last long. There used to be a women's group who met in a house next to the school and prepared lunches for the students. Since the funding for this was withdrawn the students aren't provided lunch. At lunch time my two daughters eat their sandwiches and fruit that we prepare for them. Some of the Aboriginal students have lunch with them; usually they go home, but sometimes there is little food for them so they just ride around on their bikes until the siren goes for the start of the afternoon session. When the families go off to funerals they fill their cars with five to ten people so there is no room for their dogs. Each family has five or six dogs and these are left at the community. They roam the streets, looking for food. After a few days they are hungry, barking, snarling, jumping our fences, getting into our bins. It is hard to imagine how students can concentrate on their learning programmes in a context like this.

Our students love art. Our strategy, therefore, is to link as much as we can to art. For example, all the buildings are decorated with murals; the classroom doors feature local issues graphically, such as hunting, the rains and animals. The older students do mathematics using a set of activities in which answers to calculations are matched to segments of a picture that, if all are answered correctly, will generate a complete image; students then colour in the picture and put this on the wall for display. You see the walls are covered with these types of pictures. Another example is the task the art specialist has set these older students: redesign the art room to make it more like a gallery. They were offered the opportunity to look at art galleries on the internet then clean up and rearrange the furniture and walls to set up exhibitions of students' work. Students are well mannered and happily engage in such activity.

Despite the lack of food, the students are healthy. We are fortunate that this community does not have a tradition of petrol sniffing, alcohol abuse or other drugs. It is not a designated dry community, so members do buy alcohol and bring it in. There might be a drinking party that lasts for a few days. We hear the loud music all through the community. No one gets much sleep. After a few days we are exhausted and irritable, and the whole community is unsettled. This is when disagreements break out, and at times there is violence in the community. On the whole, however, compared with many other similar settings, ours is peaceful for most of the year.

I am most challenged by the task of keeping on top of all the work. This job is not easy. There are seemingly endless tasks. I make a list, and by the time I knock off two of them another ten have been added. You never get on top of it. There are so many aspects to deal with: issues with students and their learning, behavior, attendance, health, interpersonal matters; issues with teachers and their professional learning, social well-being, and interpersonal matters; issues with parents and their relationships within the community and their lack of interest in the school and their children's well-being; issues with the community as a unit and its financial difficulties and general dysfunction and finally issues with the education system and the endless demands for bureaucratic accountability. I am also a husband and a father of two school-aged girls: I love to spend time with them. I am happy to put in a good 8 hours at school each weekday but I do not believe I can or should do more than that. I hear of principals who work 10 to 12 hours a day and all weekend just to keep on top of things. I would never do that. I strongly believe that I am responsible for the well-being of my family. That is my top priority. If they are well and happy, then I can do my work. Having a wife and children helps me. It gives me perspective. This is how I balance my personal life and my professional work.

I am happiest when the school is humming along. I wake up in the morning and get up with a spring in my step. I look forward to going over to the school. I am confident that all the students are learning. Teachers are getting along. The parents are not complaining. I don't have system people breathing down my neck or demanding reports from me. I am best at getting along with people. I think my greatest success here has been to build good relationships among teachers, throughout the community and between all the students. I feel comfortable talking to parents. I walk around the houses and knock on the door if I want to talk to a family. I never go inside a house: that's out of bounds. If I see a bunch of old ladies sitting around the fire outside, I go up to them and have a chat. I like to be out, talking with the parents and families. They know who I am and what I stand for. It's humming along nicely now. But it has not always been like this.

In my time as a principal two serious incidents occurred, both of which shook me to my core and challenged me as a human being. The first happened 4 months into my first year as a principal. Two of our teachers were driving the 500-km trip to the nearest coastal town. The sister of one of the teachers had come to visit. The teachers were returning from taking her to the town so she could return home. The road is generally sound, though unsealed, and the teachers had made the trip on many occasions. Why the accident happened has never been clarified, although there was speculation that a tyre burst. The car swung out of control and rolled over five times. One teacher had her neck broken; the other died instantly. She was a wonderful teacher, beloved by all students and highly respected in the community. Her husband, who was our Vocational Education and Training (VET) teacher, was inconsolable. As a school we were devastated. I closed the school out of respect but also out of necessity: none of us was fit to face a class of students. Now we have a lovely framed photograph of her hanging in our reception area. We remember her every day. My challenge was to support our staff through their grief and back to normality. This was made both easier and more difficult because we were an extremely close group, almost like a family. Among the staff there was respect and collegiality that helped us to mesh together, in good times and then in bad times.

Although I had no formal preparation for dealing with this shocking event, I had been through something similar when I was deputy principal at M High School some years earlier. The 6-year-old daughter of our art teacher was raped by a community member down by the creek. Everyone was shocked beyond words. The principal was away and one deputy was acting as the principal. She was expected to address the staff. She could not do it. I was the other deputy principal and was called on to do it. I had to take charge. I sent three teachers home because they were not coping. I sought advice from the district office. I was advised to 'continue as normal'. However, I saw that teachers were too upset to be at school so, against my line manager's advice, I closed the school the next day. We all needed time to come to terms with what had happened, not that any of us can ever get over that.

The second incident that challenged me as a principal was less sudden, more gradual and insidious. It occurred last year, my second year in the position. I might have handled it differently, looking back even now. I expect that as the years go on and I learn more about being a principal I will realize more acutely how it could have been dealt with better. But this is what happened and how I reacted. At the start of 2008 we were short four teachers. This was at a time when we had a staff of six, before the current cutback when we lost our kindergarten and VET teachers. I had a call from a couple who was teaching at a government primary school in a wheatbelt town some 600 km south of here. They came to visit us and seemed nice enough. I was attracted to the idea of getting two teachers, a married couple, both experienced teachers, used to rural life, one a middle primary teacher and the other a VET teacher. It seemed too good to be true. It was.

They were duly appointed to the school and we began the year with most teacher vacancies filled. A good start, I thought. Pretty much from day one, the atmosphere in the staff room changed. Gone was the harmonious, supportive, family feeling of the group we had the previous year. The new male VET teacher was clearly out to cause trouble. He niggled and confronted and soon had everyone off side, with him, with me and with each other. You could cut the air in the staff room with a knife. He talked very fast and stood right up close, with his head in your face. He was a tall man, well built and a dominating figure in a room. He undermined every idea that was put up. He got involved in the politics of the community and fostered discontent among the families. Parents were annoyed with his interference. He was harsh in the classroom, and we had complaints from parents about his rudeness to their children. He openly stated that he did not like indigenous people. Now at first I thought he was just trying it on and my best strategy was to let him wear himself out. If I didn't intervene, then he would have nothing to push back on. Staff were getting increasingly unhappy. I needed to take some action. I spoke to him, asking him to settle down, get on with his teaching and stop aggravating staff and parents. He wouldn't even listen to me. By now one of our best teachers was so stressed she took a term off. I was getting anxious. I couldn't sleep at night. I didn't like coming to school. The only person who seemed able to manage him was J, my wife, the registrar. Her strategy was to bite back. He couldn't take that and steered clear of her. But it took its toll on her too and she needed to take stress leave. I knew then that I had to take action. I consulted the district director and had this man moved to nearby M High School, where I had taught previously and where the principal was experienced. The plan was that he would be able to start afresh. I heard, though, that he did exactly the same things there. That principal wouldn't stand for it. He negotiated swiftly with the department to get rid of him. He was paid out, and the last I heard of him was that he had joined the army. I wouldn't want to repeat that year. In hindsight I should have tackled him right at the start, set the standards and protected the teachers, students and community from him. If his wife hadn't been such a good teacher, I probably would have thought about getting rid of him more rapidly. I know I am a fence-sitter. I just don't like confronting issues. I still wonder if I would have the confidence to do that, even now.

I would have to say though that these two experiences – the death of our much-loved teacher and getting rid of the destructive teacher – coming one after the other so early in my career as a principal have tested me. I know I am tough. These challenges were about as hard as they get and I pulled through.

I am not clear about my future. I am never one to plan, but I do have lots of dreams. We own a 55-acre block down in the south of the state, with rolling hills, a creek and a great bog shed that we have furnished. A neighbour runs sheep on the property. We go down there for holidays sometimes and feel nourished by its beauty, especially after the harsh ruggedness of this environment. I have dreams of living there. The most important thing for us as a family is to settle down in a town with a decent school for our girls. We want them to be in one school throughout their secondary school. It has to be a good school so that they can have good career prospects. It has to be a large school so that they can build friendships with young people their own age and background. I would be unlikely to find a principal's position in such a location because what I have described is keenly sought by all young principals. I will probably have to revert to being a deputy principal. I don't mind the backward career move but I do worry whether I would be content to be second in charge after having been the boss. I am now used to being on my own. I have never had the experience of working as part of a leadership team. I need to learn how to do this and I expect I will find that a challenge.

When I leave here at the end of this year, having completed my mandatory 3 years' service, I qualify for remote teaching service leave. I could take that leave – one term – and add it to my accumulated one term of long service leave and we could go for a long holiday. We could travel around Australia. We could go overseas and see more of the world. Both of us are well paid and I worry sometimes that we are spoiling our children. Each year we have a good holiday. We have been to Bali a few times; we go to Sydney, Melbourne and, of course, down to our farm. We stay in high-quality hotels and resorts. J and I sometimes dream about buying a motel or a hotel in a rural setting and running that for a few years, just for something different. Or we could go back to Victoria to be close to our families. Both of us have siblings who are having children now. It would be good for our children to grow up with their cousins.

I talk to a number of people about my career. My wife is open to ideas, and we dream together about possible futures for our family. The principal at M High School asks me how I am going and tells me about jobs that come up. He even set up mock interviews for me to practise when I went for the job I have now. He has been a good support and friend for me. The district director has a bit of an interest in my career. When he visits, which is about twice a year, he asks me how I am getting along. In my first year I was assigned a mentor by the department. He was a very experienced principal, and I found it helpful to call him from time to time. I have a good network of mates, from my time teaching and as a deputy. I feel I can call up people when I need direction. But it is lonely here. I am the only professional male, except for our newly appointed graduate teacher. The closest like-minded male is over 300 km away.

If I were asked to give advice to an aspiring school leader in this context I would say that being a principal is tough. You have to deal with competing pressures pulling in different directions. It is a struggle to avoid getting snowed under by endless small tasks. I work hard during the week but never during the weekend because I want to be a good dad to my girls. It is hard to see the big picture. For example, the emails are relentless and it's hard to sort out the dross. The main issue for me is that the department is stressing educational leadership while bombarding us with administrative trivia. I believe that the best way to prepare for being a principal is to get on top of the trivia. Find out how to deal efficiently with the desk work. Learn the policies and procedures so wading through the paperwork doesn't get you down. I am geographically and professionally isolated so I have had to learn all this alone. Fortunately being a deputy principal in two previous schools gave me some experience. I doubt I could have moved straight out of the classroom into the principal's office, as many of my peers have done.

I need to learn how to be an educational leader. I have mastered the business of running a school but that is only a fraction of the principal's job. Teachers need support, and I am not sure how to give what is required. Students need appropriate programmes but I haven't the skills or experience to work with teachers in a way that helps them provide what is needed. The best way I could develop this expertise is to work closely with a knowledgeable and experienced principal in a mentoring relationship. I want to know more about dealing with teachers, tackling hard issues and bringing out the best in them. I guess you'd call this leadership.

Tihei Mauri Ora: Becoming a Primary School Principal in New Zealand

Reynold Macpherson meets with Keita McIndoe, principal of a rural school in North Island, New Zealand

A traditional way of starting a speech in Māori is to declare that you intend to breathe life into some ideas: Tihei mauri ora! In this chapter Keita McIndoe, principal of a 57-pupil, three-teacher, co-ed, decile 7[1] rural state primary school located in the centre of the North Island of New Zealand/Aotearoa, breathes life into ideas about how new primary principals might be better prepared for their responsibilities. Her story is set within a context in which accelerated promotion, without preparatory training or higher education prior to leadership appointments, has become the norm in recent years and low investment in leadership preparation has been overtaken by a crisis in supply and quality triggered by a bulge of 'Baby Boomer' retirements, resulting in accelerated career advancement and leader turnover, especially by Māori and Pacifika leaders.

The local context

Keita McIndoe's school is located on a quiet, tar-sealed rural road about a mile from a secondary highway that links two major tourist towns on New Zealand's volcanic plateau. A notice board decorated with Māori carving welcomes visitors. A wheelchair ramp leads visitors into an airy reception area tastefully decorated with children's art. This area provides access to the school secretary's office, the principal's office, a resource room, the staff room and three classrooms, all of which are carpeted. The internal decoration of the school is fresh and bright, predominantly in green pastel colours. Large pin boards display children's work.

The open architecture of the school features a functional assembly of pre-fabricated units and gently sloping, corrugated, green iron roofs. The outdoor areas include asphalted playing areas, a 'Learning Park', grassed sports areas and large shade trees, on more than a hectare of flat land. The school has four other standalone buildings: a library, a hall, a meeting room and a teacher's residence. The school also has a vegetable garden, a climbing frame area and sandpit for junior students and a 'confidence course' (similar to a military assault course) for senior children.

Beyond the school are rolling grasslands and blocks of pine trees broken by fault lines. Occasional steam vents indicate volcanic activity. The dairy farming economy of the area is currently doing well, primarily due to Fonterra's successful marketing of milk solids into China. The economics of forestry are steadily recovering from the international downturn, with demand growing from China and India. A short distance from the school and along the 'main road' is a minor tourist town built around its hot pools, a transport business and a dormitory town. Settlements in recent years at the Waitangi Tribunal have seen substantial transfers of land ownership from the government to iwi (tribal federations) trusts in the region, and early revitalization of the Māori economy and long-term investment in, for example, education scholarships. More then 50 percent of the school's children are Māori with 67 percent of these boys. They present as smartly dressed, active, confident, bright-eyed learners.

Keita is a Māori woman in her late 40s. She is married and the mother of two children who have left home. Her husband, also Māori, is a foreman for a city bus company. They are comfortably well off.

The principal's office is unpretentious. She has two desks linked to form an L-shaped work surface. She has a computer that enables her to communicate online with her secretary and teachers through an intranet. She also has links to ministry databases via a high-speed network. She has filing cabinets under two other work surfaces and bookshelves. From her office she can see along the verandas outside each classroom and across the asphalted and grassed playing areas.

Keita came to this school at the beginning of 2009 as a senior teacher. Within 2 weeks she was asked to serve as deputy principal. In the middle of the second term her principal was offered and accepted a 6-month secondment into the Ministry of Education, with the permission of the school's board of trustees. The deputy principal served as acting principal for the rest of the year. The principal resigned at the end of 2009 to continue in the ministry in 2010. Her position was advertised by the board of trustees. They selected Keita, and the ministry confirmed her permanency as principal in early February 2010.

Her career trajectory has been meteoric. She taught for 7 years after teacher training, served 1 year as a teaching principal in a sole-charge (one-teacher) school, one term as a senior teacher and two terms as an acting principal before being given permanency as principal of a three-teacher school. She did not receive preparatory training or higher education prior to any of her four leadership roles: team leader, senior teacher, deputy principal and principal. Leadership learning was done 'on the job' and through short training courses after appointment, with some mentoring and networking.

Keita manages three teachers, a secretary/teacher aide and a part-time cleaner. She reports to a board of trustees, which comprises six elected parents, an elected staff representative and herself, ex officio.

Becoming and being a principal: Keita's story

My legal name is Keita, my nanny's name. When I was young, people used to pronounce it wrong, even Māori, although it is not so bad these days. I disliked it intensely when people got it wrong. My nanny was known as Kate; I prefer Katie. My parents are both from the East Coast, from Ngati Kahungunu. I am a twin, so I was named after Dad's mum and my sister Kahu was named after my Mum's mum. So we are Keita and Kahu. As an adult I have met five other Keitas.

I have maintained my connections with Kahungunu. Many family members still live on the coast. Aunties and uncles still live there. One brother lives on the Mahia Peninsula. My *whakapapa* (genealogy) means that I know where I come from. The land (*whenua*) holds great significance for Māori. My *whakapapa* gives me a greater depth of understanding of Māori children and how they think. I love teaching and came to this school because over 50 percent of the roll are Māori children. My last school was a sole-charge principal school, 98 percent rural Pakeha (New Zealand European) children. I tried it for a year and it was totally different. Prior to that I had been at a city school with over 70 percent Māori kids. When a senior teacher position came up in this school, the Māori roll appealed. I had to decide between staying in a European school as a principal or stepping down to senior teacher to be in a school with over 50 percent Māori students.

I started in this school last year, 2009, and was here 2 weeks when the principal offered me the deputy principal position. She said that my pay level would have to go up, so I said that was OK. In the second term she called me into her office and said she had been thinking about a 6-month secondment into the ministry. She wanted me to act as principal. I accepted the acting position, with reservations. At the end of the 6 months she resigned as principal and took another position in the ministry. The principal's position here was advertised. I was appointed permanent principal by the school's board of trustees about a month ago.

Looking back, I did 7 years as a teacher, then 1 year as principal of a sole-charge school and then less than a year here as a senior teacher before being appointed permanent principal. Everyone said 'Don't go to a sole-charge school. That's a lot of work'. The challenge for me was the professional and cultural isolation. I had gone from a city school with over 300 children to a school with 10 kids. I absolutely loved the teaching. It was also my first time at teaching senior level. You could see every student every day, spend quality time with them and when you set work, it was always finished. The senior kids were of similar ability and so were the juniors, so they were grouped for learning.

While I loved the teaching, the professional isolation was difficult. There was no one to bounce your ideas off. The nearest school was 20 minutes away. The school is on a back road halfway between the lakes and the coast. The community was very different. In the third term my board of trustees resigned so I worked with a commissioner in the fourth term.

At the end of the year it seemed to me that the board had not looked after me. I had done my job but the board of trustees had not done theirs. From the beginning the board gave me the impression that I was an outsider coming in. I didn't live in the community; I stayed in the schoolhouse for two terms, but it didn't work for me, so I moved back home and commuted. It was a 45-minute drive each way. Most of the Māori children in the area went to a nearby bilingual school. When I started the sole-charge position, there were two Māori children in the school, but they moved when their parents got a farming contract in another area. The sole-charge school had an all-Pakeha community and I was able to make some positive connections with many of them. The key issue I had at this school was having to work with a very small board of trustees who wanted to have 'more say' in management than I thought was appropriate.

The school community here is lovely, much more open. They were ready for a change in principals. The communication here seems to be good, and it's getting even better after two terms. It is partly because they have gotten used to me and how I do things. Also they have seen that I am an effective teacher.

In hindsight I always go back to the fact that the board at the sole-charge school was all women, the middle-aged, white females (MWFs) who loved to tell me how to do my job. We had trouble with communication so I brought it up as an issue with the chairperson. As with any issue I raised, it was very different when it was discussed later at a board meeting. After some discussion among themselves, the board chair and the treasurer said that I had the communication problem. They did not want to work on our communication and resigned.

A commissioner was appointed by the ministry, and that worked out very well; he was a really nice guy. At the end of the year it was obvious that the board members who had resigned were going to move their children to other schools. In discussions with the commissioner he advised me that my own future should be my priority. He explained that if I found another position, the children who were left, and the community, would get over it. There was a teacher in the community who had applied when I applied for the principal's position. She did not have what they wanted, that is, junior school experience. She did live in the community and had been commuting to a city school. The commissioner put her in as an acting principal when I resigned, and it turned out to be a good solution. Fifteen months down the track I believe the school still does not have a board of trustees and the commissioner is still in place.

My attitude to the whole experience at the sole-charge school was always 'What have I learned from this?' Coming here and stepping up into the acting principal's position meant making sure that my communication was effective so that the same thing didn't happen again. Before I went to the sole-charge school I thought my communication was pretty good. At the end of that year I had to say to myself, 'Was it as good as you thought? Could you have done things differently?' The experience created doubts and I carried those doubts through to my current job and worked really hard at building networks. Maybe they were right. There were a couple of things that I would now do differently. But overall, I always put children's learning first in my decisions.

Looking back, there were many signs of successful communication at the sole-charge school. The board was only three people. Initially it was four, but when the Māori family left, one of the Māori trustees left. When it came to decisions, it was always two versus one. My communication issues were with the board chair, but the treasurer always chose to follow her. They would always back each other, even if one of them was wrong.

I learned that communication and trust between a board chair and a principal must be highly effective. They have to be open with each other. The chair of the board at this school walks in and always asks if I have any issues. Sometimes I ask him if he has any issues. The communication is always open. We always go back to the line between governance and management. In my interview they asked me where the line is, and I said 'It changes'. You always have to go back to agreeing where the line is on each issue so there is no misunderstanding. It's helpful that half of the board at this school is men. They seem to be more focused on their own individual roles and on getting things done. They don't meddle in others' responsibilities.

I always wanted to be a teacher. When I was 17 I promised my father that I would be a teacher. I assumed that all parents in the 1970s wanted their kids to become teachers because that was looked upon as being quite a good career. I had got my university entrance by then and promised my dad that I would become a teacher. But I didn't. I did some of this and some of that, everything else except teaching. My mum and dad were both farming people. My father was also very clever, a justice of the peace, a toastmaster, an articulate man of the land. He was a *kaumatua* (elder) and chairman of the *marae* (meeting place) in the days when everything was based around the *marae*. He was comfortable dealing with all types of people, even politicians. So the promise was always with me, and after 'mucking about' for a number of years, I finally said to my husband when I was in my 30s, 'I want to go and do my teacher training. If I don't do it before I am 40, I will never do it.'

The decision was also triggered by a sense of security. Our children were older and the oldest had left home. We were more secure. Our relationship was good. Our family relationships and finances were good. We were comfortable. Then I remembered that I had made a promise to Dad.

I always thought I would make a good teacher. My sister had trained several years earlier as a secondary teacher, and I could see how much she enjoyed teaching. It was a significant shift because I gave up a full-time job with the Inland Revenue Department (IRD). When I told the other staff in the IRD that I was leaving to do teacher training, many of them said that they had dreamed about having other careers. They had all these things that they really wanted to do in their heads that they did not follow through on. Some of them are still there!

I gradually realized that I wanted to offer leadership as I went through the steps of accepting more and more responsibility. I went to my first school as a beginning teacher and stayed there for 7 years. I worked my way up. I became a team leader, a senior teacher and it got to the stage when I felt that I had to get out of my little comfort zone, where I knew all the procedures, processes and the kids. When I had been in my first school for about 3 years the chairperson on the board of trustees (BOT) encouraged me to stand as the staff representative. I did that for 4 years and loved it. I realized that I was learning more and more about how a school runs. If that woman had not told me to go on the BOT, I probably would not have considered principalship.

After 7 years I felt the need to get out, spread my wings, make my own mistakes and learn from them. I realized that in a big school one of the rewards you get for working well is more work. I was doing all this extra work and the benefits were going somewhere else. I used to think that the one who is getting the pats on the back is not me! It's the one at the top! I love teaching, and I'm not afraid of hard work, so I decided that I would give the principal role a try.

I expected leadership to be scary. Initially I thought that you had to know everything. I thought I could not be a principal because you have to know everything, and all I know is how to teach. That is why I chose a small school to start. I thought, 'I can't do much damage if it is such a small school!' I knew it would mean hard work, but I was used to that.

I didn't really prepare for my sole-charge principalship. I just went in and started teaching. There was no systematic induction into being a sole-charge principal. I arranged a visit to my new class in December 2007 before I came in the new year as principal. I visited the school in January. There was no induction. No meeting with the board of trustees. It was 'turn up on the first day and start'. I turned up a week early, organized teaching resources and tidied up the staff room and moved the library. My induction was tidying up the school and putting resources back where they were supposed to be.

It was great in the first term. I was focused on setting up learning programmes and getting to know the kids. In the second term I had these little niggling doubts that things weren't right. By the third term I knew that the state of communication between the chair of the board and myself was not right. I had two options: to let things carry on as they were or insist on change. That is when I decided to express my concerns to the board chair. The governance relationship was not working and it needed to work well so that I could do my job well. Honest communication was missing in the school culture. When decisions were made and agreements reached, what happened in reality was different. We never seemed to discuss the mismatch. I was looking for honesty in communication, agreements and implementation.

For example, we had a parent-teachers' association. It was run by the parents to raise funds for school projects and resources. My husband and I supported these fundraising events, sometimes standing out in the cold all day. After the event the funds raised were put into a separate bank account controlled by the parent group. They would not release money to help with learning resources and programmes. We were scrimping to buy teaching materials while they sat on $20,000, doing nothing. When I asked for meeting minutes and bank statements, they did not have any. I went to the board chair but she refused to intervene.

One board member, a forceful lady, would come into school on 'board business'. Her daily presence on site was unnecessary and during these periods she took to giving advice on teaching and other events. I felt that she was not doing her job but telling me how to do mine. She kept interfering in my management decisions. She had crossed the line from governance to become a school manager. I asked her not to do this. I also asked the chair to speak to her about her role. The chair said, 'I can't. She is my friend.'

When I first arrived at my current school, my impression was that the boundary between governance and management was very strict, very formal. I learned the word 'territory'. The previous principal and I had a good relationship, but there was always an underlying feeling that things would always be done 'her way'. At the time it seemed to me to be a power thing.

I am now much more informal as principal, more flexible. If anything, this has improved the relationships between myself, the community and the board of trustees. Honesty is more evident. For example, even when I was acting principal, I mentioned to the principal that 'the board would be silly to let her go on another temporary secondment because it was about improving her career, not students' learning'. However, it became clear that they were happy for her to go and to give her leave for a second secondment. In the end she decided to resign. These discussions showed me that there was a high level of trust and openness between us as leaders. If there is respectful and honest communication, then it takes you through any misunderstandings that arise.

Professional development helped me but always came after my appointments. When I was appointed the school literacy leader at my first school, I went on several day-long workshops that helped a lot. I did not have any professional preparation for leadership. Once I had started at my sole-charge school I did the First Time Principals (FTP) Programme. It was very interesting. You received support from the school support services, access to a mentor and attended two 3-day workshops in Auckland with other first-time principals. The groups at the workshops were based on the size of your school so we could discuss common issues. The keynote speakers presented research findings, and we followed up with group discussions. I was given a great mentor, and the networking was very helpful. Some of these friendships are still going. One of the principals in my group brought her sole-charge school to visit us here last year when I was acting principal. It was awesome. The kids loved it.

The aspects of the FTP that really worked well were the workshops, the mentoring and the networking. The aspect that was not effective was school support. I saw my school support person twice in the whole year, but I had to go to her. She never visited my school. She was always busy, probably with too much to do. If I wanted to discuss anything, because we lived in the same city, it was easier for me to drop in to her office. But she was often 'tied up' and 'booked out' for weeks. One barrier at my last school was that it was often difficult to get relievers to come into the sole-charge school. It meant that I missed out on some professional development that would have been really useful.

After I had been appointed here as a senior teacher I did the Aspiring Leaders course run by experienced principals for the local principals association. The course has four 1-day workshops spread over a year. They cover basic management and leadership issues. I enjoyed reinforcing what I already learned from the FTP workshops, picking up tips from other leaders who had been through visioning processes and strategic planning. The networking was again very helpful.

Being 'the boss' leads me to think a lot about what sort of a boss I am. Above all I try to be fair. Fairness means teachers knowing what I expect and why and, at the end of the day, being able to relate expectations back to student achievement, student learning, safety and welfare. If teachers come to me and say, 'Keita, this is what I want to do, this is why I want to do it and they can show me how students will benefit, then I usually say "Go for it!" ' At the end of the learning experience I expect them to come back to me and explain what worked and what didn't.

The teachers tell me that the change from strict to interactive professionalism means they have greater freedom to think outside the square and to try approaches that they would not have tried before. I often say, 'I don't know if it's going to work but we are going to give it a go.' Teachers change slowly. We are getting there. There is still some territorialism over resources but more thinking about using resources to help learning. There is only one teacher left from 2 years ago, so the old strict culture is going. The new teachers collaborate easily in the new culture. Parents have responded to the changes by saying that there is a different atmosphere around the school. The kids are happier. It used to be "Sit up straight", "Don't move" and the parents felt that that was unnecessary. We have an 'Ag Day' (Agriculture Day) here. After my first Ag Day the board chair said, 'I am sick and tired of hearing all about you. All I have had is parents telling me how wonderful you are.'

The cultural change has also freed up the communication of complaints. I had two parents come in separately to provide feedback on a young teacher. They took their issues to the board chair, who sent them to me. I listened, along with a board member who was there with the permission of the parents. The issue was about a very good beginning teacher who did not yet have all the strategies, knowledge and behaviour management skills she needed to teach efficiently. When I provided a summary for the teacher, she asked, 'How can they say that when they have not been in my room?' We assumed that a teacher's aide was passing on criticisms to other parents. Comments made by the parents included 'the kids have too much fun!' The teacher and I discussed some simple strategies to fill in some of the gaps in her experience. I have gotten better at carrying criticism back to colleagues. When dealing with parents and teachers, it's best to let them have their say, so they 'get it off their chest', and then collaborate with them to make improvements.

When I arrived here I was the stranger. I was soon a deputy boss, but my authority was ambiguous. The longest-serving staff member had the greatest difficulty with this, claiming not to know who was in charge. The secondment was only 0.8, so 'the boss' came in on Fridays. The boss and I had distributed portfolios, so we were clear on responsibilities, and all the staff were in the loop, but this teacher saved up her questions for the boss on Fridays. The principal asked her why she had not raised them with me during the week, and she claimed to be confused. She was pleading ignorance, but it might have been game playing.

The biggest policy issue we hear about at the moment is national standards. The government and the ministry want us to match student learning against benchmarks and report on this at specific times each year. The purpose of this is to enforce evidence-based teaching and reporting. Part of the problem with this is that students in a year group have a wide range of abilities, needs and outcomes and teachers need to learn how to make appropriate professional judgements. Another part of the problem is that teachers have doubts because there have been no trials nationally that have shown evidence of success in using national standards. A third concern is that the emphasis on standards distracts the government and the ministry from the need to provide appropriate learning resources. It also distracts attention from the need to improve the quality of teaching – investment in professional development is needed to respond to the outcomes of reporting. For me it means helping my teachers come to grips with reporting against national standards while they are still learning about the 'new' national curriculum that came out in 2007.

My big successes as a principal in this school have been in identifying the children's needs and the gaps in learning, by testing and visiting classrooms and using my experience. This has led to a much more exciting curriculum and improvements in teaching, such as education outside the classroom, to visit 'the world out there'. The two new teachers will help speed up this process. When I got here, the evaluation data stayed in a bag. It was not used to identify needs, gaps and students' next learning steps. I have introduced an 'evidence book' so that we log test data and keep running records on each child's progress.

The biggest challenge I have is that my teachers are just getting their heads around the New Zealand Curriculum launched 3 years ago, while the government is insisting that we also report learning progress against new national standards. We will get there, but it will take time. In all this, my greatest hope is that the kids will get to where they should be. As long as I can say I have done my best, then it will have to do. I benchmark everything using evidence of student achievement.

Note

1   A Decile 1 school has children from areas with the lowest 10 percent socioeconomic status (SES) in New Zealand. Decile 10 schools have children from the areas with the highest 10 percent of SES status. Decile rankings are used to adjust the distribution of resources to New Zealand schools as a form of positive discrimination.

Part 2
Americas

Leadership Based in Love of People and Place: A Novice Principal in an Economically Poor Community in Texas, United States

4

Sarah W. Nelson and Israel Aguilar meet with a novice principal in an economically poor community in Texas, United States

Chapter outline

Although technically two separate towns, Karl, Texas, and Kate, Texas (United States) are one community. In 1940 Karl-Kate was a centre for agriculture. Located in the rich farmlands of the Rio Grande Valley near the Texas-Mexico border, the area boomed with economic growth and was known as the 'Wonder Town of the Valley'. Citrus fruit, vegetables and cotton were shipped from Karl-Kate to other regions on the SA&AP Railroad. But years of bad crops, hurricanes, fires, economic recessions and an expressway built 12 miles south of the town contributed to the town's decline. Today, Karl-Kate is one of the economically poorest communities in Texas. More than half the population of 3,000 lives below the poverty line, and the businesses and industries that once provided jobs are now gone. Even the railroad ceased operations in 2000.

In spite of the economic decline, Karl-Kate is a community rich in cultural capital. Almost the entire population can trace their ancestry to Mexico, which lies just 15 miles south. Many families have lived in the area since Texas was part of Mexico. Other families have come as immigrants to work the fields and packing plants that supported the way of life in the valley. Mexican-Americans have been the backbone of the region since before there was a Karl-Kate, and this collective tie to Mexico creates a distinct sense of connectedness within the community.

Yet, until recently the political and economic structures of Karl-Kate were controlled by White businessmen and farmers. Although the area was once part of Mexico, the United States took control of the region in 1848 following the Mexican-American War. The land was sparsely populated and used primarily for ranching until the early 1900s when speculators began acquiring large parcels and promoting the area to settlers in northern states. In spite of the fact that it is a delta, they called the area the Rio Grande Valley, and thanks to irrigation, the once desert-like ranch land was sold for farming. Lured by the promotion, European immigrants flocked to the area. One settler purchased land and started a town named in honour of his wife, Kate. After learning that the SA&AP railway intended to run a line to the lower Rio Grande Valley, the settler began lobbying the rail company to run the line through Kate. Another settler similarly lobbied to have the railroad come through the town of Karl, which he had founded just east of Kate. Their efforts were successful. The Falfurrias to Brownsville line of the SA&AP ran through Kate and made a stop in Karl. The railway secured the future of Karl-Kate.

Karl-Kate continued to grow through the 1960s, in large part due to the system of racial segregation that was built into the foundation of the community. In planning for development of Karl-Kate, the area north of the railroad was designated for Anglos. White farmers and business owners were allowed to develop this area and build homes there. The area south of the railroad, which had no paved roads or utilities, was for Mexican-Americans and other non-Anglos. A few businesses in this section catered to Latinos, but most commerce occurred north of the railway. Homes in the Mexican-American community were crudely built tin structures with no running water or electricity. Latinos were permitted to do business and work in the white section of town, but were legally forbidden to occupy any building north of the rail line. When they went north, Latinos had to return south of the railroad before dusk or face arrest. Although not enforced in recent decades, this law was not officially repealed until 2008.

When Karl joined with the nearby town of Kate to create a public school system in 1929, the practice of segregation was reflected in the schools. White students in Karl went to a newly built brick elementary school while Mexican-American children went to school in converted army barracks. A similar disparity existed for elementary school students in Kate. Because there was only one high school in the Karl-Kate district, it was technically an integrated school. However, few Latino students made it to high school. Not only was the education in the Mexican-American school substandard, but because much of the work available to Latino families was migratory farming, Mexican-American children often missed months of school. In spite of this being a prevalent condition, little was done to modify the schedule or in any way address the needs of migrant students. As a result, most Mexican-American children in Karl-Kate were undereducated and had few options other than to become migrant farm workers themselves.

By the mid-1940s, under a directive from the Texas State Superintendent of Instruction, Mexican-American students who could pass an English test were allowed to enrol in the white elementary schools. While many Mexican-American students took advantage of this opportunity, many more were trapped in the army barracks where the Anglo teachers taught students just enough English to interact with Anglo business and land owners, but not enough English to allow them entry into the white school. In this way, the public school system ensured that racial segregation and economic oppression were continually woven into the fabric of the community.

Even after the 1954 U.S. Supreme Court Case, *Brown v. the Board of Education,* which outlawed racial segregation in public schools, Karl-Kate maintained separate schools for whites and Mexican-Americans. However, the Latino population of Karl grew to such proportion that increasingly more

Mexican-Americans made it to the high school. However, the discrimination continued there. Latino students were routinely punished for speaking Spanish, openly humiliated by teachers, tracked into low-level classes and discouraged from applying for college even when they had outstanding academic records (Guajardo and Guajardo, 2004). By 1968, conditions reached a tipping point. After months of organizing, students staged a walkout. More than 150 students left the school that day and did not return until 2 days later. The walkout caused considerable upheaval in the community. The school administration used every available resource to identify each of the participants and subsequently expelled them. The students filed suit on grounds that their First Amendment rights had been violated. In December of that year, a federal judge ruled in favour of the students, and Karl was forever changed.

The 1968 walkout signalled the beginning of a power shift. Anglos began to move away from Karl-Kate towards Weslaco, a nearby town that not only had a larger white population, but also the advantage of being on a major highway. Shipping and transportation by rail had already begun to decline as better roads made travel by car and truck a viable option. As the Anglos left Karl-Kate, so, too, did the businesses they owned and the jobs they offered. Some Mexican-American families followed the work. Those who remained were left to create new government and economic structures for the community. With limited financial resources and an undereducated population, the challenge was significant. Nonetheless, two decades later, new forms of commerce are beginning to emerge and young adults are assuming leadership positions in city and county government. The community is still awash in economic poverty, but there are signs that a different future is possible.

It is within this context that Xavier Rios[1] works as a principal. Karl-Kate is a unique setting in that it's located in a particular place with a particular history. Texas itself is a distinctive state within the United States. It has an unmistakable culture and history that sets it apart from other states. Within Texas, the Rio Grande Valley is a distinct region. Yet, in many ways Karl-Kate is not so different from the thousands of rural communities across the United States in which novice principals find themselves. The history of opportunistic settlers creating communities based on racial oppression is common, as is the practice of abandoning those communities when political and economic and power structures begin to shift. In these rural communities, school leaders play a central role in reimagining the community. In this way, Xavier Rios's story is both unique and common.

An early path

Within a few years of the 1968 walkout, Xavier Rios entered the Karl-Kate public schools. The youngest son of migrant field workers, Xavier lived in a modest home on the Mexican-American side of town. Although he travelled with his family to work the fields and often missed school, Xavier knew education was important. His eldest brothers went to school during the 1960s when few Mexican-Americans made it through high school. They continued their education by joining the military and earning certification as law enforcement officials. Xavier saw them as role models. Conditions in the schools had shifted somewhat by the time Xavier entered high school, but Mexican-Americans continued to face discrimination by teachers. Systemic barriers worked against the academic achievement of Xavier and other Latino students. Xavier watched many of his friends become discouraged with school and choose other paths. Xavier knew leaving school was not an option for him. His family expected him to complete high school and go on to college. While it seemed to be destiny that his older brothers went into law enforcement, Xavier and his siblings and cousins who were closer to his age went on to become educators.

For Xavier, the goal was to not only be a teacher, but one day a principal. This path was set the day Xavier met his high school principal, Joe Ramirez. Mr Ramirez was the kind of principal who knew his students well. He used this knowledge to connect with students and inspire them to do more. He encouraged them to join clubs or sports teams to ensure they stayed involved and on the right path. For Xavier, this meant joining the debate team. One afternoon during Xavier's freshmen year, Mr Ramirez approached Xavier in the lunch line and said, 'You are going to debate camp this summer, aren't you, Xavier?' Wondering how Mr Ramirez knew of his interest in debate and believing that no one ever said no to Mr Ramirez, Xavier agreed that he would go to debate camp. And Mr Ramirez made sure he did. By the time Xavier was a senior, he had participated on the debate team for 3 years and was a skilled debater. He was grateful to Mr Ramirez for encouraging him to join the team and he knew debate skills would help him in college and in his chosen profession. More importantly, the attention and care Mr Ramirez gave to Xavier conveyed a confidence in Xavier's potential for success.

Being a humble man, Mr Ramirez did not always understand the impact he had on students. Xavier recalls standing in the cafeteria one day during his senior year of high school. Xavier saw Mr Ramirez wearing a letterman jacket with *principal* embroidered on it. Xavier told Mr Ramirez, 'One of these days I'm going to have one just like that.' A few weeks later, Mr Ramirez handed Xavier a letterman jacket with an emblem signifying the debate team. Appreciative of the gift, Xavier did not know how to tell Mr Ramirez that it was not recognition for his participation on the debate team that he sought. Rather, Xavier intended to one day wear a jacket emblazoned with the word *principal.*

Following high school graduation, Xavier enrolled in a teacher education programme at a university not far from Karl-Kate. After 4 years of study, Xavier returned to the Karl-Kate schools to teach. He became a middle school reading teacher in the very school he had attended. Some of his former teachers were now his colleagues. Because the school had recently shifted from a junior high school to a middle school model and Xavier had received training in middle grade education at the university, Xavier was soon asked to help train other teachers. Xavier felt empowered by this opportunity, although it meant negotiating the sometimes precarious terrain of facilitating professional learning for teachers who had many more years in the classroom than he did. This experience of working with more seasoned educators was an aspect Xavier would later draw on when he became a principal.

Xavier remained in the classroom for 12 years before being asked to serve as a formal teacher facilitator. In this role, Xavier provided support to teachers as they worked to improve their instructional skills in reading. It was as a facilitator that Xavier came to understand how to be an instructional leader. Working with teachers from kindergarten through grade 12, Xavier was able to see student learning from beginning to end and how teachers impact this learning. This experience inspired Xavier to pursue his goal of becoming a principal. Returning to the university where he had done his teacher preparation, Xavier earned a master's degree and principal certification.

In spite of having married and moved 20 miles away to his wife's hometown, Xavier continued working in Karl-Kate after completing his administrator credentials. For his first administrative job, Xavier was offered a position as an assistant principal at the junior high school. Xavier felt he had been well prepared for this job. In addition to the outstanding academic preparation he received at the university, he had several years of practical experience in the classroom and as an instructional facilitator. The principal Xavier was working with gave him wide latitude to work in all areas of school leadership. Xavier took advantage of this. He implemented new academic programmes. He addressed student discipline. He provided coaching and mentoring to teachers. He worked with parents, and he made suggestions for ways to improve the functions of the school. This array of opportunities gave Xavier insight into the principalship. After 12 years in the classroom, 2 years as an instructional facilitator, and 3 years as an assistant principal, Xavier felt he was ready to lead a school of his own. The superintendent agreed. When the principal of the junior high school left, Xavier was appointed to the position.

The school and community context

Trevino[2] Junior High School is a utilitarian structure reflective of a pragmatic approach to school architecture. High-set windows dot the cinderblock walls, allowing only ambient light into the hallways. Asbestos tile floors and neat rows of desks suggest classrooms from decades past. In contrast, digital projectors, interactive whiteboards and laptop computers reveal these are contemporary learning spaces. This juxtaposition of old and new, traditional and innovative, characterizes Trevino. With limited financial resources, the school must be judicious in selecting instructional materials. Purchases are made with years of utility in mind, and careful attention is paid to avoid wasting precious discretionary monies on what may be a passing educational fad. The technology and other innovative instructional tools found in Trevino's classrooms were purchased through grant-funded initiatives aimed at addressing educational inequity for Trevino's nearly 800 students, almost all of whom are Latino and economically poor.

Having worked at Trevino for several years as an assistant principal, Xavier was familiar with the school, the programmes and the students. He knew the district faced tremendous challenges, including financial exigency that led to the termination of nearly 20 percent of district personnel the previous year and the removal of the superintendent for alleged fiscal mismanagement. He knew an increasing number of students needed specialized educational services and that the issue of educating the children of migrant workers had never been adequately addressed. He also knew the district was not likely to get an influx of new resources to aid with these concerns anytime soon.

Moreover, because Xavier had lived in the community his entire life, he understood the social conditions that affected students and families. He knew, for instance, that many of his students lived in extreme poverty in the *colonias* near the border with Mexico. Built on floodplains and otherwise undesirable areas, *colonias* lack infrastructure for basic services such as water, sewer and, in many cases, electricity. Most homes in the *colonias* are owner-built and constructed in stages as materials become available. Government agencies pay little attention to whether the homes meet building standards or safety codes and show little concern for ensuring people in the *colonias* have access to basic services. Lack of potable water and sewer services create conditions ripe for disease. With few medical facilities nearby, *colonia* residents often suffer chronically from treatable conditions. For many children who live in the *colonias*, health-care services are limited to those they receive through school. The school lunch programme is also the primary source of food for many children in the *colonias*. In this way, Trevino serves as much more than a provider of education. Students and families depend on Trevino to survive. Yet, getting to school can be a challenge. When the area receives heavy rains, as it does during certain periods of the year, the unpaved roads become impassible and students must walk through ankle-deep mud to reach the school bus stop.

Other social issues affect the community as well. Karl-Kate sits along what the U.S. Drug Enforcement Agency (DEA) considers a major pathway for illegal drugs entering the United States. Certain homes in the community are rumoured to belong to drug runners. DEA raids are not uncommon. DEA agents warn school officials and parents that drug runners are constantly recruiting youth and are increasingly targeting children under the age of 10.

Close proximity to the border also places Karl-Kate on the path of immigrants moving north from Mexico and Central America. Border Patrol agents are a constant presence in the community, searching for those who cross the border without government authorization. The Border Patrol's unmistakable vehicles, distinctive green uniforms and visible weapons send a clear message that the community is under surveillance. Many Karl-Kate residents came across the border without authorization in search of jobs and educational opportunities for their children. Even those who are not immigrants themselves typically have family members who are. The presence of the Border Patrol has long been a way of life in Karl-Kate, as has movement of people back and forth between Mexico and the United States. But in recent years, anti-immigration policies, antiterrorism efforts and violence from drug wars have made crossing the border in either direction a much riskier proposition. This has created an unsettling climate, as nearly everyone in the community has ties on both sides of the border.

Xavier was aware of all of these conditions, any one of which creates particular challenges for educating children and youth. Yet, when Xavier received a call from the district superintendent requesting that he cut short his summer vacation and return to work so that he could immediately assume the principalship of Trevino, Xavier did not hesitate. While not ignoring the challenges, Xavier knew that the assets in the school and the community far outweighed the challenges. Xavier had known that he wanted to be a principal since he was a senior in high school. Seventeen years later he was finally getting his chance in the same community that had nurtured his growth from a young migrant farm worker to a professional educator. And it was in Karl-Kate that he would realize his dream of becoming a school principal.

Assets

One of Trevino's strongest assets is its teacher core. Most of the teachers in the Karl-Kate district have many years of experience. Like Xavier, most are from the community and grew up in conditions similar to those their students live in. This gives the teachers a distinct advantage because they can relate to the students and their families and can build on shared experiences to enhance learning. Moreover, the teachers serve as a living example of the difference education can make in a person's life.

The families of Karl-Kate are also an asset. Most Karl-Kate families have few economic resources, but they have deep and abiding love for family and community. This love means that children are well cared for and parents sacrifice to provide children with what they need, including an education. Although many families depend on migrant farm work as the primary source of income, and even young children may be employed in the fields, families increasingly make the decision to allow school-age children to remain at home so they may attend school regularly. Evidence of this is seen the district's attendance rate, which is consistently higher than the state average.

The students themselves are also an asset. Having come from generations of migrant field workers who work in extreme conditions, a strong work ethic is an inherent characteristic of Karl-Kate students. Xavier asserts hard work is in their blood; they have the *ganas* to succeed. And, Karl-Kate students have succeeded in impressive ways. In the early 1990s, two Karl-Kate high school teachers who were frustrated by the fact that so few of their students went to college began a programme to help students access higher education. The teachers talked to the students and their families not only about nearby universities, but also about Ivy League institutions. The teachers helped students complete applications and took them to visit colleges. They developed a strategy whereby several students in a particular graduating class would apply to the same university and attend college as a group to establish a support system. The strategy worked. Over the next 10 years, more than 60 Karl-Kate students became graduates of the most prestigious universities in the United States. Many of them have returned to Karl-Kate and are leading the revitalization of the community. Some are teaching in Xavier's school.

The first year

Being appointed to the principalship just weeks before the fall term started meant Xavier had to hit the ground running. He had to ensure staff positions were filled, students were registered and assigned to appropriate classes, classrooms were stocked and all the systems and facilities were in working order. There was much to do, but Xavier felt he was well prepared. Between the coursework he had taken and his years of experience, Xavier thought he understood the job of the principal. Add to that the fact that he was assigned to a campus with which he was intimately familiar, and Xavier had the perfect setup for success as a novice principal. However, what Xavier found was that although he was as prepared as anyone could be, he could not fully understand what it means to be a principal until he was in that role. Xavier soon learned there are aspects to the job that cannot be seen except from the principal's chair. As an assistant principal, Xavier was involved in all facets of school leadership and worked closely with the principal. He felt that in many ways, he and the principal equally shared responsibility for the school's leadership. When the principal left and Xavier took over the position, he did not anticipate a significant change. He thought he would slide seamlessly into the principalship. Xavier quickly learned there is a distinct difference between being an assistant principal and being *the* principal. Although he was performing many of the same duties he had as assistant principal, there was a greater level of responsibility and an entire realm to the principalship with which he was unfamiliar.

Constant conversation

In particular, Xavier was surprised that so much of his time was spent providing individualized support to faculty members. There seemed to always be a teacher waiting outside his door to speak with him and another requesting an appointment. Xavier could easily spend his entire day engaged in conversation with faculty. As an assistant principal and instructional facilitator, Xavier was used to talking to teachers. But conversations in those roles centred on how to improve classroom practice or how to address student discipline issues. The conversations he was having with faculty now were different. They were much more personal and tended to focus on larger and more long-term issues, such as career planning, goals for the future and earning advanced degrees. In addition, although the conversations were about professional issues, they often involved personal matters. Xavier found himself privy to a level of information about the faculty he had never had before. At times he wondered why faculty shared so much with him and felt a bit uncomfortable being the recipient of such information. These were people he had known for years, and yet, he had not known them in the ways he was getting to know them as a principal. He had new insights that helped him to better understand the people he was working with. He also understood that the faculty was look-ing at him in a new way as well. Xavier discovered that the principalship is a unique position and part of the uniqueness is that faculty and staff see the principal as an advisor and confidant. Although not a role he had anticipated, Xavier embraced it. As teachers came to him, Xavier listened, offered reassur-ance and gave guidance. In this way, Xavier expanded his understanding of what it means to be a principal.

From peer to principal

Because Xavier had spent his entire professional life in Karl-Kate schools, he had an established relationship with almost every person on the Trevino campus. He had served as the assistant principal for 3 years. Prior to that, he was a teacher colleague with some of the faculty. In a few cases, Xavier had even been a student in teachers' classrooms. To move into the role of being principal to former peers is not easy. There can be resistance on the part of some faculty to accepting leadership and direction from a former peer. The new principal can also be too forceful in asserting himself as the leader. This combination of resistance and force can create significant tension that detracts from the work. Yet, Xavier smoothly negotiated this transition in large part due to the approach he took. Standing before the teachers in one of the first faculty meetings he held as principal, Xavier acknowledged the contributions the teachers made to his development as an educator:

> I feel like they have not changed. The one who has changed is me. Some have said, 'I remember you as my student and now you are my boss.' That is more of

a compliment. I also compliment them back and say, 'I couldn't have been here without you putting forth your effort'. I have said in meetings that I was prepared. I was an excellent reader and writer. I learned math, and I attributed it to all the staff we have here. I saw my first grade teacher substituting for us the other day and I thanked her.

Xavier also believed it helped that he knew from an early age that he wanted to be a principal. Throughout his career, he was mindful of the kind of leader he aspired to be and he worked to develop the knowledge, skills and disposition to become this kind of leader. He did not want to be the kind of leader people feared. Rather, he wanted to be the kind of leader people wanted to work with and felt confident following. At each stage of his career he tended to relationships and his own growth and he tried to act in ways that were consistent with his notions of effective leadership. Perhaps most importantly, he recognized that he was in a leadership position from the beginning when he was a new teacher helping to train experienced teachers. He did not wait to become a leader. He was a leader in every position he held.

It depends on how you conducted yourself beforehand. Since I was 18 I always knew what I wanted to be so, I conducted myself as a peer leader. I did not boss people around. When I worked with teachers, we did implement that team system where everyone had responsibility and you knew everyone's potential. You knew their faults and their work habits and their positives. So it goes back to emphasising those positives and eliminating those negatives. It's something unstated 'I know what you are capable of doing and I expect you to really work at that high level' as opposed to 'I know what you are capable of not doing and I don't expect that from you.' So there is advice to give out to someone going into the administrative field. It's know exactly what you want to get into and conduct yourself in that way because by the time it is time to lead your peers, you have already led them.

Xavier believes that because he conducted himself in this way, the prior relationships he had with the faculty and staff helped him in his first year as principal. He attributes the success he had to the trust he and the teachers shared. Because they trusted one another and they already knew him as a leader, he and the teachers were able to be honest about their needs and how these needs converged. According to Xavier, 'It all just fell into place' and set a positive tone for school culture.

Collaboration as a cornerstone

Building on the relationships he had with the faculty and staff, Xavier encouraged teachers to work collaboratively. He knew from his work as an instructional facilitator that without purposeful attention to creating a climate of collaboration among teachers, a divisive and competitive culture would likely form. He wanted to avoid having cliques of teachers work in isolation from one another. Xavier intentionally created opportunities for teachers to work together and put systems in place that gave the teachers authentic pathways for collaboration. He also modelled collaboration as a leadership style. Although he 'took hold of the reins' when this was required, he did so sparingly. He gave the teachers license to make instructional decisions and sought their input as much as possible on matters that affected their work and the school as a whole. He attributed much of the academic improvement the school experienced in his first year to this collaborative approach, which pretty much helped him to 'set the tone for the culture and helped us implement initiatives from one day to the next with ease'.

A work ethic formed in the fields

Hard work also plays an important role in Xavier's leadership style. As a child who travelled with his family to labour long hours in fields far from home, the notion of what it means to work hard is seared into Xavier's being. He knows that his life is different not only because he has worked hard and proven himself, but also because generations of his *familia* paved the way for him to have a different life. Xavier feels the weight of this responsibility. He understands that working a 12- or 15-hour day in an air-conditioned office is nothing compared to picking cotton in the scorching Texas heat. Many nights you will find Xavier in the office until 10:00 p.m. and back again at 7:00 a.m. the next morning. But Xavier also knows his parents and grandparents did not sacrifice so that he could spend his life in an office. Family first means Xavier is conscious to routinely leave the office at a reasonable hour so he can be home with his wife and children. This is important not only for Xavier's family, but also as a model for the Trevino teachers and staff. They, too, have parents and grandparents who sacrificed so that they might escape fieldwork. Building a culture that honours the previous generations means finding a way to balance the many responsibilities of running a school with the most important responsibility – *familia*.

Leading forward

Xavier knows the history of Karl-Kate and he knows the community is in the midst of an important shift. The schools will play an essential role in helping the community envision a new future. Xavier is both inspired and somewhat overwhelmed by this.

> What I'm seeing is that a lot of society's needs are being addressed by school now. We are becoming a one-stop shop for resources. Any of the community's problems we will try to solve them here. It's a big task, but it is the task of the modern school. Eventually everything hits here.

Xavier fears that the school may not have sufficient resources to address the deeper social ills, such as the drug trade, which preys on young people and lures them with better economic prospects than what the community currently has to offer in terms of jobs. At the same time, he is hopeful.

> You have to understand. Our community, like many communities around the world, it is a community with a lot of potential and only education can unlock that potential. Since most of the jobs are out of the area, people have to go and work somewhere else. A lot of times they end up moving somewhere else, and that's where we sit. But a lot of people are coming back, and we look forward to seeing the business grow and our community get better.

Xavier is hopeful not only for the community, but also for himself as a school leader. He sees himself as having found his place in the world. He is eager to continue learning and growing each year as a school leader.

> It's a really good feeling. This is really where I wanted to be. But as a principal there are still things I am learning every day. To be a successful principal, you have to take every year like it's your first. So every year, you learn something new, you try to do something better . . . . I look forward to all the challenges heading my way because there is so much more potential. I am a man of the people. The struggles that the students go through is my potential and I seek to unlock that. I hope to teach them the viable skills they need. Of course we ask that once you get those

skills, you come back and contribute to the community. It's a great feeling to contribute back. I felt I got a lot out of the district and I've come back. And if I make a difference, then to me that is success.

Notes

1   Xavier Rios is not the principal's real name.
2   Trevino is also a false name.

Reference

Guajardo, M. and Guajardo, F. (2004), 'The impact of Brown on the Brown of South Texas: a micropolitical perspective on the education of Mexican Americans in a rural South Texas community', *American Educational Research Journal*, 3, (41), 501–26.

Changing School Perspective: A Challenge for an Elementary School Director in Mexico in Her First Years

5

Gema López-Gorosave, Charles L. Slater, Susana Martínez Martínez and José María García Garduño meet with Rosa Eaton Guerrero, principal of Estado de México Elementary School

Chapter outline

The border of the Mexican state of Baja California is the most frequently crossed in the world, and the city of Tijuana is the principal point of coming and going between Mexico and the United States. Baja California is a magnet for the poorest people from central states, who arrive with the intention of crossing the border. At the same time, economic activity and scientific development thrive. Visitors and retirees are attracted from other countries. This confluence of traditions of native peoples, those from other states and those from other countries make it a cultural mosaic.

Nearly 500,000 children are in elementary education in more than 1,500 schools located around coasts, valleys, mountains and deserts; one-quarter of them were born in other places. The average level of academic achievement is slightly higher than the national average. However, the results vary widely among private and public school students, indigenous students and those who have recently migrated to the region. Private schools represent a small portion of the total number of schools, and their students score highest on national and international measures. The lack of equity in the quality of services is one of the principal educational problems. The gap has increased between private schools and public schools for indigenous students.

A scenic road along the Pacific coast connects the northern and southern regions of the state. Vacationers, long-term visitors and retirees find the section between Tijuana and Ensenada to be one of the most desired areas. The ocean and the hospitable climate are major attractions. However, the violence unleashed by organized crime is a major threat. A visitor starting at the border crosses military checkpoints and goes through three tollbooths before arriving at the port of Ensenada; it is the oldest city in the state with approximately 300,000 inhabitants and the second-largest number of Americans and Europeans after Mexico City. Ensenada also has the largest number of researchers per capita in Mexico because of the presence of universities and research centres. However, the major industry is tourism. Most arrive by car or bus and a few come on luxury liners that arrive two or three times a week. Ensenada is known nationally for the quality of wine and variety of gastronomy. It hosts the races Off Road Baja 500 and Baja 1000.

On a hill overlooking the bay is a neighbourhood that was originally populated by poor families. With the passage of time, the magnificent vista and central location transformed the character of the area. Today, the neighbourhood is a combination of luxurious houses with multiple levels and large windows along with more modest houses. Thirty-six years ago, a small elementary school was built in the centre of the area. The students come from local families of modest means as well as families from nearby areas that form a circle of abject poverty around the city. Most of the 163 students in the school suffer from educational deficits and social problems associated with poverty.

Estado de México Elementary School is encircled by a cyclone fence. It is kept clean despite the lack of water and extensive steep and irregular grounds. A small space with tables and benches provides rest and shade under two trees. There is a soccer court, a basketball court and a multipurpose cemented area. There are two buildings that house six classrooms, a library that also serves as a teachers' lounge, bathrooms, a storage room, the office and a school store. Some classrooms contain software, almost all have shelves to store materials and furniture adorned with drawings and signs. The inner office has a small desk, chairs and filing cabinet; the outside area has two desks, a large table, a copier, a computer, printer, filing cabinet and space for coffee.

There are six classroom teachers, a teacher responsible for the national reading programme who assists all classes, two physical education teachers, an administrative assistant and the director. There is also a teacher who provides administrative and teaching assistance.

Rosa Eaton Guerrero is the director of the school. She assumed responsibilities at the age of 47 after 23 years of service as a teacher, teaching consultant for the district and school and teacher trainer. She came to the position at the invitation of the school inspector who suggested that she work in the school where she served as teaching consultant because of an illness that prevented the appointed director from serving in the position.

Rosa has served for 3 years with a *comisión* that does not guarantee permanence in the position. She was able to count on the support of the school staff as she assumed the functions of school director for the first time. On a fresh, sunny day, accompanied by singing birds, the director shared her story with enthusiasm and passion.

Early life

I was born in Ensenada, but my parents were divorced, and I went to live with my grandparents in a small village near the city. My grandfather was one of the founders of the cooperative where I attended school; I was happy in the country. I developed a love of reading from my grandparents, my mother and my teachers. We had a library of 300 books in our house. I completed middle school and high school in Ensenada but continued to live in the village. After graduation, I studied accounting at the University of Tijuana, but I was still a small-town girl.

The traffic flows rapidly in Tijuana, and the customs of the people are very different from those in Ensenada. For me the contrast was enormous since I was not even raised in a small city but rather in the countryside. I lived alone in Tijuana, I was completely innocent, I saw things that did not fit with the values that I was raised with and I was afraid. I felt good in school, but not in the street. After a year and a half, I returned (without graduating); it was a family scandal that bothered my mother. Before she left for work, she got me up and said that she did not want a parasite in the house and insisted that I should study.

I was getting top grades in school, but at that time, I didn't know exactly what I wanted to do. My sister attended normal school and told me to enrol to see if I wanted to be a teacher. When I finished, I could work and pursue another career at the university.

Discovery in San Vicente

I never thought I would be a teacher. I was not a child who played the role of teacher with dolls or with my friends. My dream was to be a public accountant, but I followed my sister and entered the normal school. It wasn't bad. When I graduated, I obtained a teaching position in the village of San Vicente, south of the city. I continued to live in Ensenada and began to commute to the school each day by bus. The schedule was difficult; I had to be at the bus terminal at 5:30 a.m. and returned home at 7:30 p.m. I had to take the return bus in the afternoon because my colleagues who lived in the city left at noon before I finished teaching. After I got to know teachers in nearby schools, I was able to ride with them. Most of the time, they still didn't pay us, or if they paid us, the salary just paid for transportation. We were often delayed by field labourers working along the road and arrived late for school. Soon we learned all of the schedules and how traffic depended on the planting and harvesting seasons.

When they gave me a first grade class, I thought: what am I going to do? How will I teach them to read and write? I started to work, and I was always well prepared. I think I was innovative. I began to teach a story, analyze the sentences, words and syllables and brought in the animals of the story. December arrived and the students could not read; Holy Week arrived, and still, my children could not read. The children in the other first grade could already read. I didn't know that a method of teaching could delay student reading. The truth was that teaching was not for me; I was a failure. I thought about leaving the class. What's more, they hadn't paid me; they were 7 months behind.

When classes resumed after Holy Week, several students started to read, but not all. I was the first teacher to arrive and the last to leave; it stressed me a lot. What did I have to do to teach them all to read? When I achieved it, I felt a grand satisfaction. Then I realized the significance of my work; don't worry if I start to cry (Rosa begins to cry). When I remember and retell what happened, I become emotional. When you realize that your work has results, you feel enormous satisfaction. It doesn't matter that children, parents or the director tells you that you are the best teacher; the greatest satisfaction is when students learn. This is the value of the work.

With this experience, I discovered that I was a teacher; I discovered the beauty of the profession that brings much personal satisfaction and that there is no greater stimulation in teaching than the response of children to your efforts. I am not Catholic, but I repeat the biblical passage, 'Let the children come unto me.'

I began to excel working with groups of children; I always put in extra time working after school with children who needed help. I liked to work with students who were behind in their studies. Sometimes, my colleagues would be upset because they felt it reflected poorly on them.

I had an experience with a student in sixth grade who was passing a paper with drawings of sex organs of boys and girls. I realized that something had happened; I asked for the paper, looked at it and said to the protagonists that they had disappointed me. I began to walk towards my desk, and the children started to cry and couldn't stop. They felt that they had shown a lack of respect because they had tried to fool me with the drawings.

Rosa's educational preparation

In my third year in San Vicente, my first son was born. I decided to move as close as possible to the city. In the middle of the fourth year, I went to Escuela Maneadero in the village where I was raised. I was very happy there. I taught classes to the children of friends from my childhood. Later, they offered me a transfer to a large school with 18 teachers in Ensenada. I was the youngest; all of the teachers had extensive experience, but since I had a bachelor's degree from la Universidad Pedagógica Nacional, I earned a higher salary because of academic preparation. It was easy to teach because this school had extensive resources. The students were middle class and upper middle class. Many had parents who were professionals.

I continued to study at the Universidad Pedagógica where I did well and had excellent professors. I gained confidence and overcame my shyness. I realized that knowledge gives confidence. I graduated with honourable mention; my final paper dealt with the theme of how to teach children who have been mistreated physically and emotionally. This work drew the attention of the inspectors who invited me to be a teaching consultant in the school district. A little later, they asked me to work on the Programa Nacional para la Formación Permanente del Profesorado (National Programme for Teacher Formation).

I took the new experiences in teaching as a challenge. At the same time, I was invited to work at the normal school where I had completed my preparation. I had already changed my point of view and was convinced that the preparation of teachers was crucial to a good society. I designed in-service courses for teachers and carried out many academic and administrative activities. My professional development depended on my double commitment to teaching in elementary school and the normal school. I had to be consistent between what I taught future teachers and how I acted as a teaching consultant or director of a primary school.

I was not a born leader. I was a timid child, although I always got the highest grades. In the Universidad Pedagógica, I started to acquire tremendous confidence; I realized that knowledge gives power. The more informed you are, the more persuasive are your arguments to defend your beliefs. Here, I experienced change. I entered the university as one Rosa and left as another very different Rosa. Before, I was not able to speak in front of others. After my knowledge and mastery of subjects at the Universidad Pedagógica, I enjoyed expounding in front of my colleagues. The mastery of knowledge secured my professional confidence.

I am liberal; I formed part of the Asociación de Liberales de Ensenada where I share ideas with teachers and professionals. I like the philosophy of Comenius, [1] who says that you must teach all without reference to social class. I love books and knowledge.

The story of Jonathan

When my second child was born, I could not commit to working extra hours as a teaching consultant. I had to limit my schedule. I was responsible for visiting schools, and my official schedule specified that I would leave the school at 1:00 p.m. Nothing was further from reality. Although I really enjoyed the work, I had to set professional limits to take care of the baby. I asked for a change of schools and returned to teaching in the school that faced the problems of urban children who came from lower classes. These children lived in a port city but had not seen the ocean; their mothers worked all day Monday through Saturday and took care of the house on Sunday; most of the mothers were illiterate, and many children were on drugs.

One time I took a student named Jonathan to the doctor because his mother could not take him. He had hearing problems. When the doctor examined him, he heard noise in his stomach. Then he asked the boy if he had had breakfast.

He replied, 'Nothing.' The doctor asked him if he had eaten dinner. The boy replied, 'Nothing.' The doctor told him that he could not believe that he did not at least have a can of food in his house, but the boy said, 'No.'

The doctor asked me to communicate with the mother and explain the urgency of treating the boy. He said to take him to a hearing consultant. The mother never took him, and the boy lost his hearing. These cases hurt. The atmosphere in this school did not revolve around the children. The teachers in the school were not able to work with the parents to attend to the children. I didn't speak the same language as the teachers. It was very difficult for me to work there.

Students who have repeated a grade and are at risk of failure can participate in a programme called Atencion Preventiva y Compensatoria (Preventive and Compensatory Attention) in which they can complete two grades in 1 year. Jonathan was my student in fifth grade. The teachers in sixth grade have the last word as to whether a student advances. They asked me if he should advance to sixth, and I thought he had performed well in class and done well on the grade-level examination.

Two factors influenced what happened to Jonathan: his socioeconomic level and being held back in previous grades. However, I was completely surprised in a meeting when the two sixth grade teachers denied his admittance, saying that he was too much of a problem and that he did not have proper school materials, such as a uniform. But the strongest argument was against his mother. They said she was an ignorant person who worked in a nearby *maquiladora* and had four children each by a different father.

This really bothered me, and I responded to them that we should forget the mother because he would have her until she died. We could not continue to blame Jonathan's performance on his mother, but we should worry about how the school could help him. Unfortunately, the director supported the sixth grade teachers and decided that he would have to continue in my fifth grade class.

In May of the next year, the sixth grade teacher expelled Jonathan for a minor infraction that I don't remember. In my opinion, this student had been labelled and singled out by various teachers more for his social condition than for low achievement. I could not believe that with only days until the close of the school year, he would not obtain his elementary school certification and, most likely, would not continue his studies.

I spoke with the sixth grade teacher, and she agreed to have a conference with him. I went to his house and spoke with him about returning to the school, and he came the next morning.

Meanwhile, the school director was upset because she did not want Jonathan to continue in the school at all. We had a dispute and in the end, she acceded because I advocated for the rights of children and said I would probably make a human rights complaint. This situation could have affected my future career, but it was worth it because Jonathan was re-admitted and finished his elementary education.

Today, Jonathan no longer attends secondary school. I had anticipated this situation because he had everything going against him, his social, economic and family situation, but most of all, I think the school failed him.

Estado de Mexico Elementary School

This situation forced me to ask for a transfer to Estado de Mexico Elementary School where first, they gave me a second grade class with eight to ten students who had not yet learned to read and write. I worked hard with them and noticed the difference. In the next school year, the director assigned me to the fifth grade. There were various students who did not know how to add. I worked extra hours, as did the students, and they did well on tests on Spanish and mathematics. Afterwards, the director invited me to work as technology and teaching consultant at the school. She wanted someone who could manage plans and programmes of study, who could facilitate courses for teachers, who knew how to develop long-range plans, who could serve in her place if she became ill and who could carry out other duties. I accepted.

One problem I faced had to do with a new software programme that was delivered but not installed. Those responsible for the technology had not installed it for 3 months. Finally, when they did install it, it didn't work. For a total of 6 months, I kept insisting that they solve the problem because the school year was ending and the sixth grade students were not going to be able to use the programme, but they paid no attention.

One day I was desperate, and I mailed a letter to the president of the republic. I wrote that it was a shame to invest so much money in equipment that didn't work. To my surprise, he responded. Here I have the letter in which he ordered me to attend to it immediately (Rosa hands the letter to the interviewers). I called the technology office, and they spoke more moderately, and the next day they were solving the problem. I told the technologist that he had left me no alternative; I had talked with him on numerous occasions and he had not solved the problem.

Transition to the position of director

The director of this school had a serious health problem. She was sick for 3 years and I substituted for her. When her illness first became serious, the inspector asked me to assume responsibility for the school. At first she made a verbal offer, and then she extended an official *comision* (a temporary appointment as school director) that formerly charged me to run the school. Thus I arrived at the position of director; I did not seek it; I was not prepared to do it; I had served as a technology and teaching consultant, conducted workshops for teachers and helped with administrative work, which I carried out well. I had friendly relations with the faculty, but as director, I encountered other demands.

The fact that I was friends with teachers gave them room to think that they could arrive late or make decisions without consulting me. In the beginning, it was 'stretch and relax'. I had to make my colleagues see that there was authority and that they could not make decisions that affected the school organization without consulting me. They needed to inform *el Consejo Técnico* (the technical council that advised the school director) so that it could deal with problems and review implications of the activities that were organized for children. Everyone could not just do what they wanted. It was difficult to manage the situation without being imposing, but I remained firm. We had various incidents and difficulties. Now it is clear that there is authority in the school, a person who has responsibility, and that people serve under the director and the council and cannot act on their own. They have to consider the total organization of the school and the programme. Here no one can act alone because we would fall into anarchy.

Problems faced by students

As principal, I attended to parents, teachers and children; handled complaints and distributed resources. In the school there were problems with reading comprehension and children with real family problems, like Jesús, who had infected eyes and pulled out the hair on his head. His mother was an alcoholic, and he was abandoned by his father. Thus we attended to the academic and the personal. All of the children had medical insurance so that when a mother did not take her child to the doctor, we would take him even though one should not take a child out of school without the consent of the parents.

We had another student who was beaten at home. If we didn't get support from the mother, we had to report the case to Sistema Municipal de Desarrollo Integral de la Familia (the City System for Integrated Family Development) so that they could take the children to a shelter for attention. What would happen if we left these children in their homes? They were going to enter a middle school of 1,500 students in a class of 45 to 50 students with teachers who come and go every 50 minutes and with companions who make fun of them and desert them. Who would care about them?

We already had a student who worked as a prostitute for her uncle. We referred her to a shelter. We had to take her out of a family that was harming her. We sent her to another place where they would keep her until she attended middle school.

Other minor problems were identified and resolved easily. One time, I realized some left-handed students used table desks for right-handed students and vice versa. I asked the teachers why this was happening. They told me that they didn't have enough furniture when the reality was that the furniture was poorly distributed to classrooms. It was so easy to ask the administrative assistant to distribute what was necessary. It was an initial communication that did not have to be repeated.

Delegation

There are two consultants in the school: one is a teacher with 33 years of service who supports the office. She does not use the computer, but she works well with numbers and school accounting. She is honest and implements rules and regulations. She contributes to the administration of the school, and she does it in a good mood.

The other consultant is responsible for the Programa Nacional de Lectura (National Reading Program). She is a diabetic with frequent complications, but when her state of health permits, she works in the reading centres, and she does it well.

When I began to cover the director's duties, I encountered student medical problems and illnesses, and I realized the value of making decisions. When the former director returned for a few days, she rejected some of my decisions and accepted others. She was not concerned about health issues in general and did not feel that it was a school responsibility to attend to a student with a serious illness.

In a sense, the school suffered a little bit during this time when the former director was not completely gone and I was not yet totally in charge. I wanted to share decisions. Soon, I took full responsibility for the school programme and the distribution of resources. The authorities expected immediate responses, and I took the reins. They extended an indefinite medical leave to the former director, and she did not return to the school. The former director was not academically oriented. She made decisions herself and directed activities.

It is important to look for people to whom you can delegate academic functions. I performed well when I was the technology and teaching consultant in the school because I delegated academic work to teachers and learned from the experience. Other directors neither do instructional work themselves nor leave it to the consultant to do. They have their own manner of acting.

Relations with teachers

I have a bachelor's degree in language therapy and another in Spanish. This is a higher level of education than most teachers who have preparation from a normal school. Being director has occasionally been a lonely position. My hope was that no one would leave the office feeling resentful, but it is impossible to satisfy everyone. The goal must be to treat everyone respectfully. I saw myself as a director in the same way that I saw myself as a teacher, that is, as an example of ethics, responsibility, honesty and justice.

Some teachers must be re-directed. I supervised a good teacher with many years of service, but there were complaints from parents. I think she was tired of working with children and lost patience. I was able to arrange a position for her outside of teaching. This suited me because I preferred that she leave the classroom so that students would not have problems.

At times, I could not avoid being discouraged, especially when I ran out of strategies to redirect a teacher whose attitude did not contribute to the mission of the school. Sometimes I had to take severe measures. It is something that I took time to think about; it is not the way I would like to resolve a problem. I always talked about the conflict with the Consejo Técnico de Directores (the Council of School Directors) in the district composed of 18 directors and the inspector. We functioned well in dealing with these types of problems. If you had to make a drastic decision that affected a teacher but benefited students, you could count on the support of the inspector.

There is a veteran teacher who we have not been able to incorporate. She has two shifts (most teachers in Mexico teach one shift in the morning and a second shift in the afternoon). She appears to be angry with everyone. I don't know how I am going to solve the problem of her attitude. I listen to her, and my mind is working on a solution, but the challenge continues.

A director will always find several types of teachers: those who are responsible teachers, those who are members of the old guard, those who do not want to develop further but rather continue using the same method, those who come just to complete their schedule and those who are disposed to try new things. These teachers may be positive or negative. The positive teacher works extra hours, takes work home and urges other teachers to work more, but the negative teacher may want to be the director and manoeuvre outside of the group. I wanted to include them all and make them feel good about the direction we are heading.

The truth is that sometimes I become tired because we don't achieve everything after I have tried plan A and plan B through plan Z. I cannot be the therapist, but I have to continue to bring the group together. The norms that unite us can stretch and loosen, but you can only carry so much until you break.

One problem that we have had as teachers is that we think that all of the deficiencies of students come from the children, themselves, and their families. Since I was a consultant in the school until the present time as director, I have tried to help teachers recognize their own weaknesses.

Another situation that I was unable to affect as a consultant was that teachers see the bimonthly semester examination as the only valid measure to evaluate the student. Every 2 months, they take a week to prepare for the examination to obtain one single grade. For 2 years, little by little, I have changed this framework. There are teachers who now say that the exam is not everything. We have introduced continuous evaluation. The truth is that the teachers still resist completing the daily lesson plan, but we are closer to meeting the needs of the students.

Standardized evaluations tell us that we have low levels of reading comprehension. We are making progress in addressing the problem of how to teach children to read. If we make advances on various rubrics, two teachers will receive compensation from the government for student results on La Evaluación Nacional de Logros Academicos en Centros Escolares (The National Evaluation of Academic Achievement in Schools).

I like to cite the example of a teacher in a meeting who commented on the case of a student whom she was unable to help. She asked that we give her some ideas. I like the humility of this teacher who dared to ask for help and to say, 'I don't know what to do.' Then everyone started to offer an opinion and reviewed the performance of the student because everyone had these experiences with students as well as more severe cases and everyone knew the names of the students we were talking about.

I no longer feel alone. When I feel bad about a conflict, I visit with teachers and tell them the problem.

Formation as a director

Although you learn to lead through handling problems day to day, I realized that I needed to prepare myself more for the position. You need to have preparation to serve as director: workshops to manage conflicts, administrative preparation and, more than anything, academics and pedagogy because one who goes into administration can become distant from the teaching mission of the school.

At first, it seemed that being in charge was like *teléfono descompuesto* (playing a game of telephone in which messages are distorted as they are passed from person to person). Everyone came with a comment or complaint about someone. With time and professional development, I was able, little by little, to change the attitude and perspective of the teachers so that everyone was working together on the side of academics.

As I said, I was shy. I was not a born leader, but I developed leadership. I took a series of workshops on the development of director competencies. I learned to see events objectively and avoid frustration in situations that are resistant to change. I am able to take time, study and understand before making a judgement.

I took another workshop on the history of the director position and the evolution of the teaching profession. It is important to know the history of how the profession developed. Something that has influenced my management style has been contact with other directors that I had when I was a teacher and consultant. I learned to observe different forms of leadership, see the difference between a director who just filled out administrative forms and academic leaders, like my school inspector and the director of the normal school.

My inspector, Profesora Yolanda Aburto Márquez, is enthusiastic. She has 36 years of service, and she continues to enjoy attending conferences to develop further. She also liked to teach courses. I remember one occasion when I asked permission from Professor Yoly to attend a conference on teaching. I told the inspector that if she could not grant permission, it would not be a problem.

She responded, 'Rosita, you don't know what I would give to see the majority of my directors come to ask me permission for more preparation. Clearly, I give you permission.'

These examples motivated me.

Relations with parents

Good relations are important to attract parents to the school. In the past, parents did not stop at the office and children were afraid to enter. This situation has changed, not through preaching, but in my way of being. The office cannot be a barrier between teachers and children or parents. If a woman arrives, I say, 'Come in' and offer her a cup of coffee. I invite her to be comfortable and talk. When a student comes to the office, I come out and say, 'How can I help you?' All they usually want is a soccer ball or a basketball, but they used to have to ask permission. We no longer do this. They enter with confidence and leave the balls in place without fear from the office.

I believe in discipline and order in school projects; in setting realistic goals and in analyzing the advances of students, teachers and parents. Parents participate in several school groups, one is the Asociación de Padres de Familia (Association of Parents) and the other is the Consejo de Participación Social (the Social Participation Council). The Proyecto Escolar (School Project) must be approved by the Consejo de Participación Social. Parents participate with teachers, ex-students and community representatives. The council has not functioned as I had wished. The members make decisions about the school in an atmosphere of harmony and respect, but it is not easy.

The parents elected a retiree from the United States who came to live in Mexico as their representative. He did not understand Spanish very well or the culture, or the problems of a school in Mexico. Neither did he understand his role as a parent. He was upset because children did not attend classes when the teachers had professional development. We had designated days as specified by the national policy of the Secretaría de Educación Pública (Secretary of Education) or in the case of the state the Sistema Educativo Estatal (State Educational System) and the National Union.

The parent assumed the posture of a boss. He ordered the school consultant to note the hours of my coming and going, who attended and how much time each person was late and why. He also wanted to make decisions over expenditures. He did not understand that the amount of each expenditure was specified by the government. I explained to him that 60 percent had to be spent on infrastructure, 20 percent on materials, 5 percent on professional development, and so on. I told him that his attitude offended me, but I opened the door to participate together, not on the margin. One day, he held a meeting of parents without advising me. He wanted to use the library, but it was occupied with an activity of FORMA (Entrepreneurship and Development Training Center), an external public programme that gave group therapy to sixth grade children and their parents. This bothered him because he did not understand that the school is an organization that programmes activities in advance.

The parent meetings were not well attended. About a quarter of the members came to meetings. Some worked in *maquiladoras* (U.S. companies located in Mexico to take advantage of lower wage rates), and if they came they would lose 150 pesos, a day's salary. When the teachers made appointments to meet with parents to hand out grades, they had better participation.

We had a community dimension and social participation project for parents to come to the school. I wanted them to reflect on why we were not functioning the way we should in this atmosphere. I wanted to persuade them to increase their commitment to the Consejo de Participación Social. We needed to overcome the idea that it was enough to be named to the council. It needed to be transformed into new forms of administration and participation.

Goals

To be a director is an opportunity to put my ideas into practice, an opportunity to intervene with children to achieve acceptable levels of learning. All of the children of the school deserve the opportunity to discard the stigma of being destined for failure. We know that the majority of our students finish elementary school and half finish middle school. This is a problem that is much discussed by teachers. I have to motivate teachers to reinvest in the problem, and everyone has to motivate the students. They have to see ahead and realize that the school gives power and knowledge. We work so that the school will be a space where children realize that there is a door to achieve a better life, but also it depends on them to open it.

I like it when teachers comment on the changes and physical improvements in the school or the activities of the children outside of the school. All of the activities are important, but I prefer that they comment about improved levels of educational achievement. We cannot be a light to the street if our house is dark. It is here, in the school, where we can improve achievement, and this happens when the teacher has a true commitment. A good teacher teaches even under the shade of a tree.

These days, the elementary school director faces more demands than ever before. It is not easy to assume leadership, to spin like a top all day, attending to 1,000 things. It is a lot of work but I enjoy it. The teachers of first and second grade always want me to see what the students are doing. Sometimes, I have 1,000 things to do, but I always go and put on my best face because it would be disappointing for them if I didn't appreciate their work.

If there is direction, there is responsibility. When there is a correct direction, the people of the school do not act only for their own interests. In school, decisions are made collegially in the Consejo Técnico Escolar. The school operates democratically and has acquired prestige in the community. There is neither violence inside nor any graffiti on the building. We are not victims of vandalism as happens in other schools. This is an indication of respect. It is a reflection of the work achieved by the personnel of the school. We know all of the students, and we can almost say that we know the problems of their families. We monitor these situations in the meetings of the Consejo Técnico Escolar. We still have challenges, but there has been a decrease in the resistance of some teachers to turn in their daily lesson plans, a most important tool when a teacher is incapacitated, retires or changes schools. One can review the plan and continue the way in which the teacher was working with the class.

Finances

I feel that finances distract me from what I like to do. Sometimes what stresses me is handing in documentation, especially when I receive notice that says I should have submitted papers yesterday. But I do want to complete paperwork when it reflects positively on the school.

I prefer to spend time in classrooms. Classroom visits serve to inform me about a teacher's work, the level of performance and the engagement of the students. To observe every day what happens in a school, from beginning to end, permits me to intervene and improve the attention of students and elevate the academic level of the school. I don't do it to look good to superiors, but rather, because the rights of children are central to the functioning of the school. But school finances are important too, and managing them is my responsibility as director.

Until last year, the government provided 400 pesos annually for each student, but they distributed the funds in portions: one in March, another in June, another in August and the last one in October. They imposed expense rubrics and limits: 60 percent for infrastructure or remodelling of the school building and the rest divided in percentages for human consumption of water, cleaning materials, telephone and internet and professional development courses. Sixty-four thousand pesos per year does not cover everything. Thus, you have to find other sources of funding, such as re-enrolling in the Programa Escuelas de Calidad (School Quality Programme).

I have had to find other ways to address the problem of infrastructure. The ceilings of the classrooms were rotting. They were a threat to the students and teachers. I took photos of them and sent them to the authorities. When they saw them, they became frightened.

My strategy worked. Officials from the programme Escuela Segura (Safe Schools) certified the danger and helped me to obtain funding of 400,000 pesos to redo the roofs, basketball and soccer courts, steps, sidewalks and fence. Deterioration of the physical plant is natural, but when there is no maintenance, deterioration becomes a major problem. Thus resources to maintain it in good shape are necessary. The truth is that advancing in this direction is a distasteful, bureaucratic battle for a director.

There are many limitations of personnel, infrastructure and autonomy to decide how to distribute the budget. There is insufficient participation of parents, bureaucratic government programmes that we have to carry out and students with difficult family situations. And still, most classes are increasing their scores on standardized national examinations. We also increased and diversified our financial resources and community assistance. We have a Beca Progreso (scholarship) of 400 pesos for each student. The Programa Escuela de Calidad brings in 36,000 pesos per year. The support of the Instituto Naciona de la Infraestructura Física Educativa (National Institute for Educational Infrastructure) brought 400,000 pesos for remodelling. The resources of Escuela Segura paid 8,000 pesos. In the community the support of EMPRESER (an organization to promote entrepreneurship and small business), an organization certified by the Secretaría de Economía (Secretary of the Economy), brought free assistance to mothers who wanted to undertake a business. All of this is the work of management. You have to look for these funds.

The school has a high level of educational achievement. It is in 125th place out of more than 1,500 schools in the state. It is in eighteenth place among slightly less than 300 schools in the municipality of Ensenada. In general, there is a positive trend showing an increase in evaluation scores, but we also have challenges. Increased professional development of teachers has permitted us to move away from traditional pedagogical frameworks, little by little.

There is an educational movement, inside and out. The director of another elementary school asked me to bring together the personnel of our schools to work towards the reform of education. I am excited because she has enrolled in a workshop with me. It is very good to know the experiences of other schools and share curriculum change efforts.

I have achieved my first goal that the majority of teachers turn their attention to themselves and their practices before examining those of students. The internal discussion of pedagogy based on interviews and questionnaires has permitted us to diagnose our needs with more clarity to design our own plan. We have centred ourselves on our own weaknesses. We have recognized that teaching is more than just reading to students, and we do not motivate students unless we recognize our own weaknesses. The achievement of seeing our own weaknesses before those of students has been a real change of the axis and conception of school personnel. It is curious, but what it signals is that the learning needs of students come first in the school. Only in this way can we value our strengths and weaknesses as a faculty.

The future

I have been offered transfers to other schools, including a new private school that would pay a higher salary, but I prefer to stay in a public school, not only because I enjoy it here, but because the teachers chose me and we have projects in progress. The private school is attractive because it is more demanding and teaches English as a second language and classes in technology, but I believe there are better teachers in public schools. Most importantly, I believe that this is where children most need our work. As director, I have to motivate them.

My plan is to compete for the position of permanent director, but I hope that the ex-director of this school retires. I don't want to get a place in another school. My points on the *escalafón* (career ladder that determines promotion) give me good possibilities of staying at this school with a *plaza definitive* (a permanent position).

We will start a project during the summer vacation that came from an idea that I got in a workshop about sustainable development and financial culture. Many parents of this school are single. Most of them provide domestic help or work in *maquiladoras;* some live with their own mothers and others don't have employment. Thus, we want to elevate the level of income of these mothers who are heads of families.

I have already suggested the idea to women and others who are interested. We would involve them in an economic project and at the same time contribute to the care of the environment by recycling aluminum cans, glass, cardboard and plastic. We would contract with an organization that assists this type of project called EMPRESER. We know it would require a certain investment. The school would loan the space for a collection centre that we would help them convert for a small business. While the teachers worked with children on ecological themes, we would change trash cans, paint them to facilitate classification and promote the collection centre. The children would bring the materials to the school and deposit them in the collection centre. The project should contribute to the elevation of the mothers' salaries and at the same time care for the environment.

I remember the first time I did a socioeconomic study to identify which business would be the most profitable. I analyzed several possibilities, including the collection centre, a sewing workshop, a food stand and a paper shop with making cards or notebooks of recycled paper. Then I discussed these ideas with teachers and interested mothers. We saw that the most viable project in the short term was the collection centre. It required less investment; the principal promoters would be the children from their homes; the mothers would learn to administer the business to the point of being totally in charge. They would form a micro-business. This is a project that could have a grand impact on the community.

My dream is that my work will serve children to move to higher levels of scholarship, that they will open doors and advance, that generations that we prepare will be more participative so that our presidents will not be elected by 30 percent of the citizens, that the new generations will change the national framework by fighting for equality. I believe that I can have the best school in the world if we all commit to it.

My personal future is not clear. I had to abandon my studies for a master's degree. I felt proud to have been accepted with a scholarship as a graduate student at the university, but I became ill. I am a breast cancer patient. I had relapses, many surgeries and metastasis to the liver. The illness weakened me, but now I am strong. I don't know if some day I will re-enter a graduate programme or if I will maintain my professional skills through workshops. What I know is that I want to dedicate more time to my family, and I want to travel. I love to travel, get to know other places and other persons, other ways of thinking and test new waters. What I have clear is that I want to visit Portugal. I have always wanted to experience it. Why not go visit?

Note

1 Czech teacher, educator and writer, 1592–1670.

6 'Something Greater Was Happening': A Novice Principal Reflects on Creating Change through Building Community Relationships

Diane Purvey and Charles Webber meet with Tsutsweye from the Secwepemc Nation, principal of Quiq'wi'elst (Blackstone) School

In the middle of the twentieth century a working gold mine capped the top of the Deadman Valley, also known as Skeetchestn. Apart from a few ranches at the top of the valley and a thin network of dirt roads that connects homesteads and fishing resorts, there is nothing much beyond the village of Skeetchestn itself. It is, in other words, not on the way to anything. Moreover, it is the only settlement of consequence in this narrow, near-desert valley in British Columbia, about 10 km up a winding country road from an intersection on a hairpin turn on the Trans-Canada Highway.

Skeetchestn is a First Nation community located in the centre of a long rectangular reserve created in 1877. Pushed back from the frontier of their traditional territories along the Thompson River, this community belongs to the Shuswap Nation Tribal Council. Reduced by smallpox and Gold Rush–era disruptions to a population of only a couple of hundred, the Skeetchestn have recovered dramatically in the last 40 years. Their struggle against the inequities of the Canadian Indian Act, which limited their ability to do much more than feed themselves on subsistence farms, has been a long one but it has been capped of late with the creation of a band school: Quiq'wi'elst (Blackstone) School. The school was established in 1996 and, like most band schools in British Columbia, it has a mandate to meet the demands of a provincial curriculum but also to contribute to the vitality of indigenous culture and the preservation of the Secwepemc language, Secwepmectsin. A small number of non-aboriginal households hug the dramatic cliffs and hoodoos that rim the valley and head north from Skeetchestn to the abandoned mine – their children are also among the students at Quiq'wi'elst.

This is a place to which few Canadians will ever travel. Located in the heart of the arid Thompson Plateau, it is located approximately 50 km west of the city of Kamloops. It is startling in the beauty of its rocky perimeter and the long, green, irrigated farmsteads surrounded by unforgiving dry lands and sagebrush. The relative isolation of the valley has been its community's strength and it is not surprising to find that gritty toughness in the determination of Quiq'wi'elst to make a difference.

Tsutsweye (a pseudonym, the Shuswap word for butterfly) is in her second year of the principalship of this rural First Nation school. Of the 58 students in the school, all but 10 live on the reserve and are First Nation. The school has 5 classrooms with 7 teachers and 12 other staff, including cooks, bus drivers, support workers, an administrative assistant, counselor, custodian and a librarian.

Although Tsutsweye is of aboriginal ancestry she grew up off reserve in the city of Kamloops and attended public schools. However, all of her teaching and administrative experiences have been in band schools.

Tsutsweye's story

Early life

I'm just in my second year of my first appointment as principal. I'm 38 now, so I was 37 when I first became a principal. I was a kindergarten teacher for 4 years at another First Nation school in an urban setting. I was a teacher at another school, also a First Nation school, where I spent 2 years as a kindergarten teacher and then 2 years as a fourth grade teacher. This is my ninth year in education.

My interest originally, when I returned back to school, was to make a difference and to create change, especially within the First Nation population. I came to the realization that working with adults and moving them forward and creating change was a lot more difficult than with children, so I decided that working in education at the K–12 level was an excellent opportunity to effect change.

My first career choice was that I wanted to be a counselor. I just knew I wanted to make a difference. I completed 1 year of college prep because I had been out of school for so long and took psychology and sociology, but it was a visit from the Native Indian Teacher Education Programme (NITEP) that introduced me to education and kind of pulled me along in that direction so that's where I ended up.

I had a son. I was involved in sales and had a lot of interaction with people but I always was drawn to helping people. When I decided to go back to school, my intent was just to go get my bachelor's of arts and head off into counseling. The college prep programme I took was a First Nation access to trades and technology programme. It helped me to develop a sense of cultural identity because growing up we weren't really taught about our culture. I grew up off reserve. It was an opportunity for me to develop myself as a person and learn more about my culture and my identity while pursuing my education. My culture is Shuswap.

I did things a little backwards. It was a little bit more challenging going into university with a child. You go in thinking you can provide a better future for your child, so that was a big motivator. I enjoyed doing sales work and interacting with people, but I wanted more. I wanted a career and not just a job. My introduction to the First Nation programmes was when I came to the realization that's really what I wanted to do. I look at both my parents, and my dad was an extremely strong person, very much a leader in terms of his personality. My mom is an amazingly strong woman, so when I look at both my parents I see leadership skills within them. They always encouraged me to reach, to go for those dreams and to do better. Academically, I was the second high school graduate in my family, my extended family as well. My aunt had completed a bachelor's of arts degree, and I remember going to her graduation. She was a single mom as well, with four kids, and I remember watching her and thinking that if she can do it I guess I can. My parents were always supportive, but when I look back I would never have thought that I would go to the University of British Columbia, never in 1 million years. If you asked me 20 years ago or even 15 years ago, I would never have thought that I would pursue an M.Ed. It's ludicrous.

When I checked on the university preparation programme it was to do better for my son. I didn't want to just get by. I wanted to do better for him. He was 2 1/2 years old when I went back to school.

Professional preparation

In my first 2 years of teaching I had a mentor teacher and I shadowed everything she did. That was an excellent tool to build a base for me. But then after 2 years, you kind of start to develop your own way of doing things, your own priorities about the way you want to do things.

She was a kindergarten teacher in a First Nation school and worked across the hall from me. She was also a First Nation woman and she guided me through everything I needed to do because, of course, my bachelor's of education was in teaching intermediate grades. It was never on primary, so when I had my first job offer as a kindergarten teacher I looked at the principal and thought, 'Are you crazy?' Because I really didn't see myself working with kids that were so young. It was a challenge and it was a big learning curve.

After my first 2 years, that's when I started to have a voice in education and became very interested in not just teaching kids, but being more involved in the school programmes and doing things that were going to move the school forward. I knew that I didn't want to be just a teacher. I knew that I wanted to be more than a teacher. I knew that I wanted to stretch and to grow and to challenge myself. So after 2 years I knew I wasn't going to just be a teacher. There was so much more that I could do while teaching. I was always interested in what went on at the administrative level and would spent quite a few hours talking with administration and just kind of picking their brain to understand why things were the way they were.

When I moved to my second school I was fortunate enough to have an administrator who allowed me to spread my wings and take on projects and push the envelope and question things. I knew then that leadership was a goal of mine. I didn't know in what form, but I knew that I wanted to do more.

I applied for my first principalship position, which was really silly. It was 6 years after being a teacher. It was a principalship position that came up at the school I was working at. So I thought, what the heck, I'll throw my name in the hat. I think I did it to show them that I had an interest in more. I didn't really expect to get the position, but I wanted to make people aware that I wanted more.

Each of the administrators that I have worked under taught me a lot. For the most part, these were things that I wanted to do right, a lot of good, positive teachings. And there were a few things that I learned that I didn't want to do. It's all a lesson. It's important that you experience those things so that you can define what you want to do, what kind of leader you want to be or don't want to be.

Informally, I spent a lot of time speaking with administrators to understand what it is they do. I was fortunate enough to work with administrators who would have that conversation with me. Then I applied for the master's degree at the university, and in one course they asked how many of us were planning to go into leadership and I knew it was a building block to leadership so I put up my hand because I knew that's where I wanted to go.

After I applied the second time for a principalship, they called and scheduled me for an interview and I did my research on possible interview questions. And I actually came across the set of questions that they used. I sat with past administrators that I had worked under and talked to them about questions. They really helped me prepare for the interview. Then off I went and when I interviewed I was very, very nervous because it was something that to me was very unrealistic. When I put my name forward, it was basically to let people know that this is where I'm heading eventually. To be called in for an interview was a shock. I found that, for the most part, if I just spoke from my heart, I was fine. The preparation portion of it was good for me, but I thought it was first and foremost important that I spoke from my heart. So that's what I did, and it was a long interview process.

This was my first interview for a principalship. I was somewhat familiar with the school because it's in the same nation as my own ancestry. Once I was done with the interview I went away and a month went by. The administrator who was leaving called and asked me a few more questions and told me I had the job. I was shocked. I had felt that I had said everything that I needed to say but, most importantly, that there was nothing that I regretted or wished that I had said differently. For me, at that point, it was more about the experience. I felt that I had really spoken from my heart so there was nothing that I would change from what I had said.

In terms of speaking from the heart, they were talking about behavior issues and staffing issues so my way of dealing with that was, first and foremost, about how you treat others. From my own experience in working as an educator, I observed different ways I had been treated and what I found appropriate and what I found less appropriate. It was important for me to make sure that the foundation of building a relationship with the community, with the children and with my staff was a big priority. The rest of the administrative duties would follow, but if I had that base, it would make the rest of the administrative duties a lot more attainable. When I spoke from my heart it was in reference to a lot of my interactions with staff and students and community, how I felt that was an extremely important part of leadership.

Personal motivation

Before I even finished work at the school I was currently working at, the community of my new school hosted an awards evening and invited me to attend, and that's when they introduced me to the community. It was just an amazing evening. I was absolutely terrified and I had to speak to the community. I thought, 'I don't know about this. I'm still in teacher mode!' It was a really unique evening because one of my former administrators was actually there that night and he was one of those who had spent a lot of time with me prepping for the interview. It was an incredible moment to be introduced to the community in such a manner. They had a big dinner that night and the warmth of the community . . . my home community is just 20 minutes up the road. A lot of them knew my extended family and were really able to connect me to somebody, which was really important. It was a warm and welcoming event, a nice way to be introduced to the community. When I say 'community' I mean the actual entire reserve, everybody. There were anywhere between 200 and 300 people there. It's actually a community award dinner where they recognize the students who travelled into the district schools as well as students at the community-based school.

At the beginning of the last school year we didn't have a lot of parent and community involvement. It wasn't until the latter half, probably about March, that things began to change. We had a great Christmas concert. We had tons of parents there, but you are going to get that at Christmas time. We had hosted a literacy and math fun night and we had 40 to 60 people show up and we thought, 'Okay, this is good.' Then we did a science night and we had over 100 people show up, so I thought, 'Okay, this is really good!' At our year-end awards ceremony we had a few hundred people show up. And then this year we had our back-to-school Angel Street event, which was part of a programme to highlight the need for intervention in domestic abuse. We did not know how many people were going to show up. There could be 30, but I also knew there could be a couple hundred, so when you do the organization, you go with a couple hundred.

When Angel Street event first started, it was just a school. I think there was hesitancy and some people wouldn't come up to the school. And then people started coming up, and I would have parents come by and talk about parenting issues and sit and have coffee. It was really relaxed. The Angel Street was a really big thing. The school was not just about the school anymore. It wasn't just the place where kids were learning to read and write. It became more. It changed what the meaning of that school was when we put up those Angel Street signs. It wasn't just the place of academics anymore. It was so much more. Something greater was happening up there.

Also there was a lot of work in the community because there was the creation of a social task force and so I sat on that committee because it was important. I wanted to make a difference with the kids, but to some extent I had to take a few steps into the community in order to do that. Domestic violence at that time of the year was very big; it was growing. There was increased substance abuse and other problems.

The school was taken to a certain level under the past principal, and now I feel like I'm challenging it to go to the next level and offering something. Not better and not more. It's just expanding what was there.

No teachers at the school applied for the principal's position. There is a teacher who has been there since the new building, for 7 years, and he's a phenomenal teacher. I asked him if he had applied for the principalship and he said he had no desire. He said he watched the past principal go through what he went through and thought, 'No way!' The amount of hours that the past principal put into that building was incredible and he was there for 5 years. To follow in his footsteps was extremely difficult because of the hours he put in. I did do it the first year. I worked just as hard and long. It was normal to work until 10 o'clock and then drive home. I don't do it now because of my health, my family, my son, balance. There's more delegation going on and I think that first year the learning curve was so large and now I'm a lot more comfortable. For me to do a proposal doesn't take nearly as long now. I'm not teaching this year because it was not feasible; it just wasn't in the best interests of students. The responsibilities and the connections that I have to community issues were growing, and it was very difficult to teach and to administer and implement a lot of the social things that I wanted to implement. This year we are under recertification for First Nation certification, so we are going through an assessment process. It takes the entire school year to build the document they send to your reviews of all your policies and programmes and so forth.

Funding proposals go to the First Nations Education Steering Committee and the First Nations and Inuit Youth Training Programme. My support staff are largely funded through special education dollars. I'm fortunate in that the community I work in does offer financial support to the school, which is actually, I'm coming to realize, quite rare. I don't go to them for huge amounts of dollars, but when there are things that I need I talk to them and they are helpful. The purchase of the school bus came from the Social Development Department of the First Nations Band, so there are things like that that happen. I'm extremely fortunate that when we work on proposals for projects, quite often it's a shared venture.

In terms of learning to write proposals for funding, I am ever so grateful for copies that were left behind because that was my base. My first official final report was tricky because I was nervous. It was a big project and it was done through an aboriginal language initiative that goes beyond the school to bring elders together for monthly meetings to develop curriculum. I would use the reports that were created before my arrival to guide me towards whatever they were looking for. I was fortunate because an education proposal is quite different from a business proposal.

We have to seek outside funding sources. I haven't worked in a district school, but from my understanding, the financial end of a public school actually doesn't occur at the principal level. The financials of public schools occur at a higher level. In order to run and maintain programmes that meet the needs of the students, or even build on the successes of the school, you have to bring in programmes. In order to do that you need the dollars, so you do the paperwork. Language and culture is a big element in First Nation schools and we don't get federal government dollars for language and culture programmes.

You don't think that when you are going to administer a school that you are going to solely be responsible for the financial end of that building. I think that's where the difference lies in working for a district versus working for the First Nation school. I run the budget. I make the budget. I find the money for the budget. To write proposals and implement projects and then do the reporting on top of all your other administrative duties, and I was teaching as well. I had no idea how to run the school budget. I had no idea how much education cost, not a clue. A lot of the training that I did with the previous principal was a lot of budget stuff because I did not know how to write a proposal for a project to save my soul.

If I ever decided to go work for the district, I'd probably get bored. It's very different, the sense of responsibility that you have working at an independent/First Nation school. People laugh when I tell them I'm a principal because they say 'Oh, you have an easy job,' and I say, 'No! You should see my bookshelf and you should see the projects that are constantly on the go.' And it doesn't help that I have my own initiatives and my own drive, and then you have students, and I'm ever so fortunate that I have a really good relationship with students.

It's not like students get sent to the office because they are in trouble. We usually go sit in the staff room and have a conversation about what's going on in their lives. More times than not, the students are not sent to the office because they are in trouble; they're in there because they want to visit with me. I came in at lunchtime and two students were sitting there and I asked, 'What are you doing?' And they said, 'We are not in trouble. We just wanted to visit.' I said, 'Okay.' That's something I hold up high. When the kids come in, they look for that morning hug from you or when there is a Sticky Note on your desk saying, 'Hello, Ms Tsutsweye', it's a very different relationship, so when there are any issues that do creep up, your ability to deal with them is so much easier.

The job has changed me because it has put me in a position where I can do more. I'm in a position where I think I can implement greater change. As a teacher you can implement change at a classroom level if the administration allows you that flexibility. But now I'm sitting in a position where I can say, 'Yes, we can do this.' The proposal writing and all that other stuff, it's overload and it's a big responsibility and it's not the most fun part of my job. The thing that makes me go back every day is the fact that I'm in a position where I can really make change, where I can move things forward.

Going back to why I became a teacher, I knew I could make a difference. Now I'm just doing it at a different level. In my last 3 years of teaching I was at a level where I was really frustrated. I felt that my wings were being snipped and I needed to change that. I knew then what I wanted to do as a leader and what was important. Do I think that the opportunity would come at the age that I am? No, I didn't. I figured that it would be a few years down the road, to be honest. I did. I like the shock factor that it has on people who walk in the building. I used to be embarrassed and really shy about my young age, but now I have fun with it. They come in and ask for the principal and I just had to sit there and say, 'I am!' I'm a little bit more comfortable now with the position and feel more confident in the direction I'm going.

I'm fortunate, too, because we have a strong connection to Thompson Rivers University and a lot of the different initiatives that have come forward. Working with a social work professor on Angel Street was just incredible. It was everything I wanted for our school. To be in a position where I could say 'Let's do this' and do it to the level that we did was very meaningful. Now I am working with the same professor on the child advocacy group for aboriginal children in care. Sometimes I look at all of the projects and initiatives and I think, 'Am I crazy?' When is enough, enough?

Academic preparation

We were the first cohort in the master's group. I found that a lot of the programming had to do with leadership, so it was everything I could want. In one of the leadership courses, taught by the district superintendent, there was a class where we talked about the different types of leaders. They had us create a visual representation of the type of leadership that we would impart. I remember choosing a butterfly, and I still think about it to this day. I don't ever want to be the kind of leader who says this is what it is and this is what we are going to do. I would rather sit at a table and have everyone come together to make that decision. By identifying the different types of leadership roles, actually pinpointing the characteristics, just reaffirmed for me which direction I wanted to go and what kind of leader I wanted to be.

The butterfly is transformative and it is not about the leader at the front. The leader kind of sits with the group that's moving. It's not about me sitting in front and making decisions. It's about the team coming to a conclusion. I can throw out ideas explaining why something would be important, but part of the transformative aspect is moving people along, really making sure you are building that momentum within the staff that you are leading. I probably had a conversation with my staff about a month and a half ago about the butterfly analogy because I really believe that education is not stagnant. Education is always shifting shape and going through a transformation mode. It's always evolving. Therefore as educators we have to make sure that we are evolving. What I bring to the table, all these projects, and say look at this, I really encourage my staff to really push the envelope in their teaching and to really think outside the box. Don't go to your filing cabinet constantly. Build to be better.

Those who prepare leadership development programmes should know that having a strong leadership course is an important element. There were a lot of things that we did that weren't always textual based. To step outside the box and create images was something that I never forgot as a leader. I always turn back to that butterfly and ask, 'So what did that mean?' I can't remember all the elements that I included in it, but when I go back to it and look at it, it was something that no book, honestly, could've given me. It was a personal relationship with leadership that was built. For me, I am very much driven by the social-emotional aspects of children as well as their academics. Having an opportunity to be better informed on social issues and diversity is a huge advantage. Going into leadership with that clear understanding of yourself makes it easier. It does. Travelling through those challenges, it gives you something to turn back to and to say, 'Hey, why am I doing this again?' You don't realize that when you're sitting in there, going through it, listening to them talk about leadership. You don't realize it, but I think that when we created that visual representation of what kinds of leaders we wanted to be, that was a very personal connection to leadership. I don't know that I will ever forget that. If I forget that, I shouldn't be here any more.

First Nation identity and work context

Before I went into the First Nation programmes I knew I was First Nation but I did not have a strong sense of identity. My mom is First Nation but my dad was non-native. We never grew up with any sense of First Nation identity. I was taught the family values and morals and everything else that went with it.

A lot of the work I do is in a First Nation setting and it's kind of what you do. The various projects that I've been involved with all have some sort of attachment to First Nation in some way, shape or form. A lot of the things that we do in First Nation education would be just as beneficial for non-natives. The whole belief system of being First Nation – your morals, your values, your teachings – are good for anybody.

In the First Nation culture, people my age and younger identify themselves with who they belong to. So when I did my introduction to the community it was, this is my grandmother, this is who my mother is, this is my father, just really drawing the connections. Within First Nation communities linking a person to somebody, usually an elder, somebody older, another generation above you, gives you an almost automatic line that travels between you and that person. Your relationship building is already started when they can identify you with somebody who they know, so it was extremely important. When they connect to your prior generation, your extended family, it's a way of saying, 'Okay, well then you have these kinds of values, these teachings to some extent' because I have some people say, 'I know who your uncle is,' and so at least it gives you a frame of reference for them, not so much of yourself, but for them.

My family, just like any other First Nation family, has our issues and there are some family members who are still struggling with healing and so forth. When you get identified with those family members who are struggling . . . I kind of joke around about it because I love all my family and I recognize and acknowledge and accept wherever they may be in their lives. Also, you almost don't have your own identity, so you fall under the identity of your family instead of as an individual. That can be difficult at times. I know that when I worked at my first school it wasn't within my own nation and at that point in time, I went in with my own identity. There was no correlation or connection between communities. I felt I was very much on my own two feet and at that time in my life I really needed that to happen. When I came back home and worked within my own home nation I realized that I was going to fall under the identity of my family again. But by that point you've taken the time to strengthen your own identity. You deal better with the grouping of identities. Do I sometimes fear that if I do something wrong that some of the elders are going to call my grandmother up? Yes! I do fear that, but I also know too that if that were to ever happen a conversation would follow.

In First Nation, the women are the caretakers and they really are the ones that make some of those really hard-edged decisions. But they're also the nurturers, very much so. Aboriginal women in general have a strength that's just phenomenal. To endure what they have endured and to continue – they don't have to have a B.Ed. or an M.Ed. – they work to educate their youth and to nurture and guide them. The women take care of everything. It's the women who do the work.

My leadership style may be like that to some degree because that's what I do, I take care of things. It's that nurturer element. I think it's like that across many arenas for First Nation women. They have a strong presence in healing, things and activities that promote healing.

The first year I tried not to be too different from the previous principal. But I was very driven by the social aspect of education and that was important to me. I think he had good relationships with families and so on. I think it was important for me as well to build that relationship base with them, to let them know that the school is very much an open door. I tried to make it a little bit more relaxing, a little bit friendlier, although I didn't have to do that much. It was just to build on what was already there. I think that my involvement in the social issues of the community – what goes on in the community – has a direct link and a direct impact on my students and they bring it up to the school. It's not like they leave their little bag of social issues and family at the door. They bring it into the classrooms. You have to give it a voice. You have to acknowledge it and you have to give them the space to have the dialogue about what they're experiencing and what they're hearing before you can even get to the academics.

And you have the government coming to the school as well, with social workers coming into the school. I'm very hard-edged because I think that prior to my arrival they would come in and kind of do what they do and they had no sense of accountability to the school whatsoever. I was very adamant that that was not happening. If they come into the school, then they need to respect the space that they are in and do things in a good way. I had certain ideas of how things should run socially. More importantly, we should be working as a team and the social workers should not just be coming in and scooping, taking the information and running. The first year I spent a lot of time building the relationship, outlining some sense of respect between organizations, a set of expectations when they enter the building.

It was difficult at first. There were a lot of phone calls back and forth saying, 'Your worker came in and did this and I don't appreciate it.' Then, at one point I said, 'I'm sorry but I'm not obligated to give you a space to interview these children when you come in. I mean I'm obligated to allow you to interview them but I'm not obligated to give you a space. So how about we all just get along and make life easier and I'll give you a space and you come in and be respectful and all will be well!' I met with government representatives. We sat and had a meeting and I said, 'How about we do this? Why don't we talk about how things are going to be? Let's not talk about everything that's gone wrong. Let's talk about how we see this unfolding for this next school year and that's what we'll do.' In that way I don't think I'm a typical principal because the social issues I feel are very much a part of my responsibility and a part of the teachers' responsibilities. We are all there for the best interests of the child. It's not all about the academics. Academics are important, but so are the social-emotional elements. It makes life a lot easier when all organizations are working from the same page. It's important for us to work together.

Now when social workers come to the school, our school counselor sits in. There's a lot of dialogue between the social worker and school counselor. There is shared information. When we have health and wellness workers who come in, they sit down and we talk before they go in and visit the kids. Then we talk after they visit the kids. We have a direction. We have a path. We know what they're working on. We know what the issues are so we can also get some things into play. It's a much friendlier relationship, much friendlier. The hesitancy to share information isn't there anymore. Now I'm not always phoning their office to give somebody heck any more. I'm phoning because we need help and we just kind of work together, and that's how it should be. When you're dealing with children in care and issues that surround the possibility of children being placed into care, you either risk damaging whatever relationship you have developed with the families or they put trust in you to go above and beyond what's right for their child, and even to them to some extent.

Support network

My family is very important to me and moving back home was a very big deal for me. I moved back because my dad was not well at the time and it was important for me to come home. My family was a great, great support through all that I have done. I honestly believe that without their support I would not be where I am. As much as I would want to claim my own identity, the reality of it is that it was through them.

In terms of other support in my life I spent the entire summer working alongside the principal who was leaving. He stayed until about mid-August and we worked side by side. He walked me through all the different things, all the different elements, all the things that he did. I was extremely fortunate that he was willing to do that. I had copies of literally everything, all the different projects and proposals, everything. He actually constructed a little booklet for me; it was a principal handbook. He never totally finished it, but it made a huge difference for me. It's on my shelf. I don't turn to it as much now. The first year there was a lot of reference to it but also a lot of phone calls. He was still available, which was nice. There were a lot of phone calls back and forth, a lot of emails. I had questions. There were tons of questions. As the year went on the emails started to grow further and further apart. I actually ran into him at a conference just a couple weeks ago and I still had a few more questions, even after a year! I was really very, very fortunate. It was difficult too because when I started the position the administrative assistant stayed and that was very nice. That offered additional support to the principal's office but then just about a week before school was going to start there was a death in the community. It was a boating accident. An elder had fallen into the water and they were searching. Most of the community was out on the river, including all the workers who were supposed to be in the school. It was about a week before the teachers were coming back, about a week after the principal left! There was a lot of stumbling around that week about what to do, but it was good too because it gave me an opportunity to be in the building on my own, and that in itself is a valuable experience to kind of sit by yourself in this building that you are now going to be an administrator in. It was very empowering but it was also a very moving time to watch the community pull together the way they did and to see them go through the loss, but do it in such a manner that was just amazing. It was a difficult but very moving time.

Sacrifice

When I was working on my master's in doing coursework, a lot happened in that timeframe. I made a lot of sacrifices in order to continue with programme and, to some extent, I still feel that those pieces are not resolved for me because I lost my dad during the first week and still continued through it. I actually had to leave his bedside to come and start the M.Ed., with his approval, which was very important to me, but that's an unresolved piece for me. I left his side and I'm still sitting here with something that isn't finished. Until I'm finished with it, leaving his side means what? It has to mean something, so it's important to me to complete my M.Ed. And then I want to move on to a doctorate, which, to me, will expand on the work I do in the social-emotional level and the different social issues.

I talk to my family about my future plans, not so much friends. I'm also fortunate in that I have a lot of people who, on a professional level, have a belief in me that I can do things, which helps. I look in the mirror; I look at my age. I'm very young in education. I don't feel that people discredit my thoughts and my opinions and my beliefs, which makes a big difference. Had I felt that, I wouldn't be so strong. And I wouldn't feel that sense of encouragement. When I have that sense that people believe in me, then I can do more, I can do better, I can go to that next level. I tend to take that belief as it's almost my obligation to do so.

The toughest part of my job has been the change in my life. It had a great impact on my son. A lot of time is spent away from home – a lot of hours. He's 17. He'll be 18 at the end of January and finished the twelfth grade at the end of January. That first year of being a principal, I was very absent and it was very hard on my family, my extended family, very hard. I mean I think they still struggle with that. I don't get to see my family the way I used to and spend the time with them that I used to spend. I can blame it on the job and my responsibilities, but I think it has more to do with my ability to balance things. I really work hard to say at the end of the day I've done all I can and be okay with that. That's one thing that's different from teaching where you do your day plan. You can lay it out for a week. You can lay it out for 2 weeks. You feel a sense of 'it's done'. With an administrative position, it's never done. It's never finished. I really struggled with that during the first year. I have my checklist and I expected to get through that checklist by the end of the week but guess what? It's never finished! Now I'm much more realistic. I have my weekly things that I hope to accomplish. I have my daily things that I really work to accomplish. I could very easily stay there till 10 or 11 o'clock at night. I allow myself maybe one night a week where I do stay late on site. I do bring some work home with me, but a lot of times it's not so much in the evenings that I do it but I might get up earlier in the morning so that I have that time with my son or with anybody else, my family, my friends. I'm learning slowly but I still hit the bumps. The last month was go, go, go, go, work, work, work, and it was a hard month. Sometimes I come down for a day, luckily on the weekend, where I kind of sit and care for me, you won't see me. I'll just sit and recoup. Then I get up the next morning and off I go to start again. My son and my family, it's had a huge effect and sometimes I'm angry about that. Sometimes I go to work and I'll be down at the Band office and I'll think, 'I'm more than just a principal. There's more to me than this.' And that's kind of my rebellious way . . . But ultimately the only one I can blame for that is myself. But still, you want to do more, you want to do better, and that's drive. As an administrator you owe it to your staff. That's an important piece in this.

And my staff give a lot in all of the different projects and things that I brought into the school. I'm very fortunate that my staff understand why we're doing things. In return, when I start to see my staff waver, I tell them, 'Off you go. You have appointments. You have to take care of yourself. If your kids need you, go take care of them. If you need to go take a day for yourself, you need to do that.' But you don't have anybody sitting above you telling you, 'Off you go'. There's never a good time. Any time I'm away from the school, I feel guilty. I try to do better.

I don't know that it would be any different in any First Nation community. I think that when you administer in a system that's outside the district it's a very different experience. I don't know that I was 100 percent prepared and, honestly, I don't think there was any way that I could be prepared for what I walked into. But, I definitely don't think I would've chosen anything different. There are those days when, like I said, I think, 'What am I doing?' But, for the most part, when I look at the kids and I look at where the school's at and I look at my staff, I'm proud. I'm proud to say that I'm there now. I'm not this timid little principal who was so eager, so worried about what everybody else is thinking and working to improve myself. I think that in that first year of being an administrator out there, a lot of things happened in that community, I mean a lot of big things, and I think that school really took a strong role in leadership in the community and in trying to promote a healthy stance. I'm proud of that and I'm proud of the position that the school has taken. In the same breath, I'm lucky. I have a staff that are along for the ride and that's important. There's no way that I could've done that by myself. There's absolutely no way.

Future plans

I unintentionally cycle every 4 years. My first teaching position was 4 years. My last teaching position was 4 years. So 4 years here before I move on? I don't do it intentionally. It's just what happens. I think my aspirations are to continue to work in a school setting at a community level, but I also have a strong desire to work at a provincial level. But I always see that as something coming down the road. I would eventually like to have a role with First Nation education in British Columbia. And it was funny, I was in Victoria for some training and I walked outside the Parliament Buildings and I said to a friend of mine, 'One day, I'm going to be in those Parliament Buildings.' I do have those hopes and dreams. Do I imagine myself being a principal until I retire? No, because I almost stumbled into that arena at a very young age and I think I still have a long way to go. I do look at myself and say, 'What next?' I do see the challenges. I do have aspirations for a doctorate, a couple of years after I get through the research for my M.Ed.

Part 3
Asia

'Our School Is Our Independence': A Novice School Director's Perspective on School Leadership and Post-Conflict Reconstruction in East Timor

Reynold Macpherson meets with Paulino de Carralho, director of Aileu Village School and Paulino de Jesus Araujo, president of the School Parent Teachers' Association

Chapter outline

Introduction

Paulino de Carralho's account of becoming and being the director of a remote village primary school in the youngest country in the world is embedded in a context of post-conflict reconstruction.

One of the most complex challenges for school leaders in Timor Leste is the language(s) to be used locally to enable learning and manage schools in a national education system. Most people, especially those in rural areas, speak their own ethnic language at home. These ethnic languages signal very early migration and settlement patterns. Tetun is spoken by most Timorese, in most districts, and is regarded as the original lingua franca, but there are exceptions, and a primary school director has to be verbally fluent and culturally adroit in terms of local ethnicity, as well as in national aspirations expressed in Tetun, to navigate through intense and continuing rivalry over scarce resources. A director may also have to provide leadership across an East–West political fault line in Timor Leste that was originally generated in inter-tribal historical times.

Other deep schisms were created by the countervailing forces of colonization and resistance. Portuguese was the first language of colonization and was the language of government and education. The authority of the Portuguese rulers, however, was relatively weak outside of regional centres. They reached accommodations with the *liurai,* the traditional Timorese rulers, and focussed on growing and extracting coffee. Following occupation by Japanese forces during World War II, the Portuguese returned, but left in 1974 when economic and political crises in Portugal forced it to give up its colonies. Indonesia then annexed Timor Leste and ruled from 1975 to 1999, but faced a gradually escalating insurgency.

Colonialism had nurtured a societal capacity to resist imposed change, to the point where it became a valued national trait. Portuguese became the language of resistance during the Indonesian occupation. Many of the current political leaders were educated during the Portuguese colonial era and spent most of the Indonesian occupation in Portuguese possessions such as Mozambique. Portuguese language is, therefore, seen as a marker of national identity and both Tetun and Portuguese are now recognized as 'official languages'. Bahasa Indonesian and English are accepted as 'working languages'. To the consternation of many primary school directors, who are neither literate in the language nor inclined to be so, Portuguese has recently been re-introduced as the basic language of education, starting from the lower grades of primary schooling. Teachers' explanations and school directors' instructions may be in Tetun, yet many schools still hold on to their Indonesian textbooks, and most of the new textbooks and policies will be in Portuguese. While discussions about teaching and learning may be in Bahasa and Tetun, formal documentation in the ministry and minutes of executive meetings are in Portuguese.

Another challenge for primary school directors is that Bahasa is the second language of colonization. It was the language of government and commerce for 24 years, the language that most East Timorese have been educated in and is the language that most still prefer to write in.

The final language challenge for primary school directors is that English has played a major role in government since 1999. The United Nations (UN) mission that managed East Timor's transition to full independence in 2002 conducted its affairs in English, and the UN mission that returned in 2006, when internal factionalism undermined the government's capacity to maintain internal security, restored calm using English. English became the language of peace and, by association, prosperity. Alongside Tetun, English appears to be emerging as the second language of choice of many young Timorese in Dili, the capital of Timor Leste, especially among the computer literate. Language policy appears to be an intractable problem in education, particularly the absence of a common language to teach teachers with and a lack of teaching resources in any language.

Other major challenges are the poor quality of education in terms of teacher capability, teacher qualifications and the curricula at various levels of learning. There is also high absenteeism of teachers and students, high attrition rates, high repetition rates, high adult illiteracy, a gender imbalance with only 30 percent of teachers in primary schools being women and poor classroom facilities. Teacher–student ratios are typically about 1:40 and with about one-third of the population of school age, the system needs hundreds of newly trained primary teachers each year.

The local context

The main road south from Dili zigzags up the face of a steep and dense eucalyptus forest for about 30 km, before crossing a rugged mountain watershed. The bush thins out dramatically and becomes much like a steep, dry and red earth Australian landscape.

Another 17 km of narrow, partially sealed and badly potholed road gradually drops into the fertile highland district of Aileu. The main town, also
named Aileu, is only 47 km from Dili, but it takes an hour and a half driving
time. Aileu is a town of sharp contrasts. It is surrounded by intricately watered
rice fields, vegetable market gardens and rich bush. It has a vigorous market
and a disproportionate number of boisterous young people with ready smiles.
Yet, some of the main buildings in the town centre are still burnt out husks.

A further 7 km into the mountains northeast from Aileu is the remote village of Aikua Rinkua. Getting there means driving very slowly up a wide and
shallow riverbed and then walking the final 2 km. Through interpreter Johnny
Viegas, the current president of the School Parent Teachers' Association,
Sr Paulino de Jesus Araujo takes up the story of the village primary school.

Paulino de Jesus Araujo, president of the School Parent Teachers' Association

We established the school in 2005. Our community realized that it was taking far too long for our children to walk to other remote schools and that our
numbers were growing. At that time I was the suco chief (village chief) and
the current school director was a teacher at another school. I called the community and the current school director together to discuss the idea of having
a new school. We decided that I should put a proposal to the Aileu District
Education Office. They supported the proposal and sent it on to the Ministry
of Education in Dili.

We waited 2 years for approval. In the third year the District Education
Office informed us that our proposal had been approved. They also sent staff
to survey our families to identify the number of children that would probably
be attending. The survey showed that our proposal met the ministry requirements. We were asked to indicate the land to build on. Things were getting
urgent, so we decided to use the home of the current school director, who
comes from our village. Fifty children attended, so we divided the house into
three classrooms and organized four teachers.

The opening ceremony was held on 25 July 2007. It was organized by the
District Education Office. It included a formal signing of the authorization
from the Ministry of Education for Aikua Rinkua to run a public school.
There were speeches by the superintendent of the Aileu District and the suco

chief. All school directors in the Aileu District attended, along with about 100 people from the community. The current school director's wife organized the feast. It was a very important day in the life of the Aikua Rinkua community.

The school is located central to the village. The parents have large gardens that primarily produce potatoes and hillside plantations that grow coffee bushes. Looking south you see large rice fields and the main road. The steep ground to the north provides us with water and coffee, and east and west are the gardens.

The community is pleased that their school is nearby. The parents feel that the government has supported their remote suco, and they feel proud that they have been able to have their children learn so close to home. They feel that they have real independence. They have independence to learn from home. They have independence as East Timorese to have education in their own village. The parents have independence to collaborate with our teachers to help direct and support our children's learning. Independence means everything to us East Timorese.

Our school has four grades. Grade 1 has 12 boys and 8 girls. Grade 2 has 9 boys and 4 girls. Grade 3 has 5 boys and 2 girls. Grade 4 has 4 boys and 6 girls. That totals 30 boys and 20 girls, 50 all together. We have one permanent teacher, the school director, a male, another contract male teacher and two voluntary teachers, one male and one female. They are each paid US$183 per month.

Our classrooms have sufficient tables and chairs for the students. They are organized in straight lines facing the blackboard. The classroom has a dirt floor; there is no ceiling, and in the rainy season the roof leaks a little, but not enough to stop the teaching and learning. We have window frames but no glass. We have doorframes but no doors. We can't lock up, but nothing ever gets stolen. The school has never been painted, inside or out. One of the three classrooms is now used as the teachers' room, for the school director's office and where the community meets.

The curriculum is based on the national curriculum: Portuguese, Tetun, mathematics, history and environmental science. The pedagogy is a little different by subject, but the teachers all use direct instruction, textbooks in Portuguese, the blackboard, questions and answers and their own teaching aids and materials. Although the textbooks are mostly in Portuguese, the teachers explain things in Tetun. We also speak Mumbai at home but it is not used at school, mostly Portuguese with Tetun. Even though the constitution determines that Portuguese will be learned, the parents are happy that the explanations are given in Tetun. We are also happy to retain Mumbai as a home language and to have Bahasa Indonesian and English used in the market and for international travel. The community down in Aileu has organized English classes out of school time, and some of our people walk the 7 km to those classes.

In sum, our school is special to us. We are interested in building relationships with primary schools in other parts of the world. The reason is that Timor Leste is an independent part of the international community. These relationships would help the teachers learn more about different countries and teaching methods. These relationships would help students learn from each other. Letters can be addressed to the school director, Aikua Rinkau Primary School, Aileu, Timor Leste.

Our remote school makes us all feel very proud. It is not in a city or in a town. It is in our community. Education is available for our children in our remote village. We have independence in our newly independent country.

Paulino de Carralho, school director

Sr Carralho is short, slight man with an intense yet gentle disposition. I am introduced to him under a large shade tree outside the Aileu District Office. He seems ill at ease until our interpreter Johnny explains that we can move chairs outside and conduct the interview under the tree. He touches the tree for assurance, sits and relaxes.

Paulino is dressed modestly and he defers readily to others who call by to greet him. He is obviously widely known and respected. He gives carefully considered answers to my questions. His wide smile and generous wit are evoked whenever a joke is made about his remote village and school. His story is anything but funny.

Paulino's story

I am 33, born in January 1976. Our country was at war at the time, although the conflict eased a little in 1980. I was told by my parents that the Portuguese were cruel, dictating how we lived. They also told me that it was the Carnation Revolution in 1975 in Portugal that led to the Portuguese finally leaving, and soon after that, the Indonesians invading. In between, they said, we had a short, sweet period of independence.

My first memories are of my mother's message being passed on through my father, after she died at the end of 1976: 'You must go to school until you get your degree.' I was brought up by my uncle and auntie, who paid my school fees up to 1990 when I rejoined my father.

The situation was very bad in our family. We had no economic support, often short of food, so I had to leave again. A priest in Manututo took me in and I stayed there for 9 years, until 1999, when the Indonesians finally left. I was educated from pre-secondary up to secondary levels in the St Antonio Catholic School in Manututo until 1995, and I then worked on in the school for 4 years as an administrative assistant.

When the Indonesians left in September 1999 it was traumatic. There was an East Timorese militia team linked to the Indonesian army in Manututo who destroyed community homes, tortured a young man and stole community property. The situation became so critical that the priests and the community all ran away to safe areas in their home villages. I escaped from Manututo by myself, walking 6 hours through the night to Aileu. I was 18, frightened and very pleased to find my father. But another militia team in Aileu supported by the Indonesian army burned our family house. So all of my family ran away to the mountains and we lived off the land. We used to creep down to our crops to collect food, but it was very dangerous and we had to return to our hiding places.

We still have mixed feelings about the Indonesians today. The education they provided, the roads, bridges and university places, we appreciate. But the behaviour of their army and their militias was not like human beings, without any respect for people, killing freely. So when the Indonesian army and their militias left, and the United Nations Transitional Administration in East Timor (UNTAET) soldiers arrived, we returned to Aileu. We found everything destroyed. It was hard to find food. We survived through the garden and the rice field. We used palm trees to build houses. In 2000 the United Nations High Commissioner for Refugees (UNHCR) provided construction materials so we could build new houses.

In September and October 2000 we collaborated to identify a qualified team to rebuild education in Aileu's subdistricts. I started teaching all subjects in a primary school in Besilau. I was not formally qualified to teach, but my education and experience as an administrator at Manututo helped me. The Ministry of Education screened us using a test in Portuguese, Tetum, mathematics, Indonesian, environmental science and History. I passed and taught at Besilau for 7 years. I was paid US$120 a month for those 7 years.

I was married in 2003, here in Aileu, to a one-time classmate in Manututo, from Emera. We had three children, two boys and a girl. The eldest is now six. We hope they will all be teachers. While I have not yet achieved my mother's advice to me, I have got my Diploma 3 in education from the Chrystal Institute in Dili and will wait for opportunities to improve my qualifications.

I was invited by the suco chief to help build a new school in my home village. I could not say no to him and my people. I was also interested because of the high number of dropouts from my village in other schools. There was no real opportunity for our parents to escort their children long distances to other schools to ensure their safety. The memory of war is with everyone. And the other reason for agreeing was about local development. Our community will grow and the local population will grow if we have local schooling. I have never thought of doing any job outside of education. It means that I can focus on service to my own community.

So when I knew that I was going to be the director of a new school in my home village, it was like a dream come true. The local community trusted me. I consulted other school directors to prepare for the role. I also recalled my experiences in Manututo and Besilau to identify what I would need to do. So, I started as a school director on the day the school opened: on 25 July 2007. At first I felt overawed by a heavy sense of responsibility. I was very nervous on the day, but all the local school directors came and offered me support. I was also strongly supported and carefully guided by Sr Augusto Manuel, our district superintendent in Aileu. He told me 'that is your village, your community, your people, and I trust you to carry the responsibility.' My wife organized the feast and she stood with me.

So the next day we started taking enrolments. It took 2 weeks to check all birth certificates and all the other details that were needed, and we submitted them to the district office. In the third week we organized the students into age groups and started teaching. The district office had delivered enough tables and chairs for the students and the teachers. I rented a car to help transport the textbooks and teaching and learning materials to the end of the road. I invited three local boys to unload the supplies and carry them to the village. I invited three locals to help teach the children; they were unpaid volunteers who had finished secondary school. In 2008 the teacher recruitment process changed. I recommended that the three volunteers sit the ministry test, but one of the volunteers failed. Currently I have three teachers that have all passed the text.

The most surprising thing to me about starting up as a school director was that I could lead as a local person. The second most-surprising thing was that the government recognized me as a competent leader. And third was that my community trusts me to lead education in our area.

So my approach to leadership is first about being a good example to the community. This means not being involved in cock fighting or gambling, always growing the respect of the community. Second, it means communicating effectively about the school's activities, such as explaining the curriculum. Third, it means delegating responsibilities to colleagues so they share in community leadership and improve their own standing in the village. Fourth, it means always checking the teachers' punctuality so that they check the students' punctuality. And yes, I copied the school director at Besilau, who always spoke to his staff nicely, with respect, and was always punctual, setting a good example. He always planned carefully for each day, each week, each trimester and each year, and shared the planning and the plans with us. In these ways he developed excellent relationships with each of his teachers.

I also watch how my leadership affects my colleagues. When they make mistakes, it is important to speak with them quickly about the mistakes, but to speak softly so they are not embarrassed and my relationship with them is not affected. I have the same teachers I selected over 2 years ago and they keep getting better.

There have been problems. The first difficulty that I had as a leader was that some of my colleagues have a poor capacity to resolve their problems with students and refer all of these problems to me as school director. Now, if I resolve a problem, I always follow up with a meeting with my colleagues to discuss what happened, so that next time they can solve the problem without waiting for me to get involved.

Another type of leadership difficulty has been about organizing the School Feeding Programme. There are people in the community who seem to believe that I am corrupt and my family is eating more than we should. This tendency is countered by meeting with parents and children to explain how we manage the food, the cooking and the sharing of the food each day. We invite local and remote parents to come in to help with the School Feeding Programme, and this generates transparency and wider understanding.

My second year as school director was very different from the first. I discovered that my voice was invited at district meetings of school directors. The district superintendent asked me to explain to other school directors how I had made some improvements. My voice was respected. And then the school was provided with a new roof, which lifted our spirits. And then our school inspector was appointed and he visited each month to talk over our problems. This helped encourage me. It motivated me to accept some of our poor conditions, make a number of improvements with colleagues and community members, change a number of administrative procedures and consider how other remote schools were doing their planning.

My third year as a school director has been very different again. Some very remote communities have moved closer to our school so that their children can have access. We believe that it is partly a result of our school's reputation improving and partly a result of our school getting support from the government. The quality of our community's educational facilities is improving and as our all-weather roads and tracks improve, our school is becoming less remote.

On the other hand, the most difficult aspects of my job are to do with access to the village, its remoteness. It is 7 km from Aileu with the last 2 km on foot. There is no electricity. It is difficult to deliver textbooks and impossible in the rainy season when the river floods and we are cut off, sometimes for months. We need a library, textbooks and graphics to help us counter the remoteness. We need high-quality pictures that show our students what life is like in other places. We need mathematics textbooks with pictures and concrete learning materials rather than trying to teach applications on the blackboard. We need to be able to talk with other teachers to share our problems and solutions that work. It is all about overcoming remoteness. I also worry at night about my colleagues using paraffin lights to do lesson preparation. The black smoke is not good for their respiration. And the cold at night makes it hard for them and the students to study.

Is being a school director a lonely job? No. It is not a lonely job. It should always be a team leadership role, a community leadership role. There should be no reason for being lonely. The most satisfying aspects of my work are my relationships with my colleagues, our excellent performance evaluations and the support we get from our community.

Looking out 5 years, I want to have improved the professional development and training in my school, especially in curriculum, pedagogy and cultural activities. The big changes I want to see include the construction of a new school to shift the school out of my home, water and sanitation facilities, solar panels generating electricity, laptops for administration and teaching and learning, a library, filing cabinets and so on. I expect my job to change steadily as better resources arrive and as leadership training is provided.

In 10 years time I imagine that I will still be a school director, providing politics don't come into play. I may well be at the same school, because it is my family, my community, in my country. It all depends on the Ministry of Education and on the politics of education. So, my advice to teachers in Timor Leste thinking of becoming a school director is to find a good mentor, build good relationships with colleagues and school directors and develop excellent relationships with their community. That is the best insurance against politics, but you can never be sure. So, I plan to refurbish my school buildings, the school gardens and the facilities for teaching and learning, especially in mathematics. I need models and objects to help children learn.

Concluding note

The interview was over. It became clear from casual conversation that Paulino had walked the 7 km to tell his story and he was now ready to return. He smiled widely at the offer of a lift. He stood and looked around Aileu with apparent satisfaction.

We took the chairs back into the district office while he waited. When we came out he was still gazing at the local landscape. Through Johnny, our translator, I asked Paulino why he so enjoyed the view, expecting him to explain his family's long connections with the land.

Instead, he explained that he did not like going into the district office because it had been built and used in Indonesian times to direct education and 'interrogate' people. To ease his obvious discomfort I asked him 'what was different about this building and his remote school?' He smiled at the reference to remoteness and replied with a gentle smile:

'There are no bad spirits in our school. Our school is our independence.'

Acknowledgement

Thanks to Johnny Viegas for interpretation.

8 'I Want to Do the Best Job That I Can, So I Worry': A Novice Principal in China Reflects on the Responsibility and Complexity of Leading an Urbanizing Rural School

Xiao Liang meets with Fan Heuli, principal of Zhatang Primary School

Chapter outline

Context

Hunan province lies in the central southern part of China. Its capital city is Changsha, with a population of some 6.5 million people. The city of Changsha is situated within a municipal area that is also called Changsha. Changsha is in the northeast of Hunan province, in the lower reaches of the Xiang River at the western margin of the Xiang-Liu Basin. It is a famous historical and cultural city. During the Ming and Qing Dynasty, it was an important rice market, and it became a major Chinese revolutionary centre during the Republican Period. During the war with Japan Changsha was a battlefield. It was rebuilt and underwent development during the formation of the Republic of China. The economy of Hunan province is now developed and is based on machinery, technology, tourism and the media and entertainment business. Changsha is now an important city in the midwest. Education has been a local government priority, and the province has a national reputation for the sacrifices parents make for their children's education.

Wangcheng County is one of four county areas within the municipal area of Changsha. In economic and cultural terms, Wangcheng County is relatively well developed. Following local government reorganization in 2007 and as part of Hunan province's urbanization process, some of Wangcheng County became incorporated within Yuelu District, one of four urban districts in Changsha City. Yuelu is located on the west bank of the Xiang River and named after the Yuela Mountain, an area of historical interest and scenic beauty. The district also got its name from Yuelu Academy, where scholars have gathered since ancient times. Yuela Academy is one of four great academies in China and an institute of higher learning, with a history of more than 1,000 years. In the twenty-first century Hunan province is still a centre of knowledge and learning because it is now China's 'Silicon Valley' with over 16 universities and research institutes concentrated there.

Yuelu District is the western gateway to Changsha with convenient transportation links. The Xiang River extends to the Yangtze and eventually to the sea. Three bridges link Yuelu with the four districts in the east of Changsha. This gives Yuelu District a strong strategic position in terms of priority development within the Xiang River Ecological Economic Belt. However, Yuelu is also an area of historical interest and scenic beauty, and administrative reorganization and the urbanization policy and process has created uncertainty and given rise to concern among school principals, teachers, students and parents, as well as general residents. There are mixed views about the changes that have taken place, because the advantages of the change are not clear.

Soon after the policy decision to reorganize local government, all schools in the area changed their name affiliations from 'Wangcheng County' to 'Yuelu District, Changsha City'. Zhatang Primary School, previously of 'Wangcheng County', is now 'Zhatang Primary School, Yuelu District, Changsha City'. 'Zhatang' was the name of part of the village before, which means 'pool of dregs' for some geographic reason. The school was first established in September 1989, and is located in an urbanizing rural area, east of

Yanjia Bridge, and surrounded by woods and mountains. The school belongs to Dongshanwan Village, Hanpu Town. The school is about an hour's drive from the centre of Changsha City.

The campus is over 1,314 square metres with an area for sports of around 665 square metres. The campus was built and renovated based on academic and security principles. There are computer labs, a school library, chemistry and physics labs, a music room, a file room, a sports facility room, a multimedia room, a labour skill room, a students' event room and a medical assistance room.

All children within the age categories in the locality are enrolled, giving three classes and 77 students. There are seven teachers, three male and four female. Fan Huali is the school principal. Huali is 28 years old, married and with no children of her own. She has been a teacher for 9 years and was appointed to Zhatang as principal in August 2009 under the 'Guazhi Duanlian' policy of the Changsha Education Bureau (temporarily appointed to a lower-level school as a leader in order for further promotion in one's career).

Huali had previously been a Chinese language teacher and director of a Chinese language researching and teaching group in an urban school called 'Yinwan Road Primary School' in Changsha City. She must have been diligent and smart in her previous job, because only those teachers and staff with 'top performance' recognized by their schools qualify for this kind of opportunity. In her previous position, she taught Chinese language to good effect using vivid and practical methods that enabled her students to develop a deep interest in learning. When she led the team for research and teaching, she had harmonious relationships with her colleagues and leaders. She also admitted that she did not spend much time 'reporting' to her leaders. Instead, all her performance was spontaneous and active.

Huali was influenced by her teaching parents when she was growing up. In 2000 she graduated from Jiangnan Industrial School with a secondary diploma and later studied at Hunan Normal University, a well-known university in Changsha City with a national reputation for cultivating future teachers. Her husband is a professor at the National University of Defence Technology in Changsha, a well-known military university sponsored by the Chinese central government. Following her marriage, she lived in the residential area of the National University of Defence Technology. Huali started teaching in 2001. After 8 years of teaching, she was appointed to the post of principal at Zhatang Primary School after going through a set of strict procedures. Every day Huali drives over 30 km of mostly rutted and bumpy roads to school. It takes her about 50 minutes to cover the 30 km.

On the left end of the second floor of the teaching building at Zhatang Primary School, there is an office for the teachers. All seven teachers have desks here and use them to check homework, prepare for classes or take a break. Huali shares the office with every other teacher. The office is big enough for seven teachers, but it is not spacious enough, apparently, when the occasional teacher–student discussion is needed. The view from the window incorporates the school playground where teachers and students gather for special moments such as morning exercises. The view from the doorway takes in all the classrooms on the second floor of this teaching building.

There is no separate principal's office in the school. I met Huali in the comparatively big and quiet computer lab.

Huali's story

I became a formal teacher in 2001 after I finished my studies. After 8 years I was appointed principal of Zhatang Primary School in August 2009. Prior to accepting this new position, I was a director of the teaching and researching team on Chinese language in another urban primary school, and I consider that as a 'small leader'; it was a more academic position. The principalship at Zhatang was offered to me after I had gone through a strict application and confirmation process. It was the first time in my life that I applied. I did it through writing application papers and other related procedures.

Honestly speaking, I was not intending to become a teacher when I was quite young. It was my mother, a teacher at that time, who recommended this career to me, saying that this job would make my life stable and enjoyable. As we know, there are two official semesters in most Chinese schools: the first semester of each academic year starts in September and ends about 1 month before the Chinese lunar New Year; the second semester starts right after the Chinese lunar New Year, basically in February, and ends at the beginning of July. Then teachers would have 1 month's winter vacation and 2 months' summer vacation with official payment. Being a teacher is especially proper for a woman since it gives you plenty of time to take care of your family. My parents also indicated that being an educator can endow me with a strong sense of spiritual achievement. I remember when I was much younger, I thought that I would rather pursue another career that is more mobile so that I could have a real taste of the 'outside society'. In my life until now, I have not had work experience in other areas. I've only been a teacher. But if there had been other opportunities, maybe I would have considered other professions beyond education as a career.

After I became a teacher, even with several years of experience, I still thought that I was not the kind of person who is suitable for being a leader. I heard from my previous leader and other colleagues who said that I was too innocent and inexperienced. In other words, I was too 'pure' to become a school leader and handle all the complexities of an entire school. They must have observed this through my daily behaviour of keeping simple relationships with colleagues and speaking straightforward words to them. However, deep in my heart, I knew that I would prefer to have a try and see how it goes. I did not believe that a person should be that 'sophisticated' in order to manage a principalship. I do welcome the challenge.

The application process was a bit complicated and serious. First we had to make a decision in the countryside to turn to *Guazhi Duanlian* under the policy of the Ministry of Education. Then we had to complete an application report. The school had to sign and agree, and then we had to send the document to the education bureau. The education bureau then considered the application, and a certain percentage of applicants are approved.

After a series of application procedures, I finally got the chance. Honestly speaking, I was anxious since if I could obtain this position, it could bring me huge pressure. I remember that my previous principal indicated that I was too young and inexperienced. Plus, I heard people say that coming to a rural elementary school to support rural education is quite relaxing. Many people regard the countryside as a place to relax and spend your holidays. But I did not want to waste time, and instead I decided to make my life more substantial and colourful as well as challenging. But unlike others who have just 1 year in countryside schools, I have 2 years. My psychological preparation was not sufficient, obviously. I was not given notice of which school I was heading for until the eve of my arrival day in school. Perhaps they did not want me to change my mind – they just let me know which school to go to one day ahead.

I did read many books related to school management as part of my preparation. But this is not called 'training'; it is in my mind 'self-promotion'. There was no regular training provided to the new principals. However, there were aspects that I considered useful in reading, such as in methods of management, including 'taking into consideration others' feelings', employee-centred theory and so on. Before becoming a principal, there was no formal training in leadership or management for me. But once I had made the decision to come here and become a principal, I intentionally imitated the way my leaders spoke, the attitude, the ways of acting and behaving. They influenced me a lot. This was my only real preparation. However, I believe that my professional experience of being a teacher and a director for the research and teaching team endowed me with a lot of insights into education, and these have helped in my current position as a school principal. I was also determined that if I encountered problems, I would turn back to books as often as possible.

Once I took up the post, there were not, fortunately, any conspicuous objections in the school, although I could sense the suspicions that some people had. Sometimes teachers did not say anything, but based on their delay in executing my policies at times, I could see that effecting change might be a longer process than I thought. Well, my idea is to construct a better school, not for the benefit of myself or the teachers, but for the students and the community. Therefore, I have no fears. However, I still wondered, as a completely new principal, would my idea be an idea only, or would it become true at last?

Once I started my work as a principal, the most apparent transition for me was having to make decisions. Previously I kind of relied on others to make possible and right decisions, but now everybody else counts on me. This was the biggest change for me. I could see the expectations in the eyes of teachers. The whole school is dependent on my choices rather than on other people's recommendations or even their own inferences.

Since I came into this management work, I certainly would, according to both teachers' and my own expectations, wish to make some positive changes on educational ideology in a countryside school. And I hope to bring countryside children some urban educational ideology and enable them to enjoy the same quality of education as children in urban schools. Comparatively speaking, with regard to hardware, including school infrastructure and facilities, or software, including school regulations and team spirit, current urban schools in Changsha, or even in China, possess much better and of course more advanced conditions. Surely I had some indication that the parents would think about the reforms I wished to make in a doubtful way. Teachers would also hold a 'wait and see' approach towards my decisions. They have hopes on me but they did not have trust in me at the very beginning. I knew I had to do something, to take some effective measures and let them know that changes could happen and these would be in favour of them and the students. In spite of having no conspicuous oppositions in my school, I always recall the anxiety and suspicion existing among my teachers and staff.

Zhatang Primary School is the only school in Dongshanwan Village. Dongshanwan Village was incorporated by Zhatang Village and Dongshan Village several years ago in accordance to the township policy. Also due to the decreasing number of kids as a result of the Chinese 'one-child policy', the former Dongshan Primary School was cancelled and there is only Zhatang Primary School left. But not all resident kids come to our school since there are other choices in the neighbouring villages. The school's history and availability in the neighbourhood draw a large amount of attention from general people. The parents expect the school to provide basic and necessary foundational knowledge to their kids and also to teach their children how to behave in this society. There are no other real expectations. In order to understand more about parents' thoughts and ideas, I make use of the frequent birthdays or weddings and some other gatherings to communicate with them. In addition to this, on my way back and forth from school to home, I always meet some parents and stop and have a chat with them. This kind of exchange of ideas is not difficult, and there have been no problems. I think that the parents accept this school and me as its principal.

Inside the school, there is not a very well developed ideological environment among teachers since most of the staff are older and I believe that they are at a stage in their careers where they are less motivated to engage in further studies, research or exchanges. In addition, this school, although it has a relatively long history, has not established itself as a campus with its own culture. All of this is somewhat disappointing me and the situation is far from my ideal. Age and life experience sometimes make people too proud or too content about themselves, I think. My job is to try to motivate them in aspects of teaching and learning so that their students may benefit more from their education in our school.

Looking back over the first year of being principal of the school, I have mixed feelings. I recall that after my application was approved, I felt huge pressure and a certain degree of anxiety. Though this is not a critical post, it is a brand-new environment and I knew that I would face many new challenges. My family, my colleagues and my leaders set great score onto it; I am afraid of people blaming me or accusing me of not doing my job well. I was also afraid that 2 years later the school may not have changed at all, or it would have become worse after I took the position. How miserable that would be!

When I was appointed and finally reached Zhatang, it was not relaxing at all. One problem was that I had not realized that is so far away from my home and the city. I think in my heart there was a little bit of regret, since the geographical distance was much farther than I had thought. But there was no going back. There were no other choices and the decision had been made. The town school management authority leaders and the previous principal instructed me a lot about the school, and with almost total innocence, I started to really learn about the school from the moment I first set my foot in it.

On the first day I came to Zhatang, our upper school principal Mr Li introduced me to others, and then I made a brief self-introduction. I began to understand about parents according to what the teachers said and to understand students through my personal observation and participation in the classes. I personally teach the Chinese language classes and also I regularly observe other teachers' classes and made a policy of observing classes among respective teachers. I also asked students to offer feedback for improvement.

In order to facilitate the understanding between the school and parents, in this past semester I held a parents' meeting. It was interesting. Before this parents' meeting, I believed that rural parents did not attach great importance to education. I was wrong. They pay much attention to education; the only dilemma was that they do not know how to deal with their children's education and support their learning. They not understand the correct ways to cultivate them. The reasons might be their lower education level themselves, and they may lack information in this relatively remote area in the countryside. But with their earnest approach and sincerity, everything could be much easier if we want to initiate reforms towards a better school and a more excellent education.

During the first few weeks I felt that the pace of the school was slow, including that of the teachers and students, and this was much different from my previous schools, much slower. And their politeness, behaviour and study habits were kind of unsettling. For example, in my previous school, the teachers would enter the classroom right after the bell rings, but here in the countryside the discipline is not that strict – although the bell rings, teachers might still chat for 1 or 2 more minutes and then meander off to class. And usually when we assigned some tasks, they acted slower than I expected. These were the kinds of habits that I could not get used to.

In the transition from being a class teacher to a principal, I felt and experienced more complicated interpersonal relationships, too. When I was a director, I was dealing with people as well, but now I face more people and the matters that I am supposed to manage are more problematic. But this proved to be helpful in improving my capabilities of doing things. After I took the position, in the adaptation process, I found that my role here is different from the role I had in my previous school. I have to be a leader; if staff did not know how to do something, I would teach them how to do it; if they were unwilling to do it, it is fine because I would finish it by myself. Many teachers cooperate with me now since they know that I am simply taking over the position here for 2 years. As a younger woman, I am ready to do so much for the development of the school, and I think they felt embarrassed at being the real master of this school and the older generation of the school. They began to put more devotion to this process of turning an idea into reality.

With the increasing communication with teachers, I found that the changes that happened were astonishing. Now they are actively making contributions to the school development. Their roles have been transformed. I played some role here, but now everyone is playing a part.

Changes had to be made and still have to be made. But with continuous self-encouragement and group work, the process is no longer a sole process. There are pleasant changes for everybody to see and feel. It is the reality. On the one hand, student behaviours, such as being polite and their approach to study, have been elevated. I think that the students now have a more genuine interest in studies rather than taking study as a task only. On the other hand, teachers have more passion towards the school's operation and have shown increased concern. Besides, we have held events such as parents' meetings and the sixtieth Anniversary of Young Pioneers celebrations. My idea of improving teachers' educational ideology and implementation efficiency, enabling them to use computers effectively, internet resources and other modern education technology, is being fulfilled step by step.

Luckily, there have not been any tense interpersonal relationships between me and teachers. But there have been some situations when there is only one person – me – who is working on a particular task. I was frustrated, but we had to move on. Teachers see this and sometimes they want to be of assistance; it is only that they did not have the ability to help in certain areas. If this happens again, the situation would remain the same.

Of course, I am more often enjoying my work. When I see teachers are involved in the reform and innovation process, I am enjoying it. Except that sometimes I am sad to see teachers' unsatisfying work pace. There is not any surprising thing for me to experience here. And I think every step taken is as planned.

There have not been many unsatisfying points worth mentioning. What I am most concerned about is elevating teachers' skills and comprehension. I am also happy about the support from the leaders above and related organizations. When I experience difficulties, I sometimes seek help from my previous principal, previous colleagues and current village leaders, through which I gain more experience of school administration and improved educational understanding. I learn, too, from urban teachers teaching temporarily in the school. Village leaders also help me with solving some practical problems.

I would say that my leadership and management style is 'democratic'. When in situations where I cannot be completely democratic, I will hold meetings to have further discussion from others, at the end of which teachers will figure out an approximate direction. If there are still disagreements, the solution is 'minority obeys majority'.

Compared with the previous principal of the school, I think that there are not so many differences. But according to our teachers, the previous principal would do whatever the funding allows for the school but nothing more. She would never do something extra. I, instead, would be much more proactive in fundraising work and in rationally allocating the funds.

As far as I am concerned, there have been positive responses from the teachers involved in this school. They say that there are changes, and they have been very cooperative. Parents have also responded very well, perhaps because they have had their very first parent meeting and got a close look at the school, which is their kids' daily environment. I think they believe that this principal is a perfectionist and thinks about the students' interests first. Like me, parents want the school to be better and better. And they want their children to be more effectively educated.

Honestly speaking, my decisions were not always accepted or understood by school employees at first – they could not get used to it. I still want to bring some advanced approaches from the city, but they have been accustomed to many aspects and they have limited abilities. But they are not resistant. It is not that they do not cooperate; they are kind of not willing to do things.

I would say that the community of Dongshanwan Village, as well as Hanpu Town, tend to accept our school much more than before. They definitely have witnessed its improvements: students' progress, parents' meeting and a change in the school environment.

However, that is not to say that there is no pressure. There is pressure for sure. Some older teachers are less motivated, and a lot of tasks have to be completed by me and the director of teaching affairs. This is a mental stress for me, too. I want to do the best job that I can, so I do worry. I worry about the long-cultivated habits of teachers such as delaying tasks, which makes it difficult to achieve many of my ideas in the school. In addition, some relationships with institutions outside of the school have given me sleepless nights. Now it's better as I have been working here longer. But there are still too many things in my mind at the same time. I sometimes regard myself as not being an appropriate candidate to be a school principal, because I take others' feelings into account too much. I suspect that in many cases I should be more powerful and make every task more achievable. I think I sometimes lack that kind of forceful determination.

School affairs have influenced my life a lot since I became principal. I put a great deal of energy into school management. This position has also had some negative effects on my health and moods. If you ask me whether I am tired because I am a woman, I don't think so. Instead, I think that being a female principal can make you more sensitive and give you a sharper perspective when making decisions – and it makes it easier to communicate with teachers and parents (she smiles). Still, when I am facing problems by myself, with no outside support, I would definitely feel helpless and lonely. But I am also pleased to see the progress students are making in their studies, the improvements of teachers' passion towards the school and the school having a higher reputation in the parents' eyes. This is why I repeatedly say that I have mixed feelings.

Until now, if there is a typical difficulty, it has been to help teachers learn computer technology. They do not think this is highly useful for them. They have relied on books for too long. I always create chances to hear from teachers, such as regular meetings. Talking to parents is also part of my job in order to gain opinions and suggestions.

In the remaining years while I am a principal here, I plan to focus on students' academic work. Simultaneously we will organize a variety of activities to further facilitate students' comprehensive cultivation. My idea is to train excellent school graduates and therefore help the countryside to develop in a faster and more effective way when they grow up. Recently our school was assessed to be a 'qualified school' by the city education bureau. Next year we are building it into a provincial 'qualified school'.

I am pleased that we can, in most cases, obtain support from teachers and parents. Together with all staff in the school, I intend to help students improve their study habits, to help teachers learn more advanced education ideas, to help parents realize the importance of school education of their kids and encourage them to cooperate more with us.

If there is another chance, I would choose to be an ordinary teacher. During the time when I am a school leader, I meet financial troubles with the tight school budget and there is also the inconvenience of transportation. When problems such as misunderstandings between me and other teachers occur and we cannot resolve them, I will report them to related leaders to understand more about teachers. This might help me to some degree, but not completely.

I hope in the future I will be able to invite some successful and experienced principals and teachers to share some of their experience and perspectives with us. Also we should provide some opportunities to visit other schools for the purpose of learning and exchanging ideas.

After these 2 years, I could still be a principal in some school, since I have contributed much to improving this school and its atmosphere, and this has been recognized by both leaders and the community. Of course, speaking of my personal reasons, such as personality, if I am not suitable to remain a principal, then I possibly would become an ordinary teacher again. If I am a principal 2 years later, I will choose another school. I hope that the next school I will go to will have more young teachers and staff. I have consulted my family and friends in this respect.

I don't think being a school principal is the 'best' profession in this world. In order to make the school a different one, a more outstanding one, in terms of teachers, students and other factors, is not be an easy task. I understand that there are several 'musts' to fit a person for this job: a noble personality, a knowledgeable mind and a willingness to learn. Well, experience is accumulated through life. If I continue to be a principal after my 2 years at Zhatang Primary School, there is likely to be more pressure to cope with. If I find it difficult to cope, I will be a regular teacher again.

Part 4
Africa

Life in the Principalship during Challenging Times: A New South African Principal's Perspective

Kobus Mentz meets with Cedric Matroos, principal of Frank Joubert Primary School in Port-Elizabeth, South Africa

Background

Frank Joubert Primary School is situated in Schauderville, a suburb of the coastal city of Port-Elizabeth in the Eastern Cape province of South Africa. The school caters to students in grades 1 through 7. There are 582 students and 18 teachers in the school. The city of Port-Elizabeth forms part of the Nelson Mandela Bay Metropolitan Municipality. The municipality has a population of about 1.3 million. Port-Elizabeth was established by British 'settlers' who arrived around 1820, but the area was first settled by hunting and gathering people ancestral to the San, thousands of years before that. As is still the case with most of South Africa's cities, the suburbs are inhabited mostly by people from the same racial group. Schauderville was established as a suburb for so-called coloured people – a descriptor still used many years after the dismantling of apartheid and an official term used for the purposes of the national census.

The population of the suburb of Schauderville could not be described as either affluent or very poor. Most of the roads are tarred, but the houses are small and built of concrete, with small gardens that in the main are not cared for very well. A few blocks of flats can be found in the area, and these contribute to a fairly high crime rate, although in the South African context this is not particularly high. The school buildings are well cared for, and the uniformed cohort of school children were found to be friendly and outgoing during my visit.

Frank Joubert School is an English medium school, although Afrikaans and IsiXhosa are the mother tongues of a large number of students. The principal, Mr Cedric Matroos, is relatively new to the position, although he is an experienced teacher, head of the department and deputy principal. He knows the area well, having grown up in the Port-Elizabeth area.

Mr Matroos is responsible to the school governing body (SGB). In South Africa, SGBs play an important role in the management of schools. SGBs consist of the school principal and representatives from parents, teachers and students. The majority of members must be parents. SGBs are responsible for determining the school fees and a number of other management tasks. They have no jurisdiction over the teachers, who are employed by the provincial departments of education.

Language rights are protected in the South African constitution. Students have the right to be educated in their mother tongue, where this is practically applicable. In practice, however, the language of instruction used by the majority of schools is either Afrikaans or English. Indigenous African languages are used as the language of instruction in schools with a majority of black students in grades 1 through 3. After third grade English is used in the classroom. This is a cause for concern, as most speakers of indigenous African languages are not ready for the sudden change in the language of instruction after third grade. This contributes to poorer results among black students when compared to the results of white students. Parents in so-called township schools who can afford it send their children to schools in more affluent areas. Frank Joubert School has seen an influx of Xhosa-speaking children from neighbouring townships as a result of this.

Cedric's story

I started my career here at Frank Joubert Primary School in 1978 as a physical education teacher. I did a diploma in physical education and also in political science; I did a 3-year course in political science at the University of Port-Elizabeth. I didn't complete the degree, but I completed the section of political science. At that time, there was a lot of political upheaval, so I didn't continue with that. Instead, I concentrated on the school itself. My main subjects were physical education and natural science from Standard 1 to Standard 5 boys. Those are the two subjects in which I specialized.

At the moment, I have been a school principal for almost 4 years and this is my first post. This principal's post in this school was not the first one I applied for. I applied for two other posts for which I was short-listed but I didn't get the job.

I started teaching in 1978. I became a teacher because my father was a teacher and he insisted that I to go to college. As a teacher I was reluctant in the beginning. My biggest ambition before starting to teach was to be on the ships. I was even accepted into the mercantile submarine, but because of my father's insistence, I started teaching. After 2 years, I acclimatized and got used to it and started to love it.

The idea of going on a ship probably seemed more of a dream or an adventure for a young person, because you sit back and travel to many places on earth, but when you get back, there is nothing to come back to. So I did not have any other work experiences outside of education when I started teaching.

Before I became principal my previous leadership responsibilities consisted of belonging, in the old regime, to the South African Primary Schools Sports Union, of which I was the soccer chairperson, national soccer chairperson, and the sports coordinator between the Nine Codes, including winter codes and summer codes. South African 'coloured' primary schools had an umbrella sports body that catered to all the sports, which included rugby, soccer, netball, hockey and volleyball in the winter during the week. At that stage there were 16 provinces. During the summer we had athletics, swimming, cricket, baseball and ladies softball. That lasted for 8 years until unification.

In terms of leadership responsibilities, I didn't have any aspirations to become a leader or a principal. I had an aspiration to cultivate sportsmen, to emphasize sport instead of the administrative side of the whole structure. But what happens while administrating sport is that you come in contact with different principals and you learn from them. Afterwards you find yourself in leadership positions because you must escort provincial teams and attend provincial meetings and there you learn a lot. I think that was where I learned about being a leader and gained negotiating skills, in addition to the content I learned in college, and I applied these when administrating sport. So I was involved in sport and actively involved and taking leadership positions there.

What led me to become a school principal was the fact that we needed people in leadership positions that knew what was going on in sport and knew what was going on in education. There was a difference in 1986 between the various education departments that had an influence on the sport. The national budget between the different races was not the same and something had to be done in education to fix it. I learned that I needed to listen to other people's perceptions on sport and integrate these perspectives with how we and the black man see it. This integrated meaning then needed to be implemented in education first to serve the community as a whole. At that point I was interested in becoming a principal and I wanted to make a wider contribution to education. I wanted convince our black counterparts not to partake in federations, that school sports only must take place in schools so that schools control the sport and not the South African Rugby Union, or South African hockey for that matter.

My decision to seek a post as a school principal was influenced by the background and history I gained in leadership experience with my involvement in sport. I was against apartheid and was disappointed when the African National Congress (ANC) started with the negotiations about how school sport is controlled. We sent the president of the South African Council of Sport (SACOS) to speak to the ANC [1] about the differences in sport, but they refused to speak to SACOS. And then they formed the National Sports Council, so they performed. But I realized that to get between the three groups, the only way that we could solve our problem was through education.

I think I was influenced in terms of being a principal by several school principals. During my time administering sport I was in the company of several high school principals, one of whom is now an honorary doctorate at the University of Port-Elizabeth and two of whom are judges now. Being in the company of these white people, I learned leadership and negotiation skills and gained insight. Insight was something that was lacking in the coloured community because impulsive decisions are often made without thinking about or realizing the implications of decisions on children. So the experience I gained from my involvement in sport influenced me to apply for a principal position.

I prepared myself to become a principal through the process of learning to listen and giving each person the opportunity to reflect his or her own opinion. I have learned you must negotiate, but you must stay within the Schools' Act. I have also learned to be open to correction and to listen to the majority of people and what they think is right or wrong. I did not have any formal training to become a school principal except a few courses or workshops that the department runs, but these were not very useful. Basically, my experience as a sports administrator and involvement in school sport and the South African Soccer Federation prepared me to become a principal.

My thoughts and feelings when I was appointed principal were of pride. I enjoyed the cooperation, harmony and interpersonal relationships with school staff. I welcomed the decision when they appointed me. Some new principals may feel threatened, but I didn't feel threatened because the staff accepted me from day one. I was aware of the culture, the nature of the school, but it was not a new situation. I didn't make a lot of changes because at first I think you must try and go on as the previous principal did. You must be very diplomatic when you change something because you don't want to upset the equilibrium, but I am still gaining a lot of experience now.

The benefit of knowing the community and the parents is that you are aware of their personal lives, but sometimes I think it is better to be part of cross-pollination because as principal you know the circumstances of these people and you tend to become subjective when you apply law. I didn't take any special measures to get to know the parents and students because 50 or 55 percent of them were in my class and I had great respect for them. I knew them well and I'm on a tight ship with them. And they knew how I worked. I'm not a dictator or a Hitler.

I had no induction from the department, not even workshops. The transition from teacher to principal was not very dramatic or traumatic. Before I became principal, I acted as principal for 3 months because the principal at that time, it was a lady principal, was on leave for a hip replacement. Because I knew that I was going to get the post, I had no induction because of the system that we have in place. But what surprised me was the lack of support from the department. The Eastern Cape Education Department is in total disarray. I think this school is better organized than the district office is because of various factors such as financial, bad appointments and nepotism. But the district office, for me, to describe it in one sentence, is in absolute chaos. I do understand that it is a difficult province because it is responsible for a large rural area, but many posts are not filled at schools for principals and administrative posts and sport staff at the district office. These posts are budgeted for but they are not filled.

I think that the main difference between the classroom and being the principal for the first few weeks or months was that I missed my class and the children. The first year I couldn't get used to it and I took three subjects. Then I discovered in June that it was not going to work. The next year, I scaled it down to one subject.

Coping with the first few weeks was a challenge but by the end of the first and certainly the second term, I got used to being the person responsible. I realized how important it is when you're making decisions to work together with a management team. Problems are always solved when we reach and make a decision together. Then we go into a staff meeting and take a direction. It is important that the principal is linked to what's going on in the classroom and he has to know what's going on with the content and what's in the classroom. So the learning area heads and phase heads are extremely important parts in the whole system. If they are not operative, then the school will collapse.

My approach to leadership is that what's right is right and what's wrong is wrong. And never the two shall meet. Everyone must follow and be aware of the rules. When it comes to reasonable requests, I always accede to those. For example we have a very low absentee rate, so if someone asks to take leave, it is not a big problem. My leadership style and approach is not that much different from the previous principal because many of the things that she introduced in the school I inherited and still apply today. The previous principal was a woman, as I said earlier, and she still ran things under the old regime. Then we had an influx of new teachers. When things changed in the teacher union, she couldn't cope. She tried her best and she was a good principal, in fact, I inherited a lot of skills from her. So I took what I've learned and added on to that.

There was only one staff member who had a problem when I was elected principal. Because she had her degree and studied as a librarian and she was good at what she was doing, she thought that she should become the next principal. I felt for her. Next year she will be finishing off and I will give her a golden handshake, but that's how the dice fell.

At first the parents had a wrong impression about what a school principal's job consists of. They thought a principal is meant to be a chief accounting officer, that he must be a parent and that the principal should not teach. So I arranged a meeting with the parents and explained to them that the South African Schools' Act stated that a principal can be a teacher and does not work with the finances. One person came and asked me for a receipt for a debit order and I had to give him a whole procurement lecture as well as a treasury lecture. At that stage I think my image in the community was not that good, but now I think I have remedied that by having closer contacts and more communication with the parents and more newsletters. In the past I had only two newsletters per quarter-term, now I have one at the beginning of the term, in the middle of the term, before the exams and at the end of the term.

The main challenge for the parents is the influx of black students (Xhosa speakers). The Xhosa parents also use the school as a springboard for the children so that they can attend the English high schools later on. Our registration is more open now and our sessions will begin in August to give the local community enough time to register, but the feeder area comes in January when the school opens and then they want to come and register. The Xhosa people from the western and the eastern suburbs come to pay the annual school fees early, and you accept them in good faith, because it is fair that first come should be first served. Some local parents are not comfortable with that. I also feel uncomfortable about that, but if the local parents don't react to the advertisements and the newsletters, I can't do anything about that.

I have taken measures to engage with the parents and the community by giving them the opportunity to exercise their language rights. The majority of the community speaks Afrikaans, but most of the children have English classes. English is not their mother tongue, but the parents prefer their children take English. I feel upset about the children not being taught throughout their school years in their mother tongue. The Xhosa children are taught from grades 1 through 3 in their mother tongue and suddenly they are taught in English in grade 4. But the department does nothing to get those children back to the schools in the townships so that they can be taught in their mother tongue.

The culture of the school was at first equal in terms of language with a 50–50 split between teaching in Afrikaans and in English. Then the influx began with the Xhosa children. I want to revert it so that it becomes 50 percent Afrikaans and percent English again. In the past we played sport against the seven schools in the community and then the representative team played trials against other schools, but now the sport totally collapsed because the federation wants us to play against far-away schools like Gordon's Bay Primary. The federations don't take into consideration that we don't have the financial resources to play against a far-away school. When the community schools played against each other, you did not spend any money. So I have implemented some changes, but I want to see language change as well as the sport.

I did initiate a few changes within the first year that I became principal. We had more regular assemblies, which are on Mondays and Fridays. I am not ashamed to say that I have copied some of the strategies that the former (all-white) ex-Model C schools used. Next year I am planning to implement a new way of administering the school and to use more strategies in the classroom. For example, I want the children to write tests more regularly and to introduce class inspections. So I have copied a lot from the so-called white, model-C schools. But I did not make many changes in the first 2 years except to introduce more sports teams and I engaged some private hockey and netball coaches. Other than that I realized that there's a difference between the school organization of the model C school and our school. That was the type of change that I made. The teachers were positive about the changes I have made.

I had some unsuccessful experiences as well. As an ex-physical training person, I wanted to keep physical education on the timetable as well as handwork and needlework, within the curriculum, within the confines of the Outcomes Based Education (OBE) system. I couldn't do that because the new OBE system that was introduced did not lend itself to that. If we had more resources to engage more teachers at our school, we could have had that type of subject. The teachers were also disappointed because many of them are specialists in that type of knowledge. I tried to introduce it, but it did not work. I also tried to imitate the ex-Model C schools by giving incentive bonuses to the teachers, but because our resources are limited, I couldn't. And to get sports and physical education and handwork classes back, and to get moderation, teachers need incentive bonuses, not necessarily from the state, but paid from the school fund. But unfortunately in my 4 years I could not convince the SGB or the department to provide incentive bonuses for the teachers, because their view is that teachers get a monthly salary and that should be sufficient.

Communication with the education department is the biggest challenge for me. You can, for example, submit one letter and afterwards they ask you to submit the same letter with a petition. I think the link between the education department and the schools should be improved. I do not think the problem starts with the officials at the department, but the fact that the education is politicized. I think that the communication with the department and the politics of education are the two major problems. We mustn't think that people are being appointed on merit. The higher positions are political appointments. In the news this morning, the ANC stated that they will continue appointing their leaders to strategic positions. I don't think that education should be run by a politician. There is nothing I can actually do about the two mentioned problems because communication is kept to an absolute minimum. There is a curriculum unit, an exam section, schemes of work and a support group, but there is no coordination between those sections. They do not work together. For instance, in the Eastern province, we are writing the common exam. Now the new ruling is that children are writing two exam papers per day (Grades 3, 6 and 9), for example, on life skills and life orientation in the morning and arts and culture in the afternoon. This decision comes from the superintendent.

I don't think that there is anything that I would have done differently in my first 2 years. I would have loved to have more SGB teachers to alleviate the workload in the classrooms. But because of a lack of funds that was not possible.

I still enjoy my job tremendously. Of course it is a challenge, and I do have ups and downs, but there are many positive aspects. I would say that the most positive aspect of the job is working with the staff. If there is a problem, they come to me. I think our school is the best-regarded school among the eight in the community. The thing I'm not happy about is the support I receive from my employer, but I turn to the other eight schools in the community if I need support or advice. We work together as a network and they are my mentors. Twice a month we have a meeting and talk about our concerns and we seek advice from each other. I don't always follow their advice, but this method seems to be working. I network with them because we are all in same adverse economic circumstances in Schauderville.

There is good communication between me and my staff and they are well structured. The problem is that we, me and my staff, can't come to grips with the new curriculum statements of the OBE. We had a debate a week ago and the teachers said that they want to go back to the old curriculum and that they want everything as it was in the past. In the past there was only a record book that the principal signed. Now the teachers complain about the assessment standards and learning outcomes because it confuses the teachers who are working at the classroom level. They also complain about the high administrative load. So this is causing some unpleasantness among the staff because they can't get to grips with the new curriculum.

Another source of dissatisfaction, apart from the communication aspect, is the tension between the SGB members and the school principals. The problem is that sometimes the SGBs try to control the school and are under the impression that teachers work for them. And that causes problems within the school. Perhaps the SGB acts in that way because it wants to dominate, or perhaps it is a sign of ignorance. I don't know. But in our schools it sometimes seems as if no one wants to work together. With my sporting experience, I read and discussed about a thorough study of the Australian model. In that model, I must say, the Australian schools are well organized but it is very expensive model. In terms of academics and sport, I can't even see that that type of thing will ever be reached here that was reached in Australia. But if we are not going to work on a strategy to improve our schools in academics and sports, I think we are going to have major problems. I think next year's twelfth grade, when they leave school and go to university, they are going to experience difficulties because they can't read. I lie awake at night thinking about the tension between me and the SGB. I think the whole thing about the role of the SGBs in education will need to be re-examined sometime. Their role must be redefined and it must be clear. The SGB must make calls because I see it as a major threat. Fortunately I work with one or two persons whom I can handle, but if I have to work with an SGB member who is totally ignorant within the next 3 to 4 years, who doesn't know the South African Schools' Act and who acts dominant, we are going to have a serious problem. And in fact, schools are more and more engaging lawyers when they have such major problems.

I also stress a lot about the parental involvement. If ten parents attend parent meetings per class, then that it is a major success. And the parents that do attend are usually not the ones you want to speak to.

Being a principal has changed me in some ways. I do feel lonely sometimes as a principal because I'm sitting in the office and have to solve certain problems on my own.

I know that I have to be careful and be aware of my position. I cannot partake in social responsibilities or recreational activities within the community anymore because I have to be a role model. I think I am coping with the demands of the job. I would give myself between 65 and 70 out of a 100. If I had to have 90, then I must be a rector or something. When I am on holiday, for the past 3 or 4 years, we have gone to Cape Town and stayed in the hostels there. This year we're going to Durban and then we're going to Johannesburg. When I was just a teacher, we normally took the caravan and went to the local beach. But now it feels as if the community always has an eye on you. So if you want to enjoy yourself, you have to break away. This job also has an effect on my personal health and my general well-being. When I was a physical education teacher, I could run the 400 metres, but if I have to run now, I will get a heart attack.

Looking back, I think that the accomplishments I have achieved in my first year were managing to generate more funds for the school, for instance, the office machinery. There was also not anything that I would have liked to have done differently in my first year. I am satisfied with what I've achieved. Looking to the future, my vision for this school is to give the community a better product that compares to the ex-Model C white schools. To have that better product, we need to have teachers that are on the ball and know how to teach. My vision for the school is to extend the school hours, and to do that we need to pay the teachers more with incentive bonuses. It is also for the safety of the children because otherwise they will stand on the corners of the streets. My vision is shared with the staff and some parents, but we don't have enough resources.

One of my priorities for the immediate future is to fix the school grounds so that home sports matches can be played. One of the other desires, one that I would like to initiate next year maybe or the year after that, is to implement special classes at the school. We have a need for that because we have children with learning barriers and difficulties. We have got well-trained teachers, nine of whom have received their honours degrees, and the parents are willing to pay for the special classes. We have three teachers in the school who are undertaking online education courses.

With regard to longer-term goals in the future of this school, I would like to increase the number of English and Afrikaans students language-wise. The department must address the language problems the children struggle with. But the Xhosa-speaking parents absolutely refuse to enrol their children in the townships. I don't want the school to become homogeneous, but

I think it would be better for the children. The obstacle that I anticipate in making the school dual-medium in Afrikaans and English is the commitment from the Afrikaans parents. The commitment from these parents is limited because of socio-economic circumstances. A lot of drugs and alcohol are being misused.

One of the things that I wish I could have had was more knowledge or skills to administrate a school to run it more like a business because the days where schools were Christian oriented are over.

I see the role of the principal changing in the future from being school oriented to being more administrative and flooded with paperwork. The principal's only loyalties will be towards the department, and principals will be driven by the department. However, I see myself still working as a school principal in 5 to 10 years' time because I do enjoy it. Seeing that I've started here, I would love to open a new school and administer it. The only thing I think would make me resign as principal is if the whole department became politicized. I don't like it when the politicians stick their noses into each and every aspect of the school, for example, the school fees.

I talk to former principals about my professional future. Among our discussions, we also talk about the Cuban model. We are talking about the high literacy rate in Cuba and how little money surgeons are paid per month. I find that the Cuban and Zimbabwean models work amazingly for those people there, but our own model is badly influenced by politicians.

I don't think that being a principal is a very tough job, but a principal has to be very diplomatic. It is not the best job financially, but it is very satisfying. You can inspire young people to become teachers and influence them. Some of our former students are now fourth-year students at the university and they are very well skilled and they can help solve some problems, but I doubt if we can solve the political problems.

The advice that I would give to any teachers who are contemplating applying for a principal position is that they must develop their sense of interpersonal relationships, especially in our so-called non-white schools. I think that all principals must learn to have discipline and to have respect towards other people. In the army, the white people learned about respect and I think it is important to have it.

My fears for the future are the politicians. My hopes for the future are to free education from political influence. More money must be spent on education and less on ships, battleships and the army. And, as well as the contribution from the government being limited, I would like to see the legacy of apartheid eradicated.

Note

1 South Africa's governing party.

One Classroom, Seven Grades and Three Teachers: Challenges Faced by a Novice Headteacher in Tanzania

Brown Onguko meets with Tupa Lugendo, headteacher of Mandizini School

The school context

Getting to the rural and remote Mandizini School in the hilly terrain of Mvomero district is no mean achievement. From Dar es Salaam on the eastern shores of the Indian Ocean, we drive north in a four-wheel-drive vehicle, aware that the road ahead will be rough and dusty.

The ride is incident-free save for the occasional stoppage by traffic police officers. We are stopped three times. Two of the police officers at one stoppage request a ride in our vehicle as they change stations to a new site farther ahead. It is like cats changing their hiding place as they strategize how best to catch rats.

There are frequent roadside stalls selling farm produce such as maize, carrots and a variety of fruits, including mangoes, oranges, bananas and apples. After 3 hours we arrive at Morogoro and take the opportunity to buy drinking water as this is the last major town before branching off towards the remote and rural Turiani divisional headquarters.

On leaving Morogoro, we branch off in the direction of the central Tanzanian city of Dodoma. The road is generally well paved with fewer vehicles than the Dar es Salaam-to-Morogoro stretch. After passing two other roadside markets where the main commodities on sale are maize and sweet potatoes, we turn off the Morogoro–Dodoma highway towards Turiani on to a rough earth road. Luckily for us, in a few days the president will be visiting Kilosa, so the road has been improved all the way beyond Turiani. The ride to Turiani is therefore better than it would normally be.

The main economic activities along the Turiani road are rice and sugar cultivation. There is a major rice market at Turiani, while 5 km further beyond Turiani is Mtibwa sugar factory.

Eventually we arrive at Turiani and it is clear that we are in a remote outpost. It appears that all the people in this small divisional headquarters know each other, for they immediately can tell there are visitors in town. We check in at Honolulu Hotel, the venue for a leadership course, where we are to meet the next day with Dominick Tupa Lugendo, headteacher of Mandizini School. Our immediate concern, however, is the large number of mosquitoes because of the flooded paddy fields.

Mandizini School is in a remote part of Morogoro region where the main economic activity is banana farming. Dominick was promoted and transferred to this hilly and isolated part of the country without applying for it. He has a wife and several children.

Tupa's story

I enjoy working as a teacher. I love my work and have been trained for it. I attribute my vast experience to having worked for 28 years. I have been a headteacher for only 1 year. It is now 1 year and a few days since I was appointed. This was my first appointment as a headteacher. Before I became a headteacher, I had been an assistant headteacher for 12 years.

In most cases, to become a headteacher you do not apply for it. You are just appointed. I was a teacher like any other working in a school. I started working in 1981. In 1997 I was appointed to the position of assistant headteacher. In 1999 I went to college for an upgrading course. I went to upgrade to the Form Four level of education. When I left the post, another assistant headteacher was appointed. On completion of the upgrading course, I became a classroom teacher. When I was appointed headteacher, I was transferred to my present school.

The appointing office knows what they look for when appointing a headteacher. They decide who is best to serve in that position. One may be recommended by the education officials. The district education officer (DEO) decides who is fit to take the position of headteacher. The DEO is the one who signs the appointment letter. The ward officers' only recommend the candidate.

I decided to become a teacher after being advised by my parents. I had an option of becoming a policeman, but my parents convinced me that teaching was the best career. My father was a teacher as well. I have not done any other job apart from being a teacher. I just left school, went to college and then started teaching. The only other engagement I have is business. When it is farming season, I also get involved in farming because the land here is very good for farming. I lease some farms and pay people to work for me in the farm. When we harvest we get some more money.

Leadership is not something you apply for. Leadership is a blame game, a problem. If we were to apply, then many people would not go for it. If I was told to apply for leadership, I would not be ready to do that. Very few people really love being leaders. If I had the option to apply, I would just have opted to remain a teacher. However, when you are appointed, you have to take up the position; you do not refuse. You could refuse, but then your image will be dented. It is a job you are given after the officials recognize that you have the ability to do it. You take it up and if you do not make it, then you get back to your teaching position.

I have a passion for teaching. The only leadership positions we apply for are those in the teachers' association. For example, I was a teachers' union official in our ward. I was the chairman, and when I left the ward, I had to leave that position. I have held many such positions. However for headship, you do not apply for it. It is people in authority who decide that you are able to do the job. That is the difference between becoming a headteacher and working as a leader in unions and associations.

I had never thought that one day I would be a school leader. However, since the authorities decided that I should be a leader, I had to take it up. I never worked to become a headteacher. Once I received the letter, I sat down to think about it. I really wondered whether I could manage the responsibility. The challenge was that my station was very accessible and well established, and then on appointment I was posted to a remote area very far up the hills. It required that I shift my location, which I have not done yet; thus I commute daily. The distance is too long and then the working conditions are not good. Here we work with enlightened people, but there you have to work in difficult conditions. When I was appointed I asked myself many questions; then I decided so be it. I had to take up the position. You ask yourself whether you will survive the harsh conditions, then you just decide to go and do your best.

After appointment, there was no training apart from the experience I had. You get the letter and go to report and begin your work. In most cases you get more experience on the job. On reporting, you assess the environment; whatever you understand, you begin with that. Whatever is new to you, then you seek assistance from the experienced people. The first days you work with the experienced headteachers in the neighbouring schools or the school you came from. You seek their advice on how to resolve some of the issues. Your colleagues help you with ideas on how to resolve some of the issues.

I did not know the culture of the new place I was posted to. I had never lived there. I had to do my own research to understand the place before I could go. How are the people? How is the place? How do they behave? I got to know who the school committee chairman was, the local elected leader; I got all these details before I reported. I spoke to people who come from the place and even spoke to the headteacher I was taking over from. I had to sit with the outgoing headteacher to give me ideas on how I should relate with the people. He furnished me with enough details about the school.

There are many people who come from Mandizini that we live with here in Turiani. I asked them about Mandizini. Therefore, I had enough details about the school and the environs before I went there. I went to report a day before the school opening day, met the local people and started my work. I went to the school with the headteacher I was taking over from. Luckily the headteacher was not transferred from the school; he remained there. He therefore took the responsibility to introduce me to the school committee chairman, the local elders and the community and the students. I had a smooth entry because of his effort.

The transition is difficult because you come from a different area and join a new school as a stranger. My previous school was well developed and organized, and then I was posted to a school in a difficult and remote place. I was used to a particular environment and now I am in a very new environment. I keep asking myself: what am I doing here? I may just be wasting myself. I keep comparing this school to my previous school. It is difficult to settle in because the people here do not feel like school is necessary. It is like you go to school when you want; on other days people attend to their own business. Students have no uniforms. Students come in their own clothes. The students are aware that on Mondays teachers may not come or at the end of the month teachers go for their salary so they do not come to school for 2 weeks. At first I was disappointed by this. I came to school on Monday and there were no teachers and students. When I realized this was the school procedure, I discussed it with the teachers so as to come up with acceptable procedures. The former headteacher took these things as normal; it is only the newcomer who realizes these things.

The working conditions at the school are difficult because there are no learning materials. The school funds provided by the government remained in the account, yet there were no books and other learning materials. The first task I embarked on immediately on taking over as the headteacher was to work on the release of the funds by the bank so that we could buy some of the learning materials required, including books and chalks so that we could move forward. The classroom buildings are still a problem because they are just not there. We started involving parents to help in construction. We have done some construction of classrooms and now students have more space at least.

It is my intention to do my best as a headteacher. I must deliver on my work so I try my best to sacrifice so that I can surmount the challenges. I have to keep thinking of ways to tackle the different challenges that arise every day. In the working conditions in my school, I have to involve stakeholders in everything. The school community is very powerful. The parents have a lot of say and they are listened to a lot by the government. Even though the school had really gone down and teachers did not seem to be committed, they still have the support of the community. So if I just arrived at the school and told everyone to change position because I had arrived, it could not work. In everything I had to consult with the teachers and the parents to involve them in the decision-making. For example, there is a banana plantation in school and when I sought to find out how it is managed, I was told that the chairman of the school committee was the one in charge of that. He is the one who sells the bananas and keeps the funds, so when we want to use the funds we have to ask him. I enquired why that was the case. I was informed that the community is the one that takes care of the school property and if you get involved by taking over such responsibility they will let the property be stolen. They also do not trust teachers that much who are outsiders in their community. So I agreed with this position since I could not change everything immediately.

However, when I met with the chairman I asked him how much money he had from the farm sales and how much he sells the bananas for. He informed me of the amount of money he had as proceeds from the farm, then we agreed that I provide a book for keeping the records. Had I decided to take over the farm, everything would have been stolen. I got some young men who would work with the chairman on managing the sales and also appointed a teacher who would be involved in the transactions for the sake of record-keeping. We agreed that I did not have to keep the money, but we needed to know the records of the sales. Therefore, I decided that on most of the decisions we would work together and that I would give them the chance to participate but monitor the activities. So we really have to work together with the community. It should not be a case of "now that I have taken over, I will do everything."

My leadership style is participatory leadership. For example, I work very closely with the school committee. In fact, I have been letting the school committee deal with most of the responsibilities. The problem is that my school has no teachers. We have just two teachers. We have three teachers in all, but one is rarely in school. In most cases there are just the two of us in school. With only two of us in school, there is no reason for me to be throwing my weight around as the headteacher. The former headteacher who I took over from is still there so I give him space so that he can feel comfortable that he still has power. I involve him in most of the decisions I take. I give him opportunities to present his views on most of the decisions we make.

I also involve parents in the running of the school. I have been inviting them to come to school for meetings. For example, in the construction of a classroom and a teacher's house they have to be involved in fund-raising for the construction. They have hired the construction workers for the teacher's house. The school compound is very small, so I have requested the parents and the community to look for alternative land for the construction of more classrooms.

The former headteacher was demoted by the education office and remained a teacher in the school. When this former headteacher is at school, he has no problems working with me. However, the reason why he was demoted is that he drinks alcohol a lot, so most of the time he is not in school. For example, towards the end of the month, he can take 2 weeks without coming to school. That becomes a problem.

The school has 3 teachers and 126 enrolled students. The school is from grade one to grade seven. We do not have seven classrooms though; there is only one classroom, which is why we have to construct more. There is only one complete classroom. All the remaining six classes are held in the open space.

The school was established in 2002 and that is why we have grade seven this year. The previous headteacher, in my view, did not bother much about work. I think he got so familiar with the local community. He was more like one of the villagers. In most cases he would just forget about his responsibilities in school and get involved in matters of the village. In such a situation he could not improve the school in any way. In fact, people could not listen to his views because he never maintained professional distance. So when I arrived, there was a major change in the school. I had to show that things have to be done differently.

I work very well with the teachers. We discuss issues and agree on the way forward. They agree with my guidance as a way of improving our practice and the school. The major problem we have is their attendance at school. When one is in school, the other one is away. In most cases, teachers in schools in remote places get mixed up in the community. Most of the hard work done by teachers in the urban places is not reflected in remote places at all. When I reported to this school I was confused and wondered how I would survive in such an environment. I was used to doing things with urgency. It is like having been a driver of a Scania bus and then you transfer to drive a tractor. That is a problem for sure, but I am doing my best in the circumstances.

The school community is happy with the few changes we have initiated. To them it is like a blessing I was posted there. They are very supportive of my initiatives for change. For example, when we arrive with school supplies like books and request students to come and carry them from the road to the office, even the community people come in to assist. You get the elders carrying school learning materials together with the students. This is evidence that they are happy with the changes we are making in the school.

The teachers received me very well. The previous headteacher already knew the mistakes that caused him to be demoted. In fact, when I was showing signs of declining to take up the position as a headteacher in the school, he came over to me and pleaded with me to accept the position. He insisted that I should go and take over. He really influenced my decision-making at that stage. Then when I reported to take over he was very helpful in ensuring that I settled in and understood the processes in the school. He was keen to encourage me so that I do not give up, because the environment is very hostile there. On a normal day, you really wonder why you should be working in such conditions. So he really encouraged me to continue. The other teacher I found at the school is an elderly man, quite elderly actually. Both of them really encouraged me to settle in my new position.

When I received the posting letter to my new school, many people kept asking me whether I would take up the position. I really did not know how to respond to them. Some of the people were encouraging me to go to the education office and decline the posting. I did not respond to them. I just kept my cool. There were other people who encouraged me that it was about serving my country so I should take up the posting. I think word reached the school community that a headteacher had been posted there but he is not willing to take up the position. The community therefore took it upon themselves to come and encourage me to take up the position

The teachers have no problem with me at all. The only problem is that they do not attend to their duties regularly. Even if I was to become strict, I would lose all the goodwill because there are only three of us. For sure their attendance is very poor. When one requests for permission to be away, he stays away for 2 weeks. When he reports after 2 weeks, then this other teacher goes for 2 weeks. It is very disappointing and that is the problem I have.

The former headteacher had so many mistakes that the local community had been complaining about. The poor attendance of the teachers is a problem that I am resolving by speaking to them about the need to attend to their work. I have informed them we are serving people and we need to deliver on our responsibilities. We could get permission to go home, but it is not proper to take 5 days before you report back to school. If I was to begin writing warning letters to them, then we may not work well as a team. I have spoken to them, informing them that seeking permission for 2 or 3 days is okay. We have moved well and now they have reduced their absenteeism because they realize that I am in school every day so when they request 2 days they come back after the 2 days.

The school community was very disinterested in the school affairs. Most of the students had already been moved to other schools when they realized that there was no hope for their education in this school. Since we started improving on the school image, the community is sensitized and now the students are returning to the school. The parents are now responding very well. They are contributing to the construction of the school buildings. The community is now keen on developing their school. They are now fully sensitized and taking responsibility for the development of their school. Previously, they had been threatened by the education authorities that the school would be closed down. They had therefore given up on the school. The schools inspectorate team came to inform them that the school would not be closed and that was the reason a new headteacher had been appointed to the school. They were urged to work with the new headteacher to develop their school. Since they see it as their school, they participate fully in its development.

The threats of closing the school arose from the misunderstandings within the community. Development had stalled due to conflicts about the construction of classrooms. It was therefore very difficult to move the school forward. The local community leaders realized the misunderstandings in the community and kept out of the affairs of the school. Since nothing was resolved and students were leaving the school, the only remaining thing was to close down the school. Now they know for sure that the school will not be closed down.

I have not had any sign to show that the community does not accept me as the headteacher. We are just working well with the community. But there are challenges; for example, pupil attendance is dictated by the prevailing economic activities. During the planting season the students just believe that they have the freedom to be away attending to farming activities. On specific days like Friday some children stay away from school to engage in transporting bananas to the market. To them it is normal and so school programmes can wait.

With regard to school uniforms, the students just put on any clothes to go to school, which they also use to do farm work. I have to do quite a lot of work to get them to understand the need to attend to school requirements. I have to make them understand that there are rules and regulations that have to be adhered to. They need to understand that regular attendance at school is mandatory and that when there is a problem, they have to seek permission to be away. They have to understand, for example, that the right school uniform has to be used in school and the other clothes can be used while on the farm. Culturally, the older girls cover their heads with head-scarves. I have made it clear that while on the road they can cover themselves but when they get to school they have to keep them in the bag until they leave school. I have therefore tried to bring some order in the school.

I have made a number of changes in the 1 year I have been heading the school. As I mentioned earlier, nearly all the school programmes had come to a standstill, including construction of classrooms. However, over the period I have been there we have worked with the community; they have bought construction materials and they have raised money and begun construction of classrooms. The other issue is about the school compound, which is not large enough. We agreed that we have to look for more land for the school. The community have looked for land and found a school expansion site. We are now in the process of acquiring the land, and people are aware that the school will move to a new site. The changes are there and can be seen by the people.

I have initiated the changes by making the community aware of them. For example, the classroom construction: when I realized that there was only one classroom and the students were learning outside, I convened a meeting to discuss ways of solving the problem. I informed them that there was no learning taking place. You cannot use one classroom to teach grades one through seven in shifts. It was possible to teach in multi-grades of one and two, three and four or even six and seven, but it is not possible to have a multi-grade teaching of grades one through seven in one classroom. The most important thing is to educate the people. Once they understand the situation and their responsibilities, it is easier to move forward.

There is only one classroom for all the seven grades in the school. So what used to happen was that each grade would get into the classroom, learn for a short time and leave it for the next grade until all the grades had their chance to use the classroom. That was the basis for my informing the community that there was no learning taking place in such a situation. We had to do something to change that.

We have been successful in some ways in implementing the changes, though there is more being implemented still. To a large extent we have been successful in the changes because the implementation is still on. The projects are still going on.

Among the key players in these changes are the school committee members, whom I work with very closely. When we meet as the school committee, we involve the two teachers as well. When you have a staff of only two teachers, it is really a challenge. They have to participate in decision-making at all levels. We work very closely together as the staff and the school committee.

We involve the leadership of the educational zone as well in making the changes in the school. The chairman and the secretary of the zone receive the decisions taken by the school committee as part of their involvement in the changes. Most of the meetings at the zone level are held on Saturdays when I am away from the school. The school committee participates in the meetings at the zone. They sit and agree on who will do what in the projects we are implementing. They participate as members of the community for the sake of their school. When they require any clarification or they face any complications, then they talk to me. The zone leadership resolves most of the problems, including issues about fund-raising for the projects. Those community members who are not willing to contribute money are reported to the village elders. They then pay at the village elders' office.

The community is happy with the improvements taking place in their school. The major change that we are still working on is the provision of classrooms for the students. There are some challenges though. Our goal was 20,000 bricks for the construction of classrooms. However, with the proposal to look for a different site for the school, we now have the problem of moving the bricks to the new site. We therefore stopped making bricks until we have the new site; then we shall make the bricks at the site. This decision has slowed us down. Those people who were not privy to the decision could be wondering why we have not started the work. That has been a challenge.

The aspect of my work that requires a lot of effort is the provision of more teachers. Surely running a school with seven grades with only two teachers is a big joke. It is difficult to operate in such a situation. It is challenging to monitor the teaching and learning taking place in school. The children may only learn reading and arithmetic. The issue of covering the syllabus does not arise in such a situation. The district education office is aware of this staffing problem, since I have been requesting for more teachers to be posted to the school. They have promised that by July they will post more teachers to the school. That has been the greatest challenge for me as a headteacher.

I have had a number of successes. For example, there were no learning materials in the school. As I mentioned there were school funds in the bank but they were not being utilized for the benefit of the learners. Once I took over the school, we worked with the committee and withdrew the money; then we bought learning materials, sports equipment and other requirements. That is one of the successes I have had as a headteacher. These actions have even made the students appreciate that indeed they are in school.

The other success is the teachers' regular attendance. Previously the school would be on holiday half of the month because teachers had gone to get their pay and the other half the school would be on. Now students learn for the whole month. The teachers are regularly attending school now and so students are consistent in their attendance as well. The students do not have to keep asking whether the teachers are back to school as was the case previously.

The money from the government has been going to the school account, but the school management was not withdrawing the money to be utilized in the school. It is not clear to me why they could not withdraw and use the money, but the money was intact and not utilized. The money had not been withdrawn for 2 years. There is enough money on the account to construct one classroom to completion. The money had been left at the bank until the bank blocked access to the money. I am now in the process of getting the new site for the school so that by July we can request the money and use it for construction.

As I move on with the changes I am making in the school, I am learning a lot about the other improvements that are required. If we are successful in getting more teachers, as has been promised by the authorities, we will make more improvements. We shall be able to work better with more teachers.

I am happy with my work as a headteacher; otherwise, it would be difficult for me to work well and make these changes. If I was discouraged then I would not move on. Since I accepted the responsibility, I have embraced it.

My satisfaction is when I see the fruits of my effort. As people see the results of our effort and realize that there are some changes, I feel satisfied that I am achieving my objectives. For example, this year we have seventh-grade students who will be sitting for their national examinations and we are currently working to ensure that we prepare them for the examinations. Even now the schools are on holiday, but there is one teacher teaching these students. We look forward to the examination results, as they will indicate to us what we need to do in the future.

On the whole there have been no major surprises for me as a headteacher. There have been challenges but no major surprises at work because I am just dealing with the normal issues we are used to.

One of the discouraging things is the working conditions. The place where the school is located is a hardship area. It is far away. I go up and down very steep hills to get to school and there are no classrooms or teachers' houses in the school. What discourages me so much is that I cannot live there. In the rainy season there is a river that floods and forces me to miss school for 3 days. It is a hardship area for sure.

The Ministry of Education policies and regulations are not a problem at all, apart from the fact that the ministry requires that students be admitted to first grade and progress up to seventh grade. However, the same ministry is not able to provide teachers to teach these students. That is a major challenge. Surely a school with one teacher cannot achieve the objectives listed in the syllabus.

In my school's environment, I have the freedom to determine what to do. It is up to me as the headteacher to commit myself to the things I want done to achieve the overall goals of education. I have to manage myself because we do not expect the education officials to come to that school at all. It is difficult. I just have to be my own supervisor and work with commitment. The biggest challenge is the harsh environment.

Currently I have enough support from my employer. However, we need more material support for the school to achieve its mandate. We still need a lot of support. We cannot teach in one classroom grades one through seven. We need a lot of material support. If the ministry wants this school to develop, then it has to support it. When I need any assistance, I first approach the headteachers of the neighbouring schools.

On matters concerning leadership of the school, I consult the headteachers in the neighbouring schools a lot. Where necessary, I also consult the co-coordinator of education in the ward. On matters concerning the community, I work very closely with the chairperson of the school committee. The chairperson of the village is also of great help to me because on matters that seem very problematic to handle, he comes in and handles them in the best way possible. These people are the ones who are closest if consultation is needed. However, there are many people, including the village elder of the community, who are of great help when it come to general advice and are always available in school. The village elder is like the father of the school and provides all the advice we may seek. Therefore, I get advice from many people in the community.

There are no major challenges as such apart from the fact that one needs to be very keen on the job, especially concerning cases of student misbehaviour and reports of who has done this or that. I am at times required to refer some cases to the law enforcement agencies, and this being a remote and rural place, there is need to be cautious of what steps to take. In most cases, before thinking of reporting them to the police or the courts, it is better to involve the community elders, the school committee and other groups. It is better to use the time to try resolving the cases instead of rushing the matters to the law enforcement agencies. There are very few families in that place and they are all related in some way. They can easily isolate you if you rush with the cases to the law enforcement agencies. They will take it that you are not interested in their welfare but rather are out to destroy them, so they will isolate you. I am therefore cautious of that and handle the cases very carefully.

As a headteacher I have more responsibilities because previously I only worked with other staff members in the school. On becoming headteacher I have to work with the ward and district education officials as well. I have to keep moving to ward education offices and district education offices every few days. This adds to my responsibilities as a headteacher.

We are generally working very well. However, when problems arise, we deal with them as best we can. The main objective is to get the students to learn. When we are faced with obstacles that hinder learning – for example, lack of classrooms – then achieving the aims of education becomes challenging. The other obstacle is the lack of teachers. As a headteacher you have your vision for the school, but moving forward becomes a problem because of the lack of personnel.

My position as headteacher has had impacts on my life. For example, since I became headteacher, I spend a long time away from my family, unlike when I was working as a teacher. I still commute, but then I leave very early and come back very late and am tired so there is no time for the family.

My teaching role while also being the headteacher has not been affected as such. This is because in my previous school I was teaching and in my current school I teach even more because in the previous school we had more teachers. We would teach only one subject per class, but now you have to teach more subjects in all classes. I have to teach first grade and up, so there is more teaching work now for me.

I think at the beginning of my role as a headteacher, I was affected healthwise. Climbing steep hills every day has had some effects on my health. On the other hand, I like climbing the steep hills because of the effects the exercise has on the body. I was much heavier than I am now and had some problems going uphill, but since I started walking up the steep slopes, my body is in better shape. I had previously been advised to reduce my weight, so I think this has helped me.

The work of the headteacher does not isolate one at all, unless one chooses to be isolated. There are those who believe that by becoming a headteacher you are in a different category, but I do not think so. If anything, the headteacher role should bring you closer to people rather than isolating you.

In the first year as headteacher there were a number of achievements, including being able to provide the teaching and learning materials. For example, on arrival there were no chairs and tables, but within a short while I was able to procure chairs, tables, book-shelves and books for the book-shelves. I am happy with my achievements over the year. We have not achieved the number of student desks we need, but for the office we have managed to achieve a lot.

There are a number of aspects I would have wanted to achieve over the past year but I have not achieved them. For example, we had planned to get 20,000 bricks to put up a classroom building, but we could not achieve this because of the change in plans. The other issue concerns the plans to get a new school site and move the school. This did not move as fast as we would have wanted, so we are still dealing with it. These are matters that I would have wanted to move fast but the process has been slow.

The obstacles have been the procedures required in achieving these plans. You cannot just decide to do something and move into it. You must have clear procedures laid out, including having consultative meetings, involve people and go through the bureaucratic processes.

My future plan is to ensure that the school is built and to get more students enrolled. We have very few students and this is a result of the current situation. Some students go to schools far away. Therefore, I have to create an attractive school with good classrooms that will make students come to the school. So increasing pupil enrolment is one of my main objectives.

Our school vision is to create a good school with attractive buildings and learning materials. We would also like to have a self-sustaining school in the sense of having playgrounds and also a farm, as banana plantations are the main cash crop in the area. We would like to have some space of up to 5 acres for planting bananas because it rains in the area throughout the year. The school can, therefore, be self-sustaining.

We would like to have a model school despite the fact that we are in a remote and rural setting. We have discussed these plans with the school and the community and that is why the plans have been put in place. We have held many meetings and discussed the need to have the school be self-sustaining. The school should have buildings, it should have enough land and it should have its aims. Given time, the school will improve.

Our first targets are buildings. We have students, however few, and we also have teachers. There are no teachers' houses at all. If we were to get more teachers and there are no houses for them, we would be back to where we are now. So our priority is to ensure that when teachers are posted to the school, they have houses. We have to work on teachers' houses, getting more teachers and constructing classrooms, all at the same time.

Once we have school buildings and teachers, we can move to the next target, which is school self-sustainability, by planting cash crops and short-term crops for consumption in school. Our long-term goal is to ensure that the school develops in all aspects, including academic performance and national expectations. We would like to have a developed school.

There are challenges associated with my school. First of all, the school is located in an area with very few people. The population around the school is low. We might have very good plans, but then these plans may not be achieved because of the lack of enough people in the community to help in achieving them.

There are discipline challenges on the part of the students. This requires frequent consultations. We have to work on the students' attitudes towards school attendance. There are other challenges, such as the traditional practices and customs. The girl child, for example, gets married while still in school. We have to really fight off such practices. We have started making the community aware of the need to let girls complete school before marrying them off.

I never got any preparation for my role as a headteacher. My roles and responsibilities might change as we move forward. I have to be ready to deal with changing situations on a daily basis. There are new challenges coming up every day, and they have to be handled.

I am not able to predict my future in the next 5 or 10 years because I do not determine where I will be myself. I hope to continue with my work if my leaders decide that I am still able to serve as a headteacher from one school to another. It will be okay with me. If they decide that I should revert to my role as a classroom teacher, I will also accept that. If I perform well in my current role, then I will continue being a headteacher in future. Remaining in my current school or moving to another school depends on the decisions of the office. They determine whether you should be in this or that school. You may determine where you want to be by rejecting the job due to inability to perform.

I can request for a transfer to another school, but I cannot force the office to transfer me. I might request a transfer, then the office will determine if it is possible to transfer me or not. If they do not want to transfer me, I cannot force them to do it. There must be a strong reason for seeking the transfer, for example, due to sickness.

I have been working at my current station for only 1 year. I have not yet seen any reason to request a transfer. However, if a reason comes up in the future, I will have to request a transfer or leave the position of headteacher. If all goes well, then there will be no need to leave.

If, for some reason, I am transferred from here after staying for so long and have only 2 years to retire, it is possible to request the office to let me complete my service at the current station. If I have long-term goals that I have not achieved and there are chances of achieving these goals, it is possible to request an opportunity to remain in school to complete your targets in case you have been transferred.

I agree with those who say that a headteacher's role is difficult. If you compare this with a regular teacher's role, the headteacher role is difficult. As a teacher, your major role is to teach, including preparing lesson plans, going to class and teaching, plus any other duties assigned to you. That is all. As a headteacher you have more responsibilities. Apart from teaching, you are also in charge of other people. Second you have to take charge of other roles such as construction. You also involve so many people in your work through consultation. You hold many meetings with ward officials and district officials and this is more work. You are also in charge of school accounts. You have to ensure that the money is well accounted for. There are meetings at the divisional level as well. In some of these responsibilities you are forced to spend your own funds. For example, you might be invited for a meeting in Morogoro and there is no night-out money for you. You are just invited for a meeting and it is up to you to get funds and go to the meeting. After the meeting you have to get back to school and implement the instructions. As a teacher you have no idea about these responsibilities.

I think teaching is better than being a headteacher. The headteacher role is not a good job due to many responsibilities. The teaching job is very good. Once you add on the role of headteacher, it might be good but if you were an incompetent teacher and then you became a headteacher you will be a worse headteacher. So the good job is teaching, but being a headteacher is just part of the responsibilities.

I would encourage other teachers to apply for the headteacher position. If you request such a position, it means you like the responsibility and you are ready to do the job. At times if one is appointed headteacher without having shown interest, they may just handle it carelessly because they never requested it. However, if one has applied for the job, it means one is keen to do the job. Being a headteacher is a job anyone can do, so for those who would be keen for such a job, I encourage them to go for it. Those who will get the opportunity should take it up without any fears. They should accept the responsibilities and they will make it. The important thing is to be committed to the job. I think in most cases one gets appointed to be headteacher after a lot of scrutiny by the appointing authorities until they are convinced that you are fit for the job. Once you are identified as a candidate for headteacher, you should not look down upon yourself but take it up enthusiastically.

My future ambition is to achieve my goals and serve to the best of my ability. I have to operate within the guidelines provided to serve the community. About challenges, these are normal. You cannot avoid challenges. The important thing is to be ready to handle the different challenges that come up. You should be ready to resolve challenges as they arise. Challenges should not make us give up on our responsibilities.

Over the next 5 years, my goal is to ensure that the school is the best with results in all aspects, including academic achievement, school buildings and co-curricular activities. I would like the school to be a model school, to be an attractive school that people can reckon with.

Acknowledgement

Thanks to Musa Mohammed for help with translation.

Part 5

Europe

'I Think I Do a Good Job, But I Could Do a Better Job': Becoming and Being a School Principal in Scotland

11

Michael Cowie meets with Gillian Knox, headteacher of Falkland Primary School

Chapter outline

On a map Scotland, the 'Kingdom of Fife' is the peninsula on the east coast shaped like the head of a Scottie dog pushing itself into the North Sea between the rivers Tay and Forth. Originally a Pictish kingdom, Fife has a long association with the Scottish monarchy and is home to Dunfermline, Scotland's capital for six centuries.

The village of Falkland sits at the foot of the Lomond Hills in the heart of the 'Kingdom', amid rolling, fertile agricultural land. Falkland is perhaps best known for its royal palace, transformed from a castle acquired by the Scottish Crown in the fourteenth century into a Renaissance palace in the first half of the sixteenth century by Kings James IV and James V. It is a small, picturesque village with traditional pubs, restaurants, hotels and lodges. Just over 1,000 people live here. Many of the houses are over 300 years old.

Falkland Primary is unmistakably a school and could not by any stretch of the imagination be described as picturesque. It is located on the eastern edge of the ancient village and sits above the A912 main road, separated by a 2-metre stonewall and a small grass strip with a few trees.

Constructed in 1967, its box-like structure of stone, glass and pebble dash is typical of 1960s' economic architecture. The main school building houses four classrooms, library and general purpose room, assembly hall, dining area and office accommodations. The school has outgrown its original building and hutted accommodation in the school grounds now houses a nursery class, Primary 1 and Primary 2/3. There is a tarmac playground, and at the back of the school, protected by a wire fence, a large, grass playing field extends the play area in good weather.

It is the only school in the village. It also serves the village of Newton of Falkland and the surrounding area.

In the long, rectangular headteacher's office, book-shelves along the right groan under the weight of official government education publications. At the far end, sitting behind an L-shaped desk that cuts across the room like a breakfast bar, and in front of a window dominated by East Lomond Hill, Gillian has a clear view of the school entrance through the window to her right. She is in her thirties and is married with children of her own. Having taught for 10 years, been seconded for a couple of years to do development work for her employer and been an acting deputy head for a year and half, Gillian is now a headteacher. This is her third year as a head.

Gillian's story

Looking back, I don't know why I wanted to go into teaching. The funny thing is that I didn't ever want to go into teaching after going through school. It wasn't my driving ambition since I was 8 years old. I had other career plans. But a friend applied for teacher training and so I did as well and got it in and thoroughly enjoyed my 4 years, but when I left I was quite disillusioned with the whole world of teachers and schools and didn't want to be part of a community where you had to be careful about whose seat you sat in or whose mug you drank your tea out of or who you might upset or whether or not there was any brown paint in the school and all these things. These were all things I picked up on in teaching practice. One day a teacher was absolutely incandescent because there was no brown paint in the school and how could she possibly be expected to do her job without brown paint and I remember thinking, 'that's ridiculous.' So, I decided I would not go into teaching and got a job in the pharmaceutical industry as a medical representative, which I enjoyed. I did that for 5 years but towards the end of those 5 years it became boring and repetitive, and it was at that point that I thought I would go back and see if teaching would interest me again. My flat mate at that time worked in a nursery school and I did some volunteer work there and I loved it, just absolutely loved it. So I gave up my job and I went on to the supply list and started teaching and it was wonderful. I just loved it. I loved every second of it. It was so satisfying, and I loved the whole atmosphere. I loved being with children and I loved teaching. It was so fulfilling.

Fortunately the majority of my time on supply time was in one school and I settled in there. During a school assembly, I had to speak to the whole school to give some directions about something. The deputy head said to me afterwards, 'You should think of going into management', just because of the way I had spoken to all of the children from the stage, and I thought, 'Yeah, actually I could do that.' And I suppose that's what first made me think of the possibility that that this might be a career path in a few years once I'd done more teaching. I think that sparked my interest fairly early on. Somebody recognized that perhaps I had potential and I appreciated that. So by the time I came to my first interview for a permanent post, when the headteacher asked, 'Where do you want to be in ten years' time?' I said, 'Where you are.' I suppose that's the first time it had crystallized and I realized that was what I really wanted to do.

Of course, that had to go on the back burner because I needed to learn what I was doing first in the class. I've always been motivated with regard to work. I've always enjoyed doing the best that I can. When a new curriculum came along, that was great and I really wanted to learn about it and get my teeth into that. Initially it was just for my professional development and I enjoyed the results I got from my class. But then that contribution became recognized and I was asked to share what I was doing with other colleagues in school and began to be asked to be involved in working parties as someone who knew what she was doing. I liked that. I liked that feeling of knowing what I was doing now. I had been there 4 or 5 years and I enjoyed the wider involvement and responsibility. I was asked to lead one council working party and was involved in another and I didn't need much encouragement. I suppose at that stage I was thinking of building a wider range of skills that would stand me in good stead when I had to go for a senior teacher's post, which is what I was thinking of at that time. But I suppose I was thinking about being as good as I could be in the hope that this would develop the skills that would be needed one day to take on another responsibility.

Then I became a development officer. The job was advertised and then re-advertised. I didn't apply for it the first time because I didn't feel confident enough, but the second time I thought, 'I've absolutely nothing to lose and I'll give it a go.' It turned out to be right up my street and that was a fantastic opportunity to get a bigger picture of the council and how it worked. Up until then I had worked in my little bubble in school and thought that everyone taught in a similar way or everyone had similar strategies and it allowed me to see how other teachers taught and how other schools worked. It was eye opening and confidence building. It was a fantastic experience. I got to visit other schools and speak with lots of other teachers and run workshops. I got to be involved in council-wide, strategic development and that was really an incredible opportunity. I still benefit from that experience today. I loved being able to talk with other teachers about what they did and about what I was doing. I enjoyed it very much, although it was hard work.

I had been due to go back to my teaching post, but I wanted to move forward. I didn't want to go back. It's difficult to go back so I applied for a couple of jobs and thought, 'Well, you know, I'll give it a go' and was very fortunate to be given a leadership opportunity. I had done a number of courses at that time, one called 'Future Leaders', for example. I knew that that's where I wanted to go and I focused my continuing professional development on courses to do with leading and managing. I became an acting depute in an area of high deprivation in a school very different from the school I had taught in previously. It was a real culture shock because I had built up my experience working in one school and everyone knew me and I knew them and it was comfortable and we had a certain way of doing things. Moving to a new school where they did things in a different way, I had to learn how a school worked from a different perspective and to work with teachers in a different way. Looking back, I probably didn't have long enough at that depute level because I had so much to learn.

I applied to join the Scottish Qualification for Headship programme, and my interview for that was in the same week as I was interviewed for this post. I was asked at the headteacher interview if I was appointed would I still want to take part in the programme. I remember thinking, 'Absolutely, if I get the job, I'm going to need all the help I can get.' And it was incredibly helpful. It structured things around what I needed to do in the first couple of years. Some of the things I would have done anyway, but the programme supported me as a new head because it kept me on task and it made sure that I did all the things I needed to do. I wouldn't have missed it. A number of people said,

'Why are you doing that, you're a head now so why are you doing that?' But I think I needed to. Perhaps because I had such a short time as a deputy head, the programme helped fill some of what I may have missed. I was lucky to have worked with and learned from a headteacher who had real strengths, quite specific strengths, but you need breadth in leadership – you just can't focus on one area – and the programme allowed me to take a broader view.

My first day as a headteacher was one of those days I'll never forget. I thought, 'What do I do? Well, I need to meet everybody. I'll need to start meeting parents. I'll need to start getting out into the community.' I thought, 'What am I going to do for my first wee while?' I gave myself a list of tasks to do to give me some comfort. I knew I had things that I wanted to achieve. I knew I needed to get to know the school quickly and I wanted to make an impact. I had said at the interview what I wanted to achieve in the first 3 years, so I was really clear about what I needed to do. I needed to involve parents and community partners. I wanted to improve the attainment levels the school already had, and I was quite clear that I wanted to make this a really good school and have highly motivated children and staff. But then you enter a big long tunnel and realize that it's a much harder thing to do.

I had visited the school prior to the interview. It struck me as a lovely school. It's in a beautiful setting in such a scenic little village. It's a lovely size. I've never worked in a school quite as small as this. It has seven classes. It had such a lovely feel. I knew a little bit about the village. It's in a fairly affluent area although the school has a big catchment area and includes a wide range of income groups. But it's a very tight community. The people are very proud of Falkland Village and very proud of what it stands for. What I knew was that the school was in quite a good area, had good attainment and was a nice wee village school; but what that would mean for my job I didn't know.

The reality was just as I imagined it would be. But I think you start to really see the picture when you get to know a place. When I started, I met with the whole staff on the first day to introduce myself and have a wee chat over some tea and cakes. I let them know that I wanted to get to know the school quickly and that I would be in and out of classes but they weren't to worry, that was just me getting to know the children. I wasn't coming to look at them but I wanted to come into the classrooms to speak to children and find out how they were getting on and get to know them. I met individually with all the staff and had a conversation with everybody, not with any particular focus other than 'What's your experience of teaching? Where are you at the moment? What do you hope to achieve?' I also had an open night for parents, which was well attended. I think they wanted to see what the new 'headie' looked like. I used that for a bit of evaluation, with a simple questionnaire asking what the school was good at, what we needed to keep doing, what we needed to stop doing and what we needed to start doing. I used that with staff and children as well, and that gave me rich information about what people thought about the school. I also went into the community and local shops and businesses and met community leaders. I spent much of the first term doing that, just reaching out and saying 'Hello' and inviting them in, or I would go and visit them. That gave me quite a good sense of things and let people know that they could come and see me and that I was approachable. I didn't want to hide in the corner. I wanted to say 'Here I am!'

The first few weeks were quite daunting, but then I also thought, 'I can do something here.' On the one hand it was a scary prospect, but on the other I kind of wanted to take control and be the person who can make a difference. Nobody knew me and I could start the way I meant to go on, I suppose. The first few weeks were about trying to be the person I wanted to be and it was a process of self-discovery. I didn't know what it was like to be a headteacher or how the children viewed a headteacher. One of the children said to me 'You smile a lot!' and I thought, 'Well, that's good feedback' because you set the tone, I suppose, in the first few weeks and it's important to set the right tone for children and for staff and for anybody round about that we work with.

I came to realize in those first weeks that there was so much that I just didn't know. It was a case of 'you don't know what you don't know'. For the first wee while I responded by saying things like, 'What do you normally do? What normally happens?' What surprised me was that staff expected me to know how the school ran. Their expectations were that every school ran the same way that this school did, but it was totally different from any other school I'd ever been in. It was quite interesting to see that those expectations were very different. We had to have a settling-in period with me saying, 'You tell me what you do and we'll sort it out', rather than me coming in and laying down the law. I didn't want to do that. I wanted to be much more collaborative and collegiate.

It's my firm belief that people should work together. We all do different jobs in the school. They're all difficult and they're all challenging, so we need to build an appreciation for what everybody does and work together. I want to work with people before making a decision. I prefer to do that once we've had a discussion and then set down procedures agreed to by everybody. I find it difficult to make change unless everybody is on board. I think I am approachable and I've got an open door policy, which has sometimes 'bit me on the bum' because it can be too open sometimes! But I try to make sure that anyone can come in and talk to me if they feel they need to. I think the parents very much welcomed that. I like to share humour with people. It's a serious job, but there must be that lightness and fun and joy in what we do, I think, and I think the parents were happy with that. The staff were very welcoming, although my approach was less formal than the one that they were perhaps comfortable with. Although they wanted more power to contribute, they also quite liked being led and told what to do. I perhaps challenged some of the status quo and that maybe made some people feel uncomfortable. I didn't want to accept what was happening and wanted to create a sense of shared responsibility and get them to realize that it's not all down to one person whether something happens. We've been working hard over the past 2 years to build up a sense of shared responsibility, accountability and ownership and things like that. We're getting there, slowly. Everybody now has a leader-ship role within the school, which they didn't initially. Everybody now has responsibility for an aspect of school improvement or maintenance. I think it's fair to say that some weren't all that comfortable with that, but there's far more shared responsibility and understanding now of what it takes to be able to pull something together and an awareness that no one is going to come and magically do it for us. But it's been a slow, slow, slow process.

In the first year I spent time getting to know how the school ran before I changed anything. I saw quite a lot in the first year that I thought, 'Mmm . . . I won't be doing that again', but I kind of wanted to run that year getting to know how things worked. But during the first year the way we communicated with staff needed to be changed. There were a lot of complaints about communica-tion. So we made improvements, some of which were quite small and adopted very quickly. Other, more substantive changes were much more difficult and have taken a long time to get going. Even the introduction of the school diary proved problematic. Even just simple things like that took a long time. Things that were introduced were plans about who was doing what when, so meeting plans, staff communication plans, school improvement planning was organ-ized. School self-evaluation was the big thing and everybody was involved. I wanted everyone very much more involved in self-evaluation and how they did things.

But there was some resistance. I wouldn't say that there were barriers as such. What I would say is that some things take longer to achieve than others, and if you persevere I think you still get to where you want to be. I think there was a lack of understanding of it actually happening. Staff ticked the boxes on the evaluation sheets, but there's also a section on implementation and that was neglected. I had to get beyond that and try to persuade people that it was not about how much I asked them to read but about how much we can talk to each other about what is happening and make sure that everyone understands what's going on. It took a while. I had to go to people and say, 'Remember you've got to do this and remember we said we were going to do that and remember we decided this and could you go and look at that', again and again and again.

In the first year we also looked at the vision for the school. I put a draft together and asked questions about what we were going for and we condensed it down to six words. We also looked at things like uniform policy and homework. Homework was a huge thing with parents because they thought we didn't have enough homework. So we put a homework policy in place. It's consistent and that was another big thing that first year; everybody was doing their own thing, so the big push in the first year was about bringing everything together. I said, 'Do you realize we're all doing different things? Can you see that we need to be consistent and have things that work right across the school and that this would stop people complaining?' So we started putting systems in place that would make things clearer for parents and staff. That's been a bit of a theme for me – let's put in place systems that are going to work whether I'm here or not, because there was huge reliance on the headteacher having that overview. The system should work despite you not because of you, I think, and I thought that having consistency across all of the things that we do was important.

We also looked at the [parent council in the first year and moved from a parent teacher association to a parent council. So there were lots of changes. It was about opening doors and making it all clear and establishing 'this is what we do' and putting policies together, particularly in regard to how we related to the community. One of the early things introduced in the first year was what we call a shared approach, which is about how we do things here. This includes things like how we start the day, how we bring the children in, how we approach language lessons, how the jotters look, how we organize the school meals at lunchtime and so on. It was just about clarifying all of the things that happen. My frustration in the first year was being unable to find any of that information anywhere. I had no way of finding out what was supposed to happen here. I was unable to monitor anything. I couldn't make sure that things were happening when everybody did things differently. So for me it was important to be able to say, 'Right, this is what we do.' And that shared process is growing with agreement from staff. It was a case of getting people together and saying, 'Right, what do we do here? Let's write it down.' But then you have to do it. Then you've not got to mess about and make it up as you go along. You actually have to do the things you've said you're going to do.

We've been focusing on restorative approaches across the school because there was a big thing before I came about bullying. Parents were exercised about bullying and that had to be dealt with. I was keen to move away from the word 'bullying' because it's not something that encapsulates good behaviour or the kind of citizens we want. Bullying is a very small part of behaviour management, so we looked at the restorative approach and how we give children the skills to be resilient enough to cope with their relationships in a positive way.

We also worked on the curriculum and we think we're now quite far ahead with that, actually. So after almost 3 years we have a shared vision that the children are involved in; we've got consistent approaches in how we do things across the school; we've got an approach to building good relationships across the school, which is working well, with self-evaluation helping us; we're moving curriculum development forward so that we're challenging our children, especially our able children, in more innovative ways. This year we've taken a fresh look at planning and curriculum delivery, assessment and evaluation across all areas of the curriculum, so even though we started slowly finding out where we are, we've taken some big steps over the past couple of years to move those things forward.

I've tried hard over the past year and a bit to get staff to provide collegiate support and spend time in each others' classrooms and talk about teaching and learning, but I feel like I'm bashing my head against a brick wall and I'm finding it really, really difficult. We've worked on staff development with neighbouring schools this session and done some interesting twilight sessions with the university. But the staff find self-reflection and talking to each other about teaching and learning very, very challenging, so I'm at the stage now of trying to support that in a less threatening way and trying to go from where they are. But they just want it all to stop.

A couple of teachers are about 35 years old and the rest are over 45. They've not been accustomed to self-reflection through their training or experience and find it difficult. They are struggling to see the point. I go into classrooms and they know I'm coming in to look at things that have been identified previously and are set in the action plan. The idea is that I complete a pro forma showing what I think and they complete one from their perspective of what went on in the lesson, but they find that difficult. That's been going on for almost 2 years and I'm continuing to try and find a way through because I actually believe that we've got a very good staff here. They all have good skills and I would love them to share a bit more, but they don't like it. And I've still got to get a better understanding of why that is.

It's the volume of work rather than the difficulty that I find most demanding. Each individual job in and of itself is highly doable. The difficulty is when they all land at the same time. It's just the volume of stuff that needs to be done. It's about prioritizing, but they sometimes seem to be of equal importance and it's very difficult to keep all the plates spinning at the same time. I find that quite overwhelming at times. At times I feel that I'm drowning and I can't do this. I imagine the expectations of others and put them on myself. Whether it's keeping up with paperwork, answering emails, creating newsletters, writing policy documents, sharing continuing professional development with staff – it's all the little bits and the different things that need to be done. It bothers me if I can't get to the jobs I've got to do and it's that element that people, people who are not headteachers, don't understand and that is quite frustrating. And it can be things like, 'Have you phoned?' if somebody's main priority is that you make a phone call about something. But it's not your biggest priority, you've got 20 things before that, but that person keeps coming at you and you're thinking that in the big scheme of things that's not the next biggest thing. Or, sometimes my open door policy can come and bite me because I'm at the beck and call of people all the time. But I think it's important because I felt as a teacher that I wanted to be able to go and ask for help when I needed it and not have to wait. Their time is precious, too, and I want to be that kind of person, but that has created a bit of a rod for my own back because it takes me away from other things that I need to do and there's just so many.

Above all of that I need to spend time with classes. I need to spend time with the children, time with the staff, and the stress or the pressure comes from trying to get the balance right. If I'm spending too long in the office, that's unsettling. But if I spend time in class, a pile of stuff builds up behind me and I have to come back and sort that out at some point because it doesn't go away. I spend at least one night a week at school until about 8 o'clock, at least one night, sometimes two, and often work on a Sunday as well. I can't keep my head above water otherwise because I when I'm in school I want to spend time in classes or meet parents or see people that I need to see. I often don't get any of my 'work' done until everybody else has left the building. That's when my 'work', my paperwork, gets done. My average working week would be about 60 hours.

I think that by their very nature and by definition headteachers are high achievers and want to do things well or they wouldn't be doing this job. Headteachers want to do the best job they can and have no intention of letting people down, and it's frustrating because the first person you let down is yourself if you're not doing the job that you think you should be doing. We can be our own worst critics in that regard. But I want to spend time doing things that make a difference for learning and teaching. I want to spend more time doing that kind of job and less time doing administration, and sometimes that balance isn't right.

I enjoy the job. There are moments of sheer joy when I think this is the best job in the world. This is a fantastic job, but there are other moments when I think 'this is hard, this is really hard, hard work'. But I can't imagine doing anything else.

Without a shadow of a doubt being with the children is the most positive aspect of the job. Having the kind of relationship I have with the pupils. And staff, too, the staff are great, and the parents. People feel they can approach me and ask things, and that personal contact gives me a buzz. I feel I can make a difference to people, whether they're tiny wee tots, concerned grandparents or staff who are worried and feel that I can help and support them; that's the best bit of the job.

When I need advice and support I turn to other headteachers. The neighbouring headteachers are a real support. These people are fantastic and we work well together and support each other practically and emotionally. We've got that 'we're all in the same boat' kind of feeling. They are the people that I would go to first. We do a lot of problem-solving together. We do a lot of school development together as well.

I worry that something is not going to work, or an arrangement that I've put in place is not going to work or if everybody is going to be okay. The responsibilities are huge. But if I thought about the responsibilities I'd be nothing but a big bag of worries. I would be a nervous wreck. The enormity of being responsible for all of these little people and all of these members of staff, if I really sat down and thought about it, I would drive myself silly, so I have to keep it in some kind of perspective. What worries me is that, as a colleague often says, 'One day I'll be in the front of the newspapers because I'll not have done something or I'll be caught out for something.' It's not that I have a guilty conscience, it's just that fear that somebody is going to make life really hard and all of a sudden I'm going to be on the line. I wake up regularly at night thinking about work and often have to get up at 3 o'clock in the morning and write down all the things that are on my mind. I wake up and worry about what's going to happen and ask myself, 'Have I done everything? Have I done all the things I need to do?' Being a headteacher has affected my work/life balance and the job is stressful at times. But lots of people have stressful jobs and lots of people worry about things. I'm fine.

People talk about headship being a lonely job and I know what they mean. I'm not a particularly lonely person. I don't feel too lonely. I've got a great staff and the most fantastic administrative assistant who is my 'right hand woman,' so I don't feel particularly lonely, but I do know what people mean because there are certain things in the job that can't be discussed with anybody, and there are times when it's not possible to explain why I've made a decision and people have to accept what's been decided. That's when it feels lonely. There are things I can't share with anyone, but this is not a unique job; there are many jobs where those situations arise.

We've come quite a long way in the past couple of years. We've got a good team and I wouldn't want to lose any of the members of staff that we've got. Everybody contributes and we've got a growing sense of team spirit and they're a great bunch. I think the decisions and the changes that we've made have been right for the school, and it's often fed back from the parents and staff that they're happy with the changes. They like the changes in planning, the curricular change, the improved communication and the personal learning plans. I think we now have a culture and ethos around learning being important and the children are focused on why they are here and what we here to do. But I want everyone constantly asking, 'How do we make this better? How do we make it more engaging? How does it meet the children's needs?' I want those questions to be on the tip of every teacher's tongue and I want parents and children thinking about how we can help the children to be better learners. I think that is being shared, but it is taking time to build momentum. But 3 years ago, if you asked children what they were learning they might have said, 'Page 32' or 'We're doing maths.' Now if you ask, 'What are you learning today?' they'll be able to tell you. They understand what they are learning about. I think that would be the big thing, getting children and teachers focused on learning. Teachers get a bit fed up with me because every time they say something like, 'We could do this', I'll say, 'What's the purpose? What will the children learn?' Somebody said that back to me the other day and I thought, 'I must be making a difference then.' We're not there yet though.

Because we're a good school and because we've got able children, the biggest challenge for us is keeping people motivated and to keep improving and not think that we're as good as we need to be. I won't ever think we're as good as we need to be. I want people to think we need to be the best school. It's a fantastic place and the children are wonderful, but I'll know it's an excellent school when everybody is thinking about how can we do it better and how can we open up more possibilities for our children. We cannot be satisfied with good enough. Good isn't good enough. The priorities for the immediate future for me are to stay focused on how we make things better. That's what our staff conversation at the moment is focused on, and the plan over the next year is to stay focused on opening up learning and keeping people talking about quality learning and teaching and what it looks like, and to be focused on what's happening in class. My challenge for the next few years is to keep lifting the bar. Eventually I don't want to be the one lifting the bar; I'd like it to be a self-lifting bar.

I don't know if I'll still be a headteacher in 10 years' time. It's a really hard job to sustain. I think I would like to be head of a bigger school and move on and see if that was something within my capacity. I don't know if it is. There are days when I think I'm not doing this job very well so why would I want a bigger school, but there are other days when I think I'd love the challenge. But in the longer term, I just don't know if I could sustain it. It's one of those jobs that is just 'full on'. Unless I get better at what I do and get better at prioritizing, but I think there are too many things sent in the way of headteachers that really aren't important but have to be done. There's also the pressures and accountability. I accept that we can't get rid of accountability, but the way that is measured is draining on schools and their time. We need to spend more time on what is actually worth doing, which is teaching children, and not have such a heavy hand on measuring it. I know it's important to measure how well a school is doing and to report on that, but the accountability pressure is huge. I'm constantly aware of it. I spend quite a lot of time on the formal accountability bit. I do see the need for that, but I'd prefer the inspectorate and others coming in and seeing what's happening and talking with the children. Don't ask me for bits of paper – come in and get to know my school. Come in and get to know my kids. Come in and get to know me, and if I'm not doing it right tell me and point me in the right direction, or help me sort myself out. If there's something that I'm not doing that I should be doing, help me sort that out for myself.

It's a very tough job. Not in terms of how difficult each aspect is but in terms of the volume of aspects that need to be covered. One minute I could be mopping up vomit, the next I could be sorting out a serious staff issue or meeting a parent. Or I could be working with the council to develop council strategy. All of these things are really important and of equal importance and so I can't skip over the top of the job. It's such a huge job. And there's nobody else to do some of these jobs. In the school there is only me. If somebody is absent then I'm 'it'. If something isn't working I'm responsible and have to fix it. Even with a great support team it can be difficult to find time to do things as well as I want to do them. That's what makes it a tough job. And there are some tough decisions and there are some tough conversations. Strong social and personal skills are needed, and no one should do this job unless they can establish good relationships with people.

I think teaching is the best job in the world. I enjoy my job but I was more comfortable teaching. I suppose after 10 years teaching I knew I was good at that. I don't know that I've been in this job long enough yet to say that I could do it that well. But I can see myself in that position. I think it's a fantastic job. It's an incredibly rewarding job. For all I moan about how varied it is, the fact that it's varied is also a plus. I do love that. Every day is different and the different challenges make it stimulating, but sometimes it can be quite overwhelming and that's when it goes from being the best job in the world to being a really tough and challenging job. But I certainly wouldn't put people off becoming a head. I think most heads would agree that it's a tough job, but it is very rewarding.

As for the future, I hope I can be better than I am now. I think I do a good job, but I could do a better job. I hope that I won't find it as frustrating and that I won't find it as hard and that I'll be able to put in place systems that will make the job more doable for me and I'll feel that I've got a handle on it and can come in the morning and do my job and deal with the other stuff and I don't end up being buried under mounds of paperwork. I would like to be able to keep it all flowing, but my fear is that it will become harder and harder to do that. I don't have a janitor at the moment, so if a child is sick, it's down to me to clear up. We don't have a playground supervisor, so it's me that does the playground supervision. I also have to do dinner hall duty and if a teacher is absent, I'll substitute. I could go on and on and on about these jobs that have to be done. I'm the school's designated mini-bus driver and almost 'chief cook and bottle washer'. If something breaks, I go and fix it.

But I love it. I do. I wouldn't do anything else. I wouldn't go back. Even though I said teaching was the best job in the world, I wouldn't go back to it now. Even though I love teaching, it wouldn't be enough now. This is a really good job. It's hard doing it on your own and it's hard being the only manager in the school, but that's why I'm trying to build capacity with staff and help them to do the jobs they need to do. That will make my job doable and build in some form of sustainability and the development of the school won't depend on any one person. But I think it's going to get harder and harder.

12

'Probably More Than I Bargained For': A Headteacher in England Reflects on Her First Headship

A new headteacher talks about her introduction to headship with Megan Crawford

Chapter outline

Introduction

When we talk of schools in deprived areas there are many different kinds of schools in England that might have that said of them, and yet the contextual background of each may be very different. In many parts of southern England, the urban growth of the Victorian period was brought about by the railway, and the town in which Kings Primary sits is one such place. It has an established centre with a main shopping area, a leisure centre and a still-busy railway station. In the early 1960s, there was a further substantial expansion of the town, with people from London being relocated by the Greater London Council, mainly to a London overspill estate to the south of the original town. This was the first great change of the population since the Victorian expansion, and many people took the opportunity to leave London and move to the countryside. The population increased dramatically from 5,500 in 1921 to 17,000 in 1961, and there has been further expansion in recent years as the location was developed to provide more housing in the 1980s. Lately, there has also been investment in the area as part of an urban renewal programme. The area is now a mix of races, class and age groups, but it is still predominantly white, working class.

In the midst of this growing urban area lies a sprawling estate that grew up in the 1950s and 1960s, and is now very well established. The housing varies from small terraces built in the early 1960s, tower blocks that were popular at that time and slightly larger houses that were built in the late 1970s and 1980s. The estate appears at first glance to be a place of neatly tended houses and trimmed lawns, but closer inspection reveals signs of neglect, poverty and vandalism. There are broken windows and some not so well-looked-after houses. Although the latter aspects are not obvious to anyone passing through, the long-term effects of unemployment and low education expectations on the estate continue to cast a shadow over the area and its local schools. Many of Kings Primary School's former pupils have never strayed far from the local area in terms of employment, and recent downturns in the economy, both locally and nationally, have had an effect on the whole area. These challenges are similar to those that many schools face, but these were what brought the new head to the school in the first place, as she had a keen desire to make her mark and help children achieve.

In the midst of the estate, near one of the large tower blocks sits Kings Primary School. Melody Jones, the school headteacher, is nearing the end of her fifth term of headship, but there is a sense that she is only just beginning the headship experience that she anticipated when she accepted the post. Kings Primary is not its real name, for reasons that should become clear. Built in the 1960s, the school is tucked away off a main road, down a driveway with expanses of grass. The school and its grounds are well cared for. Although its leadership had changed recently, the school has an old and established staff. Many of the children at the school have parents and grandparents who attended it themselves. At the same time the school has more pupils than most schools have that join or leave the school at other than the usual point of entry. There are several other schools in the area, but the school draws on a primarily local catchment. The building is well decorated and replete with children's artwork. The reception area is clean and bright, although not large, and the headteacher can often be seen in the area. It has a large playground and good outdoor space. The previous headteacher had been at the school for a number of years, and had retired when Melody took over. This is Melody's first headship and she had planned her route into headship carefully, looking for just the right school to work in. Melody is married with no children.

The headteacher has a large, square office near the reception area. It has a desk, PC and chairs with a coffee table. It is light, bright and newly decorated. There are books on the walls, but not overbearingly so, and the whole room is welcoming and clutter free. This is her eleventh year of teaching, as she was a late entry, having worked in finance for 6 years. She had always wanted to be a teacher, but her father was against it and wanted her to have a different job, so she decided on a career in finance, a career that he approved. She enjoys working with children because she feels she can make a difference in their lives. She is in her thirties, blonde and slim, with a vivacious personality. When she was interviewed there were 280 students on the roll, with 10 members of teaching staff.

We sat down to discuss her life as a new headteacher, and it soon became apparent that the school and the role of head had turned out to be very different from the one Melody had envisaged when she took the post. Over the course of a long conversation, she talked frankly about disillusionment, personal strength and her vision for the future.

Melody's story

This is the beginning of my second year, but in a way, it feels as if it's just the beginning of my headship now. I can explain why I feel that as we talk through what's been happening here. This has been a very steep learning curve, and something that I never expected – it's probably more than I bargained for, but I am somebody who sticks at what I have said I will do.

I have found the whole thing, the business of leadership here in these circumstances, challenging, but not at all in the way that I had imagined when I took the job! It's been very stressful and difficult, and the whole experience has made me think about how people manage when things are revealed that you really aren't expecting. And as well, it has made me think about how I manage myself. When I saw the published information for this school and when I came to look around, it seemed as though it was a good, well-established school that was progressing slowly. An established good school seemed to me to be a good place to start being a headteacher! All the information I could gather about the school was positive, and it really did seem that it was a good place for my first appointment. Anyway, that's how it seemed at first.

I didn't go into teaching until later than many people do for very many reasons, although I think I had always wanted to be a teacher. It had many attractions for me even early on, but instead I chose a different career initially, in finance. I worked in finance for lots of different reasons. The main reason was probably because my father wanted me to have that career, and he wasn't keen on teaching. But I have always wanted to teach, and especially to work with children in needy areas. The catchment areas of all the schools that I've worked in reflect this, and that was one of the things that attracted me to this school. I didn't go straight into teaching though, as I say, because my father was against it, and so I spent 6 years working in a financial environment. I wasn't happy in that job really, as it never gave me a real feeling of doing something worthwhile. So, eventually, I went to university to study for a bachelor's degree in education. I soon knew that I had found the right job with teaching – that buzz in the classroom and the thought of making a difference – that was what made teaching for me. I loved it. It was a real change from my previous work with accounts! I also never wanted to teach in 'easy' schools as I wanted a degree of challenge. This is a tough area, too, but it was my choice to come here, and I knew what some of the challenges would be, especially in relation to teaching and learning. But I think I have empathy with children and parents facing difficult circumstances and with the children in particular, and I wanted to come here. I wanted to make something good for them, to build their confidence and help them succeed. It was something that I think I had done well in my previous schools.

I think I always wanted to be a headteacher from the beginning; I had that aspiration, but needed to develop and build my own confidence. After I started teaching, I guess I had gone through the usual route to headship that most people take, and quite quickly. I was a deputy headteacher, and before that a key stage manager. I was a deputy head for 4 years in a great school with an excellent head. From the start of my career, perhaps because I had already worked for some time, I've always looked for more responsibility and to be able to look further ahead, so I volunteered as a staff governor early in my career and then became a leading teacher for literacy. I loved modelling things for others – showing skills to others and planning teaching. I tried to take all the opportunities that were available to progress and develop that were offered to me as a teacher, and things seemed to naturally materialize. I enjoyed the ideas in literacy work, and the key stage manager role followed from there. I would have been happy to stay at that school for longer, but unfortunately, we had a new headteacher and the school did not want to pay for that literacy role, so I left. I don't think it was just because of that that I left though. I was becoming dissatisfied with the role in any case, but I think that was the trigger for me to look around and think about what I wanted to do next.

I was one of two key stage managers in my new school, and it was a real partnership, I felt. We worked together on the key issues, and I liked that. The school was located in a more affluent area but the children were still needy. I stayed there for 4 years before I left to take up a deputy head's post. In many ways I would say that the job is my life. I give huge parts of myself to the work and to what I do, so it was only when I heard that there was a deputy headteacher's post advertised at a brand-new school that I thought about moving on. The idea of a brand-new school excited me, because of all the opportunities for learning about leadership, buildings management and, of course, appointing staff from the start, and I was absolutely delighted when I got the job. To start with there was only the headteacher, the bursar and myself, and we worked closely together as a team. The head viewed me as a valued partner, on an equal footing, and I was able to use and develop my skills at organizing and we set up the school. It was a situation that helped me thrive as a leader. I think it was a true partnership with that head and creating everything together that gave me confidence in my overall abilities. I enjoyed and gained a lot from the wider community involvement and responsibility. I was able to see how a headteacher worked at close quarters, and the whole process of creating everything from scratch was just great. Starting a new school is a great way to learn about leadership and all the things that senior staff have to do to make things happen. In a new school you can also appoint your own staff and that can make a huge difference. I guess it was around then that I really began to think that I knew about headship, even although I had already gained the National Professional Qualification for Headship (NPQH)[1] when I was a key stage manager. I gained the NPQH 4 years before I became a headteacher, but it was working in the new school that convinced me that I was ready for headship on my own.

I had found the NPQH enjoyable and, in particular, the networking opportunities were invaluable. Participation in the NPQH programme also made me think about my future career plans and what sort of school I wanted to lead. When I had been a deputy head for 4 years I really thought I was ready for headship. In some ways that was true, because I had a lot of preparation in the key processes of running a school and had learned a lot through my previous posts. I knew a lot about running a school and all those management aspects of leadership – finance, appointing staff and so on – but nothing I had previously tackled in my career prepared me for this particular school. However, at the time it seemed like the right time to look at becoming a headteacher. I was looking forward to it.

Looking back now, I think nothing could have prepared me for what I was getting into. Nothing at all. I really didn't know what I was getting into. It just wasn't what I thought it would be. I was sure that I was well prepared through my experience as a deputy in a new school and having undertaken the NPQH programme. I had also checked out several other potential headship opportunities. As I say, I thought I was well prepared in all the things I did when looking for a headteacher's post. In the case of this particular school, I had looked closely into the school before going for the headship. I read all the relevant documentation and I visited the school. I thought that I had asked all the right questions too. According to the documentation I could find it was considered a good school with some outstanding features. The school is located in an area that I really wanted to work in and so all things considered, it did seem like the right headship for me. This picture soon changed though.

It did not take me long in the post to see that in no way did the documentation reflect the reality within the school. In fact, I spent the first 6 weeks questioning myself. After all, I was the inexperienced head – did I know what good was? Could I trust my own judgement? I looked to corroborate my thoughts so I asked the local authority to come in and do a mini-audit and this confirmed my judgement and was a bit of a confidence boost! I was even more amazed when they told me that their 'jaws had dropped' when the school had got a good/outstanding rating in the Office for Standards in Education, Children's Services and Skills (OFSTED)[2] inspection report. This made me angry because there should have been some feedback to me as a candidate for the headteacher's post, but they said they hadn't been able to pin anything down, because the standardized assessment test (SAT)s[3] results and the school performance data were good. But there were things going on below the surface of the data, and it was like an iceberg really. As it turned out, this was only the beginning of a period of deep emotional trauma for me and for the school staff, as I had to take action to deal with what was actually happening in the school. This action eventually led to the suspension of some members of the teaching staff, and a very dark period overall. I knew that when the school next had an OFSTED inspection it was unlikely to get a satisfactory report and I was in charge, so I would have to be accountable, although in many ways the situation had arisen before I arrived. However, because of the way the system works, I knew that I would be the person who would take the flak.

The whole experience was weird. When I first visited the school, it had seemed so warm and friendly, a welcoming place to be. The children were lovely, they opened doors and it was great to see children behaving like that. I believed that I could make a difference in the lives of these children. Now I know that much of it was a bit of a show, reflecting what the school wanted me to see, and perhaps what I wanted to see as well. That was a lesson too!

When I was appointed I wanted to get to know the school and the staff. I was appointed in February, and in the summer, I wrote the staff a letter telling them all about myself and wanting to know about them. I wanted to know about their hopes, dreams and aspirations for the school. I gave everyone a stamped, addressed postcard and everyone replied! That was good. When I actually took up the post the following September, we had some training days and on the second one I made an appointment to speak with every single member of staff and went through the postcard. Even with the local authority audit, I tried to put the staff at their ease, but it was about then that I began to go into my shock period as things began to unravel! My previous schools had matched my ethos and philosophy of education, but in this school I began to see incidents that horrified me. For example, a child was called an 'imbecile' by a teacher on one occasion, and that was just one example of inappropriate behavior that I came across. I felt quite numb and dumfounded and did not quite know what to do at first.

I also discovered that the data used in the school had been manipulated to show a much better picture than was actually the case. It was a shocking revelation for me and I viewed this fabrication as professional dishonesty, which I had never before experienced. But this was only the beginning of the opening of a can of worms in every aspect of the school's operations. It soon became apparent that this was just the tip of an iceberg in terms of personal challenges. I also had no support inside the school at that point because many people felt a loyalty to the previous head. New headteachers in England have a mentor head, and my mentor struggled to give me advice, as she had also never seen anything like what was being revealed. She was aghast! Another head was my school improvement partner (SIP) and she tried to be supportive, but again she had not experienced this sort of situation! I felt as if I was being battered from all sides and was so tired all the time. The only thing I knew was that the local authority understood that it was not me who had created this situation, and I held on to my belief that I was capable of taking the necessary action, no matter how difficult and regardless of any personal repercussions and what might happen afterwards.

I decided that I had to take everything in the school back to basics – start again really. I put an intervention plan in place, and I knew from the local authority audit that we were in danger of being categorized as a school causing concern when the next OFSTED inspection happened because of all the things that I had uncovered. My main problem was that the inaccurate data had informed all the previous judgements that the inspectors had made that the school was good. Even RAISEonline[4] was inaccurate because it used flawed data. I realized that this was not something that I could change quickly. For a first headship, it was very taxing. I felt emotionally beaten up and drained. I knew that if the school was judged as causing concern I would have to live with it, no matter how unfair that judgement was, as that was part of my leadership accountability. I also knew I would have to start disciplinary procedures in relation to some school staff members and that this would also be draining. Trying to see how I could support myself through this was hard, as at that point I had no one in the school I could share my thoughts and feelings with.

In addition to all of that, my leadership and management style was completely different from the previous head. The former head was the owner of everything – no one wanted to take ownership, as they had never been encouraged or allowed to do so. I was frustrated by so many things at first. For example, the teaching assistants were 'display queens' – they spent all their time on that and on tidying the school. I made them work with children, and many of them didn't want to do that so they have now gone. Many parents had been to the school as children, yet they were not allowed into the school and so another job I had to do was build relationships with the local community. The deputy head when I arrived was not supportive, and that was another nightmare. Fortunately, a new deputy headteacher was appointed this year and that has made a big difference. The way we work now is much more about partnership and support, and this includes the new teachers. I have had a clearing out of the old.

For me, I have had to think about school culture and the personal side of what it means to a new headteacher. I have had to examine myself and the pace I take things at. I am a perfectionist, but I came to realize my approach needed to be about building from where the staff are and bringing them with me. My expectations when I took the post were far too high, and as a deputy head at my previous school I had never had to face these kinds of staff challenges. I never realized I could make people think they had to be like me. The pressure began to make me feel inadequate and the pressure was piling up without me really acknowledging it to myself. I felt I had to compensate for all the difficulties and give 150 percent, and after a while the effort involved began to sap my energy and confidence.

Unfortunately, in my first year of headship I was driven by the policies and procedures related to unsatisfactory performance as I had to take action against poor teaching. Of course, the unions have been involved and even the former headteacher became involved on the side of some of the staff. I felt I needed to protect myself more as I have been too trusting, and my confidence and trust in people have been eroded. Coming from schools where I had been able to trust people, this was another revelation.

If I had to start again, I would definitely protect myself more as I think, for one thing, that I was too trusting of people. I wasn't aware of their motives and could and should have analyzed the situation more, perhaps. I was able to cope by putting in place some strategies in relation to my own well-being. For example, I now go every week to a hypnotherapist. I actually started going for fear of flying, but I have continued to go and it does help me, especially to sleep. Also, on a weekly basis, it means that I confront issues and deal with things that have affected me personally, and so I don't end up feeling rubbish about myself. I think that is something that is so easy to do in this situation, and then you just feel worse. Another issue that has hit me hard is the dealings I have had with children's services as some of the situations and difficulties that children and families have can be so upsetting – and again the therapist is my weekly workout. I do still get a buzz from working with the children, but I feel much more tired emotionally than I have ever before. I have to think about moving on and now count the milestones along the way to keep my drive going.

This post is very different from anything I have ever tackled before. I suppose a first headship anywhere can be lonely, but it certainly has been within this school in particular. But I think that headship is as lonely as you make it, and my new deputy is my right arm. My new finance officer is also great and helps to relieve some of the stress, and this prevents me from thinking that I am weak. Also, I have networks outside school that I can plug into. All these issues can pile up and make you feel worthless and inadequate – the intervention plan, the fortnightly meetings – and you think 'There is no more time, what do they want me to do?' There has been a huge change-over of staff and there are now nine new members of staff on board. It's now a very different school, but there are huge challenges ahead over the next few years locally and, of course, there will be nationally too, things that all headteachers have to face and deal with.

As an educational leader, I think I've now got to get everything to where it should be, to look at the basics again and move the teaching on. The accountability aspect and the school's performance are my responsibility, and it is for me to sort that out. My NPQH certainly did not prepare me for some of the human resources issues that I have had to deal with. By that I don't just mean the underperforming staff, but also the personal back-stabbing and attitudes of some of the staff. Good relationships were something I had almost taken for granted in my previous schools. Also, the union attitude was very difficult for me to deal with – it felt hectoring and almost bullying – and this added to the stress that I was already feeling as a new head dealing with very challenging issues.

I think you need a much clearer personal and emotional preparation for headship. The context of your work is also very important to understand. I did try, as I said earlier, to work out what kind of school this was before I took up the post. But I got it wrong. I looked for key indications such as the OFSTED inspection report and asked many of the right questions, but the main things about the context were not things that were apparent straight away, on the surface. There were issues that were hidden to the public and I had to uncover them. I think it's fair to say that this has been the worst year of my life as I have been emotionally torn apart. At the moment, I don't think I want to take on another headship. It would have to be a much more positive experience and not the same or a similar situation.

I think I will train to be an OFSTED inspector though. That could be interesting and would be a change of mode! But I will also see this one through until the end, just to know that I can do that and confirm that it's been worth it. I'm too stubborn to leave. If I were picking a first headship again, I would be determined to get to know the school much more, warts and all, and not be so trusting of people and official documents, although that's a hard thing to do. I would like to be able to emotionally switch off, and yet I think others have this perception of me as a 'hatchet head'. What they don't see is the long, slow draining of 'me' that has gone on. This has been the greatest lesson to me, I guess.

I learned how to be an educational leader with competent and thoughtful professionals, but this job brought me face to face with a group of people who didn't seem to share or want to share my values. It is those values that I have come to understand as being vital to a shared vision of a school. I had learned all that you need to know to run a school in terms of structure, from setting up a new school and from my involvement in the NPQH, but when the deeply embedded values and culture of a school conflict with your personal and professional values, that is a different matter. Finding out who to trust and who to go to in terms of support has been a steep learning curve. Headteachers in these kinds of situations need support, and I am not sure how this could best be done officially at a local or even at a national level. It is especially difficult if you are new because you have to be so sure that you are making the correct analysis of the situation and taking the right action to move the culture of the school forward. The accountability of the headteacher in a primary school means you have to deal with what you find you have and take the flak, which could be part of the reason that people are not exactly rushing to become primary headteachers at the moment!

I have needed to survive what has been a brutal time with at times only my own personal resources to draw on. I have found the support to carry on but not at the level that I would have wished. It has been a bewildering and challenging experience and a lesson in trust all at the same time. I know that this next year is going to be difficult in a different way because we will have an OFSTED inspection and will probably be categorized as a school causing concern and then we will have to deal with that. The style of leadership that I envisaged adopting when I became a headteacher is not the style that I have had to use in practice. It has meant that my leadership style here is very different from the style I would like to adopt or develop. When I was appointed I thought that being headteacher of this school would be the start of an exciting time where I could make a real difference. What I have found is that many of my core beliefs have been challenged, and I have had to learn how to draw on my own inner reserves for support. It was certainly more than I bargained for.

Notes

1 The National Professional Qualification for Headship is mandatory for new headteachers in England.

2 The Office for Standards in Education (OFSTED) is responsible for inspecting schools in England and Wales.

3 National curriculum assessments are a series of educational assessments, colloquially known as SATs, used to assess the attainment of children attending schools in England.

4 Reporting and Analysis for Improvement through School Self-Evaluation is a web-based system containing school-based data funded by OFSTED. RAISEonline provides interactive analysis of school and pupil performance data in England.

When You Enter on the Dance Floor, You Have to Dance: A New School Director in Romania Reflects on Leading an Inclusive Community School

13

Ovidiu Gavrilovici and Carmen Cretu meet with Ana Maria Doleanu, director of Ion Creanga School in Targu Frumos

Chapter outline

Introduction

Targu Frumos is located in the northeast of Romania, 48 km west of Iasi City, the major university city of the eastern Romania region, bordering Ukraine and the Republic of Moldova. The University of Iasi is a magnet for the majority of studious youngsters from the Romanian historic region of Moldova. The western part of this region belongs to Romania and has during all the centuries of Romania's existence, but the eastern part was annexed by the Soviet Union during the communist regime. After the liberation, in 1989, the region established itself as the Republic of Moldova, an internationally recognized independent state. The town of Targu Frumos is situated in the Romanian territory of the Moldova region.

There is a sharp contrast between Targu Frumos and Iasi, the county capital, but Iasi is also historically known as the country's cultural capital, and is generally perceived as a place of opportunities, with a higher quality of life than the rest of the county. Targu Frumos is a small, traditional, commercial town that was obliged during the communist years of industrialization to become an industrial city. It attracted many people from the surrounding villages, but after 1989, in the years of transition towards a democratic regime, many of the factories closed. Many of the citizens of Targu Frumos became jobless. A lot of their children were already in the town's public schools. Families strive to stay in the city; some take jobs in Iasi or they survive using their small farms in the countryside. Their standard of living is rather low, but most people really value the quality of schooling in their community.

Targu Frumos is a small, multicultural town 48 km east of Iasi City. Most of its inhabitants are Romanian, but there is also a sizeable 'lipoveni' population and a smaller number of people of gypsy/Rroma origin.

The 'Ion Creanga'[1] School, which contains grades one through eight, is rather new, founded on the place where an old elementary school caught fire. The school has 24 classrooms from first to eighth grade and four labs – computer science, physics, chemistry and biology. It is located on one of the exit streets of Targu Frumos and unlike other similar schools in town, it has a large yard, a sports hall and a sports field. It is what might be called a large school.

Being a former student of the university, Ana Maria Doleanu gladly accepted our invitation to come to the university on a sunny October day in 2010, partly for nostalgic reasons and partly because the university was in the midst of its 150-year celebration, being the first university founded in Romania. Visibly moved, the tall and athletic former student smiled warmly and told us her story.

Ana Maria's story

I recollect that back in my graduation year of 1998 I was so naïve that I chose to return to Targu Frumos to start my didactic career as a Romanian language teacher in place of opting for what was so cherished by all the graduates: a permanent didactic job in the big city of Iasi! But I wanted so much to go back home, to my hometown Targu Frumos. My parents wished to have me there for at least 1 year; we have solid family bonds and mobility is not at all high in Romania. It is customary to return to your hometown or village, if economic and housing conditions permit. So my career as a teacher in my school started immediately after graduating with a BA in 1998.

Before becoming a principal

Between 1994 and 1998 I studied at Iasi University 'Alexandru Ioan Cuza', the Faculty of Literature, and graduated with a BA in Romanian and Russian languages. My choice was not by chance; in Targu Frumos there are Rroma[2] and Lipoveni (Russian Old Believers) minorities, and my high school professor was ethnic Ukrainian and I started to love Russian language.

Later on, my master's thesis in 2009 on educational policies and management was based on a case study of my school. I benefited from direct guidance from my dissertation advisor, Alexandru Cruzan, Ph.D., from the Education2000+, who was one of the experts in charge of curriculum reform in Romania. I also highlighted the Iasi County's school inspectorate's experience with a national educational project promoted by the Education2000+ organization on 'Educational access of disadvantaged groups'.

I managed to learn how to face the challenges of becoming a school principal with strong support from my husband, who is an engineer working in the electric company in the region. Immediately after our marriage our daughter was born and we benefited from the close support of my parents. They were caring for our daughter daily and we, the parents, could come in the evening and take our little one from my parents' home. Now my daughter is seven and she started first grade in my school, continuing the tradition of bringing your children to your own school.

A project I participated in as a representative of my school immediately after working as a teacher, back in 1999, was Education2000+ 'The second chance'.[3] I benefited from a short-term membership of the school's administration committee and also from being an educational counselor, being in charge with extracurricular activities in the school, organizing and supervising special events and programs.

While in my initial studies in literature I had no idea about any initial teacher training or about an educational management career. I never thought of or planned for it. At the beginning of my teaching career I was very fond of the history of the Romanian language and I had a passion for Russian language, too. These now are cherished memories, since the new managerial role I had to take didn't allow me to continue my initial focus. I even started a 1-year specialization post-graduate program in literature, but I never graduated from it. I am sorry I did not finish after all.

In order to be accepted to apply for a director position, my didactic career had to follow the seniority normative levels: 'definitivat', 'gradul doi' and 'gradul intai' (teacher certification degree, teacher second degree, teacher first degree). I am now preparing my next stage, 'first degree' examination.

In 2004 Iasi County became a pilot county for educational reform in inclusive education. This is when our school became more involved in inclusive projects.

Becoming a school director

I am an interim school principal entering the fourth year in this position; actually, every year in the fall I am reconfirmed in my temporary position. So to speak, I am a 'new' school director every year. I have completed three school years and now I start the fourth.

I never planned to become a school director. Our school faced a media scandal when a teacher was hit by the sister of a student. She was a former student of our school, with a history of behavior problems, who had left school years ago when she became pregnant. The former school director did not want to make this incident public, minimizing the issue, but the media took up the case and the county school inspectorate dismissed the manager from her position.

So, back in 2006, during the summer, I was 'chosen' to be a school director and my colleague, the education and sports teacher, was chosen as an adjunct-director. We are of the same age, even born in the same month, and we get along very well. When we started we were, perhaps, the youngest school directors in the county; we were 30 years old. The previous director was almost 20 years older. We started as temporary school directors, initially only for 2 months, until the Iasi County school inspectorate had to organize the exam for the call for these positions. Usually this happens in two distinct periods of the year, either in October or during March–April. Due to the Ministry of Education ordinance, until now there was no exam organized. Now we are waiting to see if Parliament will pass the new education bill. I was very impressed by my colleagues who chose us as their future school principals. I owe them a lot, since they trusted me and I want to be able to give back.

I have been interim director for so long, but every year I could be replaced, but officially I am fully responsible and I have all the benefits of being in the principal's position. What I can say? What we say in Romania, *'intri in hora si trebuie sa joci'* [when you enter on the dance floor, you have to dance]. I didn't really have any expectations about this position. Initially we were told by the county inspectorate that we would fill in the position of full director and adjunct director on a temporary basis for a couple of months.

Immediately after starting the new managerial role in our school I was nominated by the county school inspectorate to participate in a training program in educational management organized by a local foundation in Iasi City on 'quality and efficiency in educational management' in 2007. That course was my first exposure to professional management information – educational management, curriculum management, leadership, quality management; we had courses during the weekends – a total of 90 educational credits. It was an eye opener! This training set up for me some directions, launched some ideas and opened some windows. I understood that there is much more to learn and that specialized information would help me in my new role.

So, after finalizing the specialization in July 2007 I started to look for more professional development opportunities. I found over the Internet the description of the Policy and Educational Management master program at Iasi University and in September 2007 I registered and was admitted. I had 1 year of experience already as an interim school director, and my master's program participation was extremely important for me from that moment on. For me it was very important that I use my school as an example and case study during the master's program.

I became richer in the professional jargon, I exercised new perspectives and new instruments of educational policies and management analysis and I started to become more certain in the way I make informed decisions. More importantly, from a practical point of view, I met many colleagues who are now school directors and we became an active and supportive network, which really is helpful and rewarding. It brought me personal and professional relationships, friendships and a very important feeling of 'belonging' to a professional group. This network of master's colleagues and now graduates is evolving and it is being maintained. From the moment you are a member of it, you don't feel alone as a school director. I really regretted graduating; we had so many opportunities to relate and to meet, being part of the academic program. Life is now busy, we don't meet as often, but the Internet 'saves' us.

The 'it' as a new director

I had to continue my didactic career to comply with the national educational regulations at that time. You cannot be confirmed in a school principal position by the county school inspectorate (or the Ministry of Education, for high school principals) if you don't have a senior didactic position (first degree of seniority). So I registered for the examination. My thesis was on the gypsies' image in Romanian literature.

At the beginning of my work as a school principal I was more emotional; I had, for the first time in my career, to make decisions that impacted not only my own work, but also the work of many, and the present and the future of the school. As a teacher you make decisions, for yourself, for the class of students, in relationship with their parents, but you did this between some clear limits and certainties. Children guide you in a way, as you guide them, too. But as a school director you deal with a lot more complexity: many persons, personalities, different attitudes and values, and you have to find a way, a way that will not satisfy all the people involved, but clearly, you take into account the opinion of your colleagues. If your colleagues invested you with their trust as their leader, you have to answer back. Collegiality is, in educational management, extremely important. It is so to me.

As a teacher, I knew the school's reality; I enjoyed working in my school's culture. But between being a teacher and being a director, these are two different worlds. As a teacher you 'executed' in a way different things, but as a director you have to be extremely attentive to the direction you move your school, what strategy you are crafting with your colleagues and teachers. As a teacher you are responsible for your students, but as a teacher you respond to the entire school as a system, and to the special relationship of the school in the community.

I think I have the capacity to adapt quickly, I presume this is the 'it' as a new director. I can say I am keen to openness and curious and eager to learn. Other things were helpful at the beginning, too: I participated immediately in specialization courses and I worked with school directors until then, so a sort of implicit and experiential learning happened, somehow.

A couple of years after becoming director I maintained some teaching load, but the third year I stopped teaching completely; now, this fall, a new government regulation specifies that a full director should also teach between 2 and 6 hours per week. So I just started teaching again.

Event organizing – tradition builder

Events are important in our school. We are delighted to have teachers who are very dedicated to organizing and facilitating students' participative learning.

Immediately after I started my job as a school principal, I think about 3 months, I organized the school's day event. It was the 10-year anniversary;

our school is very young. We thought to do it. The other colleagues were not sure if this was appropriate. It was never done before in the school. I took charge and I prepared a surprise! What was it? We created special diplomas for the 'veteran' teachers who had been teaching in the school since its dedication, including a special, personalized, friendly caricature for each of them. I also found the old videotape filmed at the opening day 10 years earlier. We copied it on CDs and we offered the diplomas while the film was running in the background. I cannot tell how much my colleagues were moved by this surprise . . . the images of the beginning, how they looked, younger and hopeful, how funny they were depicted in the caricatures, everything was sparkling and emotional.

Since then we have a tradition, the yearly celebration of the school day. Every person who has spent 10 years in our school waits for the official recognition diploma when it is time! Some time ago, asking for a memorable event in our school, everybody mentioned this 10-year celebration as 'the event'. I will not give more details about the fantastic party held after the official event, which is still fresh in our memories.

I started my work of a principal, somehow, with a celebration. And this was so unusual, since until then, it was all about planning, following the rules and doing your work. And suddenly I broke the uneventful pace. And on top of it, it was an event where the parents were also involved and participated, as well as the local authorities; today the mayor of Targu Frumos keeps his diploma on his wall in his office!

This October we are in the midst of setting up a huge 'terrible class' Halloween.[4] Already the school is filled with brown, yellow and red tree leaves and pumpkins – you hardly can see the school!

The new paradigm: the inclusive school

The school now has over 660 pupils, grades one through eight. Our school is one of the pilot schools in Romania with respect to integration of minorities. We have over 150 Rroma pupils and over 40 Russian or Slavonic Lipoveni ethnic pupils.

Also we have almost 10 percent of students with special educational needs. Due to our participation in inclusive programs we have specialized staff, such as support teachers, who work individually with such students in their school cabinet. An official external evaluation commission is assessing the educational needs of students at the referral of their parents. This creates a problem in cases of parents who are not interested in the school results of their children and who do not maintain a direct link with the school's staff.

We have about 30 children in each classroom. On top of the two to three students with special educational needs validated by the external evaluation commission there are other students without a formal evaluation but in need of special educational support. Some of these children belong to the Rroma ethnic population. Our special educator has a crucial role in the adjustment of such children and adolescents. We are very proud of having a very well-trained and talented special educator, who also graduated from the University of Iasi 'Alexandru Ioan Cuza' in special education and earned a clinical psychological master's degree.

I am especially happy with one child who was diagnosed with an autistic condition and who was not integrated into the second grade in the mainstream. Last year, nobody believed the teacher could manage to include this child, but we are now so happy to see how well this is working for him and his family.

The most important moment since I became interim director was when I decided to merge the main body of our school with the external unit of our school, a residentially segregated unit especially designed to serve Rroma students. I had this initiative: 'Let's bring all the children to the centre and let's mix them!' There was a real shock; a great shock. I didn't expect to find so many differences. Before, our teachers for grades five through eight had to work so hard with the Rroma students who joined our school to enter fifth grade; teachers of grades one through four in the main school didn't have Rroma students included; they had to adapt and learn quickly.

Rroma parents were used to bringing their children to school and having them in the segregated primary school unit. What is characteristic of them is the preference for the Romanian language, not Rromani language, to be taught in school for their children (even if they always can opt for their mother language, they prefer not to do it). Rroma parents prefer that their children be considered Romanians, not Rroma. Anyhow, in the classrooms and in the school, everybody is treated equal; ethnic background is not a discrimination criteria. We really benefit from our school counselor who organized seminaries and activities toward tolerance and multicultural understanding.

The greatest fear after including the Rroma students in the classrooms of our main school was that Romanian parents would 'sanction' this by withdrawing their children from our school and moving them to the other school in town. Well, we didn't really orchestrate the merger for the public. It was done swiftly and softly, with a great deal of internal preparation, but not so much campaigning in the community or with the ethnic majority group. Any parent who had doubts or concerns was paid a visit or was invited for a discussion with our school mediator and things were clarified. I have to mention that our school has a great human resource body: school mediator, speech therapist, support teacher[5], and we all work, in this new, modern school, with a new building, sports field, a sports hall and a lot of green around . . . we are lucky!

When we included the Rroma pupils in our main body of the school, there were some days and weeks of near chaos: the Rroma children and their parents were used to walking everywhere, anytime; it seemed that no rules was their rule. I really got involved and discussed with each and every Rroma parent and child to support and guide them to follow the schedule of classes and to respect the school norms. For me, this is very indicative of a general feature of the many large, national programs for the Rroma: most of them were directed solely towards the Rroma children, but only a few included their parents. And a lot of these projects were supposed to materially compensate for their disadvantageous economic status and, in fact, the compensation received by the Rroma students easily surpassed the level of the average majority student, creating jealousies and a new form of black market commerce in the community. I really consider that those projects directed at large target groups, many Rroma children, were not so effective; their effect was severely diluted by the lack of involvement of the families. A better result would have been if these projects would have the family as the unit of intervention. But a major result with these projects targeting multicultural issues, diversity and inclusive education is the change in attitudes, skills and knowledge of the teachers involved.

Challenges: student population decrease

The most difficult environmental change we faced in the last decade is the shrinking of the student population. This happened not only in our small town, but everywhere in Romania. For example, in 1998 our school had 1,200 students! So we faced a 50 percent reduction in student population. This is one of my main concerns.

An important potential contributor to this trend is the continuous threat that the parents who work abroad – mainly in Spain, Italy and Greece – may take their children left behind in the community to study in their work locations abroad. Fortunately, this September this didn't happen to the levels that may have threatened the student population registering at our school. Over 140 children and adolescents in our school have at least one parent working abroad. This totals almost 25 percent of our pupils! Most of these children stay with their relatives, mostly in the care of their grandparents. This has an impact on their school results and on their emotional well-being, in some cases.

Leadership style – being a 'turtle'

I started to see things differently after I became school director. I felt and I saw a direct responsibility towards others. The changes in the environment made things tough: with smaller size classes, the school shrinks, people leave and you have to maintain the position. The new governmental regulation in 2007 forbidding the school segregation a few years ago was an opportunity to include the Rroma pupils from the formerly segregated school unit into the main building. Mostly the other parents were concerned. I was very supportive of my teaching colleagues and we made it. Now we have a fully inclusive school – all our students study under the same roof!

Compared to the more direct style of the previous principal, I am a team player. We are together a school, so I think and act as much as I can as a 'we' unit. I like surprises, to get personal to people. I like to see my colleagues happy and that they enjoy being in our school. I really hate when a person has to leave. And until now, we managed to stay close-knit. Only our music teacher chose to go for a better position in a different school. I would consider our school culture very cohesive.

How the school is regarded

I see our school as 'beautiful' and rich in excellent teaching staff. During spring our school is at its peak: full of flowers and life. I remember 8 March[6] 2010: all students and their family members came to school with flowers; it was a sea of colours and joy.

Our school is well perceived; the only really difficult moment was the inclusion of the Rroma pupils from the previous external segregated unit. But I never heard a critique from somebody in the community; I can maybe put it down to reticence, especially from other parents. Lately the reticence, in comparison to the other school in town, is that the other school is central and situated among some blocks of flats, securely distanced from the main road, while we are positioned at the margins of Targu Frumos town, exactly on the main road. What are we more and more perceived like? As a stable school! We have no personnel fluctuation. Parents really respect this and in time, they show preference for our school, even if it is newer and just went through the inclusion process recently.

And we are actively recruiting students from the villages around Targu Frumos, a strategy that the other school is not promoting. And also we are competing with the high school in town, since they also developed courses for grades five through eight. But we have excellent teachers and the results of our best students are as good as the other schools.

The school is well perceived in the community by Targu Frumos Mayor House; there is a lot of pride in caring for the city's children and adolescents by the public authority, and the mayor's support is from an open-door policy to the school director nowadays, to the financial support for unexpected infrastructural emergencies that happen, from time to time. I know that this is not customary in all localities, especially in smaller villages in poorer areas of the county. We are lucky. And we worked out a partnership relationship, in time, with our leaders.

Another thing I am confident about is the difference between the school in 2007 and the school nowadays with respect to 'living its mission'. Back then, the school's mission was a mix of statements, which were staying in a drawer in the director's office. Nobody knew that it really existed, and nobody put it to work with and through the people. There was a strategic plan of institutional development that not many were aware of. Anyhow, how could you apply principles like ethnic 'tolerance' in practice, if structurally, the school admits an external unit with grades one through four, segregated, only with Rroma pupils?

Now we are the school of equal opportunities providing education **for all**. Yes, underline that in bold!

Satisfactions and dissatisfactions

I don't know what gave me the capacity to adapt to this new position. I respected step by step what was in the legislation and in the norms, and, the most important thing, I had the support and dedication of the other teachers and of my colleague, the adjunct principal. For sure, I could not stay so long in this position without that. I felt the support of the parents and the students, too. I told my colleague from the very beginning, 'it doesn't matter who is the director and who is adjunct, we are a team, we both are the directors, and that is the most important, to be a team'. We had known each other from before, but only when chosen by our colleagues did we start to work together and get to really know each other well.

I think it is important that a director come from the city or village of his or her school. The parents like to know the director, to be a fellow citizen, to 'belong' to the community. They feel safe and they are more satisfied. In addition, if the director has his or her child or children in the same school, it is perceived as a sign of credibility and validation of the school.

When I am thinking back to the first year as a school principal, I remember it was less stressful to me; this is my actual perception. Honestly! You were not really completely aware of all the responsibilities you had, and anyhow we lived the uncertainty of being or not being reinstalled as directors; my colleagues and I, the adjunct director, we believed that the 2 to 3 months would pass and a new nomination would be made by the Iasi school inspectorate. Somebody else will take over and we will simply resume our usual teaching jobs. I felt freer then. I used to go with the children in weekend trips. It was a certain joy of the moment, I felt freer, a freedom that now I simply cannot afford.

What changed after 2 years? I guess I am more aware of what is really important. I perceive the complexity and more that that, I am responsible to the children, the community and to all the colleagues in the school. With the severe student population reduction, the teaching staff is facing a new reality that nobody is willing to accept easily: each is vulnerable now in their jobs, and this is a public-sector job that traditionally was certain until pension time! And who is held responsible for the personnel reductions? The school director!

What a does a school director do? He or she needs to always have an answer and have a solution to any problem as it happens in the school. There is no room for 'I don't know'. You have to upgrade your skills, to know accountability, legislation, human resources. Everything that makes a school, a school! At a professional development workshop, discussing with my colleagues and self-evaluating myself with some instruments, I was described as the 'turtle director' – the one who really is against conflicts and keeps everybody under the same roof. I don't know if this description is entirely correct; it is rather a generalization. Sometimes you listen to the others, sometimes you have to decide yourself.

I didn't really follow a model in my management part of the career. Rather, I base my validation and ideas on the network of school directors I belong to. We collaborate and I listen carefully when we meet at some training meeting at the Iasi school local authority (inspectorate), and I can make comparisons. I think about where my school is and how I can transfer some of their technology in the way we operate in Targu Frumos. But I cannot tell that I have a model to follow. I am challenged by some ideas and methods and then I return home, and with my colleagues we try to adapt and implement our version of 'to do'.

I have had some actions that didn't work out. For example, we have to ensure the safety of the school – using a private security firm is rather expensive – and we tried to organize a parents' watch, but we had to end this. But we also had other actions of which I am proud, such as the recent initiative of developing a parents' association as a supporter of the school. Even if the community is rather poor, we believe that the 30 percent of the parents who are working abroad are interested in supporting and developing a better school for the child or children remaining at home in Targu Frumos.

Traditionally, parents believed that the school exists and you only have to bring your child there, and miracles happen. We believe and work towards developing the awareness of each parent of their special role in conjunction with the school. An efficient parent–school alliance is strategic for both of us. I know that traditionally the school was rather a closed community, a closed system, with the experts, the teachers, always knowing what they do and being aware and proud of their expertise. But in fact this 'community' remains closed and isolated, never really transparent, permeable and open to the larger community. While the existence of these 'two worlds' remains, as a backbone fact, we believe that bridges, such as the parents' association, stimulated by the interest and will of the parents who are abroad, will create a new model, a new way of interaction for all the parents with children at our school.

What I consider a real success is, for example, the case of a child who comes to our school in the third or fourth grade with important gaps in his or her education and, with the support of the teacher, of the support teacher, the special educator or, if it is the case, the community mediator, you see this child grow and adapt, and manage so that in the fifth to the eighth grade he or she had made up the developmental difference.

I think what is the most difficult aspect of my job is having to be attentive all the time to a myriad of details because you may be held responsible.

And this ties you to the school from morning to late in the evenings. And, in fact, a school director does not have a lot of decision-making power, even if you are responsible for the entire school. As a director you don't find enough legal support to stop somebody's work contract with the school. There are cases in Romania where the fired person is suing the school and the director. And liabilities are extremely severe in these cases. The most limitations a school director has are in the areas of human resources and infrastructure budgeting. But I believe that the educational reform will increase the school's decentralization. This will involve more transparency and evidence-based decision-making, but it will be for the better. If you could recruit the teachers you would like to have, if you could pay them differentiated rates, according to the value added, a lot more could be done in the school.

I think that the seniority system in didactic careers can deter the motivation of teachers: as soon as they reach the maximum level, there is a tendency to lean back. There is nothing more that a teacher can earn or be rewarded. Usually, the maximum didactic level is obtained between the ages of 30 and 40. A few are continuing with a Ph.D. but even this is no longer rewarded by the state.[7] So it is a challenge to maintain a motivated and energetic staff.

A change in the perception of the parents happened in the last 20 years: the parents now prefer younger teachers, not the senior teachers! Younger teachers seem to have another vision, new methodologies and tools. This happens in Targu Frumos at our school. I don't know if it is customary in other localities and schools in Romania.

I must say that personally and professionally I am striving to balance the two roles, and in this equation my husband – who is an engineer working at the electric company – has a crucial supportive role. Also, my parents are supportive, too, babysitting our daughter. I said 'balance', but in fact I should say that my personal life takes second place, unfortunately. I would like to dedicate more time to my family and to my daughter. I am often very tired in the evening at home. I guess a 'perfect' director should not have a child, a family, but having a child and having a family is crucial to understanding parenting and child development and to live the school years again, with your own child, as a parent. This helps tremendously as a teacher, and even more, as a director. It makes a lot more sense. So, I am negotiating every day this balance between director, mother and wife. The actual roles of my life!

I am happy that now in our school we managed to have a warm and secure climate. Our participative culture is rewarding by itself. We have a school where we start to really see and focus on our students. I wish that we could develop and get funding for more projects adapted to our needs – pupils, teachers, parents and the community needs in general. Team work and project work I wish to have more in the future than we did until now.

Being a director is like living in a crystal clear glass – everything is transparent and you may feel vulnerable at times, to the community, mass media, to everybody who is involved. I don't praise the job of a school director. I don't want to be a director. I am doing it because it has to be done and I like challenges. And it pays better, I have to admit. And I always promote this job to others: it is such a challenge . . . and it can be done!

Looking to the future – a pupils' school in their community

Do I want to stay in the principal's position? No. If there is a need, I will. But I may wish in the future to do other things. After graduating from my master's program in policy and educational management I had the chance to work with specialists from ARACIP – The Romanian Agency for Schools' Quality Assurance – in their program of training trainers for educational management counselors. Now I am a certified trainer of counselors for educational management.

Looking to the future and the new education legislative proposal I see an increase in school autonomy, especially with respect to human resource management – we will be able to recruit and select the teaching staff, while this is currently managed by the county school inspectorate (CSI); we don't know the person who will fill in a position. We have to adapt to the decision of the CSI. Also, the future law asks for continuous evaluation of the student and for the use of portfolios, apart from traditional examinations, which will impact the curriculum development: the student will indeed be in the centre of our work.

The school in the community is what I see happening more and more in the future. Though the city's economic future is by no means optimistic; the former local industries were closed soon after the fall of communism in December 1989. Unemployment is high, and it is the reason many fellow citizens leave to work in Western countries, in the European Union (EU). At least the ethnic Russian Old Believers (Lipoveni in Romanian) have their tradition of greenhouses, and this is and most certainly will stay a feature of our town. Our school is situated at the beginning of the fields of greenhouses of our

Lipoveni gardeners. But most people in Targu Frumos have small gardens and some agricultural fields surrounding our small city or in the villages in the vicinity. They survive in what we may call small-scale subsistence agriculture and farming.

I dream for a clearer vision in educational policy. A huge amount of bureaucratic assignments come at unexpected times and with immediate deadlines from the county inspectorate and from the Ministry of Education. There are many ordinances that maintain a fuzzy policy climate and makes school management difficult and risky. We live in a highly volatile and uncertain climate. I hope that the new educational law that we expect soon to be promulgated to change this state of the affairs. It will help us to reinvent the school, which will be decentralized and more student-centred in the community.

Acknowledgement

Thanks to Ms Aliona Dronic who helped with transcription.

Notes

1 Ion Creanga is the most famous writer of children's literature and fairy tales in Romania (1839–89), comparable to the Grimm brothers or Hans Christensen Andersen.

2 In Romania, the Gypsy minority promoted legislation to use Rroma as the minority's denomination and the term Rromani for the language used. Since 2002 Romania passed national legislation preventing any form of discrimination (Law 48/2002).

3 Ana Maria participated directly in the implementation of pre-university educational reform in Romania. This reform bridged the gap between European education and the transitional Romania after 1989. The major areas of the reform were with respect to curriculum development and initial and in-service teacher training and educational management training. The years of piloting and implementing the reforms were contested and resisted, but also pursued with enthusiasm and hope.

4 This is a rather new popular social and merely commercial event in Romania, practiced only in the last 15 to 20 years; children love it, making the middle of autumn cheerful and fun for kids.

5 Support teacher – specialized educator who works individually with children with special educational needs.

6 The eighth of March is International Women's Day, and in Romania the teaching staff is over-represented by women. This makes the event a very festive moment of the year, celebrating the female teachers, but also because the students are involved in preparing mothers' day celebrations and gifts.

7 Ph.D. graduates received a 15 percent monthly bonus.

14

Comparing the Experience of Principals in Different Contexts

Michael Cowie and Megan Crawford

The idea of leadership is now central in the context of principalship. Over the past two decades there has been a dramatic increase in the number of academics, educational bodies, organizations and private individuals that have become involved in what may be characterized as a leadership 'industry'. Countless books and journal articles focused on leadership have been published. Why is there such an emphasis on leadership in education? In Western countries, increased emphasis on leadership has corresponded with the emergence of 'market mechanisms' in education, the transfer of responsibility for the use of resources onto the individual school, increased accountability and answerability and political demands to improve school performance. These discourses assume that measurement and comparison will lead to improvement and have led to a preoccupation with accountability in Western nation states. From a critical perspective, it can be argued that this has led to concepts such as equality, justice, professionalism and administration/management being denuded of meaning and replaced by 'hollowed-out' concepts such as leadership (Ozga, 2000).

Nevertheless, discourses that are reflected in educational policy and practice around the world (Hallinger, 1995) have influenced how the role of the school principal is conceived and presented in many different countries (Bottery, 1999; Foskett and Lumby, 2003) and have had an impact on professional development (Gleeson and Husbands, 2003). In some countries principal preparation is shaped by the need for aspiring principals to attain a standard based on a set of competencies before being given a license[1] to become a principal. This can be controlled by the government, as in Scotland and England, or by the profession, as in the United States. The introduction of a standard can be seen in terms of attempts to control quality, specify outputs and reconstruct meaning and identity among principals, all of which are characteristic of 'new managerialism' (Clarke and Newman, 1997). Other changes also influence the life of the principal. Some are technical, such as those caused by information and communication technology. Others are due to wider issues culturally, such as migration, pluralism and multiculturalism. Principals have also become more aware of the complexity of learning and the importance of inclusion and equity, and recognize the need to work with all members of the school community and in partnership with professionals from other agencies. These pressures now place a heavy emphasis on the leadership capabilities and practice of school principals.

Following the increased emphasis on leadership and the significance attached to the role of the school principal, leadership development and principal preparation programmes are on offer from universities, local government, government agencies and commercial organizations in many countries. Aspiring school principals, principals and other senior managers are inundated with literature advocating the importance of particular models and styles of leadership as well as offers of opportunities to extend their knowledge and skills in the field, even though in much of the leadership research the concept of leadership is not sufficiently defined and remains difficult to get hold of. Grint (2005) argues that we need to forget the recipe approach to leadership because there are no 'seven-ways-to-guaranteed-success'. Our leaders' stories reflect this.

How principals are prepared, developed and supported lie within the debate about the nature of contemporary professional identity and this places aspiring and new school principals in a *complicated nexus between policy, ideology and practice* (Stronach et al., 2002). We will return to the implications of this for aspiring and new principals, and for those responsible for their selection, development and support at the end of the chapter, but with these considerations in the background, we look first to the narratives to see if there are explicit or implicit connections between the experiences of the 12 principals.

As academics we are removed from the reality of being a principal and may have a tendency to conceive of leadership and headship at the macro level. The narratives remind us that it is at the micro level, in the day-to-day operations of schools, that leadership is enacted, influenced by innumerable personal, social, contextual and cultural variations. It is therefore interesting to explore the principals' accounts of their lived reality and experience, their perceptions of key influences on their schools and their communities and their reflections on how they have developed personally and professionally. While it would be foolish to attempt to generalize or come to any definitive conclusion, review of what the principals say with regard to the multiple, heightened and often conflicting expectations, pressures and challenges they encountered as they came to terms with the reality of being a school principal reveals more thematic similarities than differences, although the particularities of each context are important.

However, we are conscious that we have value-laden axiological assumptions and that our review reflects our perspectives as well as those of the principals. Our own background, history and experiences are based on dominant Western assumptions, theories and practices, and what is expected of school principals and the cultural assumptions embedded in preparation and development programmes in the United Kingdom are likely to be inappropriate in cultures and sub-cultures where there are different conceptions of leadership (Lumby and Foskett, 2008). Moreover, with increased diversity, nations are not monolithic societies and any approach based on a single dominant culture is likely to sustain cultural hegemony and be ineffective (Lumby and Foskett, 2008).

The principals in this book came into the principalship for different reasons, but one commonality seems to be the wish to extend their sphere of influence. When they became principals they were faced with new and different challenges and opportunities. For some, it was how they expected it to be, and their experience and preparation influenced how they coped with the early years. For others, the unexpected occurred, and difficulties arose for which they were not so well prepared. Analysis of the narratives shows us how the new principals, many in a high accountability culture, faced difficult decisions for which they were ill prepared. Many of these were focused around people, many of whom have particular and embedded expectations of principals. Taking up a principal's position involves socialization into a new role and new principals must incorporate the knowledge, skills, attitude and affective behaviour required to carry out the role effectively. In doing so they must be able to deal with place, deal with people and, perhaps most challenging of all, deal with themselves (Wildy and Clarke, 2008). We start our review of the narratives by looking at why they wanted to be in this leadership role, and then discuss the socialization process and the three interrelated aspects of place, people and self in more detail.

Because we are sensitive to issues surrounding the relationship between culture and how leadership and the role of the school principal is understood, developed and enacted in different cultural contexts, we invite readers to interpret the principals' accounts and the connections that we make between them from a critical perspective. You bring to these stories your own nuanced understanding of circumstances, contexts and cultures, and through reflection, provide a personal integrative and comparative perspective that is both local and national in scope.

Why teaching and why be a principal?

All of the principals said that they came into teaching because they enjoyed working with young children and wanted to make a difference in their lives and/or serve their communities. Teaching was not always their first choice; some were late entrants and had begun other careers. Once they became teachers, the narratives reveal different paths to becoming a principal. Most found it difficult to explain why they wanted to become principals. Some had always wanted to be a principal and focused on becoming a principal at an early career stage, and talked about the opportunity to make a bigger or wider contribution. Others had not initially wanted become a principal but had always wanted to make a difference. Becoming a school principal allowed them to extend their sphere of influence. Self-belief influences personal efficacy in teaching (Day et al., 2006) and this may also be true of wanting to become a principal, because the narratives suggest that some needed to believe that they could become a principal, and secondment or being asked to take on a temporary acting role was significant in shaping the leadership aspirations of Ana Maria, Gillian, Keita and Rosa. This may be particularly true for women, as their motivation was stimulated through gaining professional satisfaction in posts that carried enhanced responsibilities and the realization that their influence mattered. Often prompted by or encouraged by others, they accepted additional responsibilities, and these development opportunities broadened their outlook and helped develop confidence and self-belief. Others had little choice and Tupa, Xavier and Paulino were appointed or invited to accept the position without having applied.

Socialization into the role of principal: preparation, induction and support

Earley and Weindling (2004) suggest that the socialization process of new principals involves two phases. The first involves professional socialization and takes place before appointment through professional development, first-hand experience derived from current and previous posts and through processes such as observation and modelling. The second phase, organizational socialization, occurs after appointment.

If we consider the first phase, the narratives reveal different paths to becoming a principal. Their routes into leadership preparation were varied. Some had attended short courses on leadership and management, or perhaps attended a series of disconnected workshops prior to their appointment or following their appointment. Xavier, for example, attended workshops, developed appropriate competencies focused on pedagogy and learning and said that these experiences helped him to see things objectively. Others, such as Fan Huali, Paulino and Cedric, indicated that they modelled their behaviour and approach on people they admired or had invested time in appropriate reading.

Of the 12, only Melody and Xavier had the opportunity to prepare for the post through participation in a programme specifically designed for that purpose, although Gillian participated in such a programme during her first 2 years in post. Ana Maria and Tsutsweye had achieved a master's degree, but few had undertaken even short-term leadership and management development opportunities prior to appointment. Those who had did not always find it as beneficial as they had hoped. Some had engaged in professional development opportunities and gained extra qualifications to become better at the jobs they were doing, but these courses were not undertaken with career advancement in mind and they had not planned their career in any coherent way. Others prepared themselves through reading, observing, modelling the behaviour of others and reflecting on their experience in different posts.

During the second phase, organizational support and the personal and professional values, abilities and interpersonal skills of new principals seem to be critically important (Aardrts, Jansen, and van der Velde, 2001; Browne-Ferrigno, 2003; Earley and Weindling, 2004; Simkins, Close and Smith, 2009). However, our new principals were surprised and disappointed at the level of support offered by their employers. Not only were they ill prepared for the post; few had the benefit of a systematic process of induction.

Most were reluctant to make significant changes in the first year and were content to assess the culture of the school and get used to being a principal for the first time. Lacking support, few attempted significant strategic changes during the first year in post as they came to terms with the demands of their new responsibilities. Many were simply preoccupied by the volume of tasks that they had to deal with.

Although committed to making a difference, few felt well prepared for the demands of the post or supported in coming to terms with the demands of the job following their appointment. However, socialization processes involve interaction with others, and neophytes do more than slip passively into an existing context (Daresh and Male, 2000; Kelchtermans and Ballet, 2002). The new principals brought with them their own set of values, beliefs and role expectations and even in the first year, although finding an appropriate balance between doing too much and too little can be difficult (Quong, 2006), small changes were made by some, often with a longer-term strategic intent.

Nevertheless, most initial efforts to introduce change met with resistance. Some talked about problems with dealing with the legacy, practice and style of the previous principal; most were surprised by the multiplicity of tasks that they had to attend to and had initial difficulties in managing time and priorities; some had to deal with ineffective staff; and some had problems coping with personal stress and the pressure involved in being a principal. These initial difficulties echo the outcomes of a literature review by Hobson et al. (2002) and problems identified by Holligan et al. (2006), as well as the uncertainty, loss of attachment and the 'shock of the new' reported in a study of new principals in Scotland (Draper and McMichael, 1998, p. 207). Some found the role transition more straightforward than others, particularly Rosa and Xavier, who were promoted internally and had a social and historical commitment to the development of their schools and communities, although even here the demands of the role took them by surprise and measures had to be taken to establish their new role with staff who had worked with them in their former role.

Looking at principals new in the post is a developing research area (Crow, 2007), but research in this field suggests that new principals change considerably over a short period (Weindling, 1999). Although our principals had to cope with a large volume of work and in some cases the resistance of staff, they talked about how they wanted to take their schools forward and began to think and act more strategically as they began to come to terms with the challenges of place and people and configure their new professional identities. Progress was seen in terms of improving their school's improvement capability and engaging with staff was a high priority. They wanted to develop the skills of the teachers they worked with, encouraging them to become more confident about accepting responsibility and about sharing decision-making. Determination to retain a strategic focus while managing the multiple and competing demands made on them contributed to the complexity of the job, but although some of those who had been in post for 3 years reported that they found the demands greater now that they had a better understanding of what was involved, they also talked about introducing second-order changes (Cuban, 1988) aimed at improving the school's ability to improve, as well as other significant changes that were beginning to produce successful outcomes.

More strategic achievements focused on specific events and outcomes and on building improvement capability were also recorded, such as developing a fully inclusive school in Romania; school in-service days to introduce new curricular programmes and ways of working in Mexico; staff development programmes with neighbouring schools in Scotland; measures to improve, establish and maintain good relationships with parents in East Timor; a range of strategies to engage 'hard to reach' parents/carers in China; changing policy on assessment and evaluation in New Zealand; establishing effective inter-agency partnership working in British Columbia and staff involvement in working groups in Texas.

But not only do principals change quickly in the early years of principalship; their needs also change in a short period (Day, 2003; Holligan et al., 2006). Most of our principals had an idea of the kind of schools they wished their school to become and had a vision of the future, but beyond talking about involving staff in fairly vague terms, the new principals seemed uncertain about goal-setting, leading and managing learning and teaching and leading and managing educational change. Most talked about the importance they attached to effective communication and about their preference for a more collegial approach, often in marked contrast to their predecessors, but appeared to be uncertain about the processes of change and how to work effectively with staff and the wider community to develop effective implementation strategies. Few seemed equipped with the knowledge, understanding and skill sets required. After 3 years in post, John in Australia, for example, felt that he could manage the day-to-day operations of the school well, but still had to learn how to lead. Although committed to making a difference, they did not seem well prepared for leadership.

This lack of developed leadership capability was confounded by particular problems encountered in dealing with an often under-regarded aspect of principal preparation and induction: the significance of context and place.

Dealing with place

Hargie and Dickson (2004, p. 226) argue that 'place identity' is an important part of self and that 'place identity' is based on physical insideness (knowing the environment in terms of physical details and having a sense of personal territory), social insideness (feeling connected to a place where people are well known) and autobiographical insideness (knowledge of 'where you come from' and 'who you are').

As the new principals settled in, they began to understand the physical, social, interpersonal and particular characteristics of each context, and were generally keen to do so. Enthusiasm, uncertainty and adjustment seem to be characteristic of the first phase of principalship (Day, 2003) and these aspects are mirrored in the narratives where the principals talk about how they began to handle the complex physical, social and cultural challenges that they encountered.

In the first year our new principals made it a priority to deal with place, and this meant that they had to engage with parents and the wider community. This involved them in dealing with a range of groups outside the school, including parents, community groups and organizations and officials responsible for school governance. This was more difficult for some than it was for others. In terms of Hargie and Dickson's components, the narratives suggest that the 'insiders', those who had lived in the school community previously or had some familiarity with it (Xavier, Cedric, Ana Maria, Paulino and Tsutsweye), had developed strong place identity as part of self and were relatively comfortable with their place in the school's environment. They had a well-developed understanding of the school and its relationship with the wider community and had a social and historical commitment to the development of both. Their narratives reflect their deep understanding of the social and economic problems of their communities as well as their commitment to community development and the lives and life chances of individuals. Each of their schools is at the heart of the community, and is a vital community resource even for those without children, and being at the centre of efforts to develop the community as a whole brought an added dimension to their work.

Gillian, Rosa, Tupa, Keita and John appear to have moved from being 'outsiders' to 'insiders' and had developed their awareness of their new setting and developed productive ways to interact in their new context. Although they did not have a deep understanding of the context and culture of their new schools prior to their appointment, they became aware of the significance of the school in their communities. Tupa, for example, had been able to gain some understanding of the context and the difficulties of the school in advance and talked about how he worked towards engaging and 'sensitizing' the community in his first year and making strenuous yet diplomatic efforts to reinvigorate the school and re-establish its place in the community. John's school was at the centre of an isolated and interdependent community, and he was careful to nurture and sustain the good relationships that existed before his appointment. Keita in New Zealand, following her experience in a single-teacher school, was careful to establish good communications and trust between the school, the school board and the wider community. Gillian in Scotland worked hard to engage with the community as soon as she was appointed and was careful to make the need to address the high expectations of parents a priority.

These differences did not necessarily follow country or language boundaries, and even a principal from the same country sometimes had difficulty adjusting to the expectations in a new area. Outsiders, such as Melody and Fan Huali, who were also coming to the community for the first time, spoke of their adjustment in more painful and dramatic terms. Like Tupa, they had also attempted to gain an understanding of the new school's culture and context before picking up the principal's responsibilities. But when Melody took measures to assess the school and its culture, she found the situation to be very different when she arrived. She used accountability measures, such as school inspection reports, to gauge the culture of the school, and found them wanting. Melody found that the management style of the previous head was very different from her own and the culture, but unlike the situation inherited by our other principals, Melody found that practice and policy in her new school conflicted with her personal and professional values to such an extent that prompt action was necessary. She faced considerable pressure but found that the wider community can be a source of support. In China, Fan Huali had little opportunity to understand the rural community that her school serves but she talked about how she realized her misconceptions when she worked to engage parents in supporting children's learning.

Dealing with place involves dealing with the particular and embedded expectations that others have of principals in the community. However, educational leadership involves working with school staff as well as people in the wider community, and most of the new principals found that leading and managing teachers was more problematic than working with people outside the school.

Dealing with people in the school

Recent conceptions of leadership propose that leadership should be distributed across the school. Distributed leadership theory derives mainly from cognitive and social psychology, both of which emphasize how social context influences human interaction and learning. From this perspective, leadership is a by-product of the interaction of people with their environment and the inter-relationships within social contexts are part of leadership activity (Spillane, Halverson and Diamond, 2004). In much of the contemporary literature, leadership is regarded as the product of the many and as an emergent property (Gronn, 2000; Woods et al., 2004; Woods, 2004) and distributed leadership is seen as a property of groups of people, not of an individual or individuals acting independently of each other. Somewhat paradoxically, this adds to the complexity of the principal's role and emphasizes its importance because it is principals who must develop the structures and culture that might encourage and sustain distributed leadership.

This challenges new and not-so-new school principals because schools are generally bureaucratic organizations with traditional hierarchies, role demarcation and status and power differentials. However, many of our new principals were attracted by concepts that overlapped with distributed leadership, such as collegiality, and several of our new principals variously described their leadership style as shared, collaborative or democratic.

One of the tasks of the principal is to create a climate in which people will want to work to the optimum levels of their energy, interest and commitment (Whitaker, 1997). Whitaker also argues that although these are not fully understood, the processes of school improvement reside in the everyday interpersonal transactions and that it is through these interactions that 'people's lives are changed' (p. 140). Our review of the narratives suggests that many of the situations that the new principals had to deal with involved complex interactions and some of these gave rise to kinds of dilemmas and tensions that have been reported elsewhere (Wildy and Louden, 2000; Day et al., 2001; Clarke, Wildy and Pepper, 2007; Cowie and Crawford, 2008).

For example, the tension that Wildy and Louden (2000) identified when new principals attempted to work collaboratively while attempting to establish themselves as strong and credible principals is also reflected in some of the narratives. Fan Huali, who described her approach as democratic, found the pace of change frustrating because her efforts were at first met with passive resistance. Rosa believes in shared decision-making, and collaboration is the 'cornerstone' of Xavier's approach, but the transition from peer to principal proved difficult for both them and for the teachers they worked with at first, and both had to take measures to establish their authority and ensure that their schools had a clear sense of direction.

The legacy of the previous principal was a problem for some, particularly where the embedded values and culture of the school conflicted with the new principal's personal and professional values. Ana Marie worked in a much more collegial way than the previous principal, but still made the major decisions. Keita noted that movement from a strict regime towards a more open culture was beginning to be appreciated, but cultural change also encouraged parents to complain more. Like Fan Huali, Gillian was at first frustrated at the slow pace of change. Her approach was less formal than that of the previous head, and her initial attempts to develop shared responsibility and initiate a system of collegial support made some teachers uncomfortable because they were accustomed to being told what to do and were used to working independently.

Improving the skills and performance of the teachers they worked with was a priority for many of our principals, but circumstances and the dynamics involved moderated the strategies they adopted. As an assistant principal

Xavier had worked with teachers to improve their teaching skill, but as principal he found that the nature of these conversations became more personal and made him feel uncomfortable. Fan Huali was aware of the sensitivities of the teachers in her school, who were older and more settled in their ways, when attempting to persuade them to adopt new methods and increase the pace of learning. She first had to win their trust and model the approaches she advocated. Paulino was also aware of the sensitivities involved in working with teachers in East Timor and monitored how his approach affected his colleagues. Ana Marie in Romania worked to change the attitudes, skills and knowledge of the teachers in her school, and Keita in New Zealand talked about ensuring that teachers were aware of her expectations with regard to teaching and learning. In Tanzania, Tupa had to deal with teachers who habitually took time off, while Gillian in Scotland struggled to persuade teachers to engage in self-reflection and focus on learning. Rosa talked about working with 'positive' and 'negative' teachers in Mexico, being discouraged when she ran out of support strategies and having to take action against teachers in the interests of children. John in Australia had to facilitate the departure of a disruptive teacher, and in England, much of Melody's first year in the post was clouded by having to take disciplinary action against teachers who were not performing, to the extent that she needed to purchase her own health support.

The tensions and dilemma reflected in dealing with people remind us that school principals necessarily work in an emotional context (Crawford, 2009). All organizations have their own well-defined roles and our principals have moved from one role to another, more accountable position. This new role requires a different skill set, but there is also the emotional aspect of the role to consider. In addition to the tensions and stress involved in making decisions that affect people's working lives, principals necessarily work in an emotional context and this can have an effect on their personal lives as well as their professional lives. For example, some of the principals talked about being tested by and learning from having to deal with the personal problems of staff, children and their families, and John had to deal with an intensely emotional event that had an effect on himself and every member of the school community.

Some individuals may find the emotional aspect easier to deal with than others. Next we discuss how the demands of the job and the emotional aspect affected our new principals' personal lives and their professional identities, as reflected in the narratives

Dealing with self

Most schools demand that principals not show their emotion outwardly, as it might be seen as unprofessional to do so. When leaders show emotions that are very different from what they feel inside, they subject themselves to emotional regulation. Hochschild (1983) conceptualized organizational emotional regulation as emotional labour, where power relations in a social system shape an individual's emotional state and require individuals, as part of their job role, to suppress their feelings and maintain a specific public appearance in order to produce the required emotional state in others. The culture of any organization is characterized and informed by emotion, but a more profound version of emotional labour may be peculiar to schools because of the variety of relationships involved and the intensity of day-to-day life (Gronn, 2003).

Research in this area now concentrates on anticipation – knowing when strong emotions might occur and being able to re-frame them in advance to be objective in a potentially difficult situation (Barsade and Gibson, 2007). The ability to anticipate such situations is likely to be particularly difficult for principals who have not yet reconfigured their professional identity.

The extent to which the expectations of the new principals were fulfilled in the early years of their appointment varied, but one commonality across the narratives is the connections between them in terms of developing an identity as a school principal. Identity seems very important to many of the principals, and difficulty in configuring their professional identities was a recurrent theme across cultural contexts.

Gronn suggests that new principals need a sense of self-belief and self-efficacy if they are to negotiate a successful transition to the role of principal (Gronn, 1999), and some found that development opportunities had broadened their outlook and helped develop confidence and self-belief. Secondment, promotion or being asked to take on a temporary acting promoted role was significant for some of the new principals, perhaps revealing a need to believe that they could become a principal and suggesting that the observation by Day et al. (2006), that self-belief influences personal efficacy in teaching, is also true of wanting to move on to headship.

However the narratives suggest that the new principals assumed new identities with different degrees of confidence in relation to key aspects of their role. Those who had always wanted to be principals appeared to assume their new identity with higher levels of confidence than others, but all were ill prepared for what the post involved, experienced considerable uncertainty, found it difficult at first to think of themselves as school principals and were surprised by the complexity of the job. Although the emotional labour required told at times, the commitment and passion of both 'insiders' and 'outsiders' is evident in the telling of the narratives, suggesting that their personal and professional lives had become inextricably interlinked. Ana Maria, Gillian, Tsutsweye and Tupu, for example, found it difficult to deal with the competing demands of home and school for their time and attention, and the extent to which their professional and personal lives were intertwined echoes Gunter's (1999) suggestion that the professional identity of school principals becomes an intrinsic part of their lives more generally.

Conclusion

There are a wide range of definitions and practices in relation to leadership development and preparation (Crow, Lumby and Pashardis, 2008) as well as different conceptions of educational purposes and how these relate to school leadership (Begley, 2008). We take the view that school principals need to be confident individuals, open to change and willing to exercise agency in dealing with the multiple accountabilities that are involved in leading and managing a school (Hage and Powers, 1992; Friedman, 2005).

Preparation for the role should therefore help aspiring principals to configure their professional identity in ways that will enable them to place themselves at the centre of any debate about the aims and purposes of schooling, equipped with the tools and ability that will allow them to resist or challenge current discourses and prevailing orthodoxies, and enable schools and communities to gain more control over practice. This raises issues having to do with cultural bias in relation to the theoretical underpinning of preparation programmes and about who is responsible for their design, development, delivery and accreditation and how they are delivered. While there may be consensus that preparation for the role of principal is important, there are considerable disagreements, often philosophical and political, about the kinds of principals that are needed, the skills and attributes they should possess and how they should be developed.

Although culture influences how the role of principal is conceptualized, the complexity of the role, the intensity of interpersonal interactions in a school and the need to mediate between multiple and often competing demands and interests are generic across different cultural settings, and school principals must therefore have appropriate educational values, be self-aware and have a 'clear sense of educational purposes' (Begley, 2008, p. 39). They must be able to lead as well as manage.

Stronach et al. (2002) discuss how professional identity is constructed in the working through of tensions at different levels of experience. The narratives suggest that the new principals were ill prepared and few had the opportunity to work through these tensions prior to being appointed. The tension for Gillian, for example, who had been a late entrant to teaching and been promoted relatively early in her teaching career, was that at first she did not feel like a principal and did not know what a principal was supposed to do. Keita thought at first that a principal had to know everything and that meant that she could never be a school principal. These tensions might have been mitigated if there had been opportunities at other levels of school leadership to test their developing skills, but, as Melody discovered, these skills do not transfer easily. Given the complexity of school leadership and the complex changes in role conceptualization and identity required in the transition to principalship (Rhodes, Brundrett and Neville, 2009) perhaps this not surprising and suggests that ongoing support and introduction into principalship could be as helpful as preparation programmes.

Our cases form a snapshot of the early experience of principals around the globe. Prior to their appointment, or even after, in most cases, the new principals had little opportunity to talk about issues that meant something to them. They lacked a reference frame to help guide their decision-making and wanted to reflect on purposes; discuss principles, values and learning needs and talk about overall approaches to leadership and management. They were also interested in how best to integrate theory and practice and how to go about developing the skills, abilities and confidence of their teachers. Most of the new principals lacked experience, had not been involved in a preparatory programme and had not had the opportunity to be involved in the kind of situated and social processes that might have helped them to construct their identities as school principals. Learning 'implies becoming a different person [which] involves the construction of identity' (Lave and Wenger, 1991, p. 53) and takes place where the social environment and the individual learner intersect. We hope that bringing together these narratives can provide a talking space for developing principals to reflect on the experiences of others and on how these accounts relate to their own personal, and unique, narrative of leadership.

Note

1 The Standard for Headship in Scotland, the National Professional Qualification for Headship in England and the Interstate School Leader Licensure Consortium standards (and resultant Educational Leadership Constituent Council standards) in the United States.

References

Aardrts, J., Jansen, P. and van der Velde, M. (2001), 'The breaking in of new employees: effectiveness of socialization tactics and personnel instruments', *The Journal of Management Development*, 20, (2), 159–67.

Barsade, S. G. and Gibson, D. E. (2007), 'Why does affect matter in organizations?' *Academy of Management Perspectives*, 59, (1), 36–59.

Begley, P. T. (2008), 'The nature and specialized purposes of educational leadership', in J. Lumby, G. Crow and P. Pashiardis (eds), *International Handbook on the Preparation and Development of School Leaders*. London: Routledge.

Bottery, M. (1999), 'Global forces, national mediations and the management of educational institutions', *Educational Management and Administration*, 27, (3), 299–312.

Clarke, J. and Newman, J. (1997), *The Managerial State*. London: Sage.

Clarke, S., Wildy, H. and Pepper, C. (2007), 'Connecting preparation with reality: primary principals' experiences of their first year out in Western Australia', *Leading and Managing*, 13, (1), 81–90.

Cowie, M. and Crawford, M. (2008), ' "Being" a new principal in Scotland', *Journal of Educational Administration*, 46, (6), 676–89.

Crawford, M. (2009), *Getting to the Heart of Leadership*. London: Sage.

Crow, G. (2007), 'The professional and organizational socialization of new English head teachers in school reform contexts', *Educational Management and Administration*, 35, (1), 51–71.

Cuban, L. (1988), 'A fundamental puzzle of school reform', *Phi Delta Kappan*, 70, (5), 341–44.

Daresh, J. and Male, T. (2000), 'Crossing the border into leadership: experiences of newly appointed British head teachers and American principals', *Educational Management and Administration*, 28, (1), 89–101.

Day, C. (2003), 'The changing learning needs of head teachers: building and sustaining effectiveness', in A. Harris, C. Day, D. Hopkins, M. Hadfield, A. Hargreaves and C. Chapman (eds), *Effective Leadership for School Improvement*. London: Routledge.

Day, C., Stobart, G., Sammons, P., Kington, A. and Gu. (2006), 'Variations in teachers' work, lives and effectiveness', *Research Report 743*. London: Department for Education and Skills.

Draper, J. and McMichael, P. (1998), 'Making sense of primary headship: the surprises awaiting new heads', *School Leadership and Management*, 18, (2), 197–211.

Earley, P. and Weindling, D. (2004), *Understanding School Leadership*. London: Paul Chapman.

Foskett, N. and Lumby, J. (2003), *Leading and Managing Education: International Dimensions*. London: Paul Chapman.

Friedman, T. (2005), *The World Is Flat: A Brief History of the Twenty-first Century*. New York: Farrar, Strauss and Giroux.

Gleeson, D. and Husbands, C. (2003), 'Modernizing schooling through performance management: a critical appraisal', *Journal of Education Policy*, 18, (5), 499–511.

Grint, K. (2005), *Leadership: Limits and Possibilities*. Basingstoke: Palgrave Macmillan.

Gronn, P. (1999), *The Making of Educational Leaders*. London: Cassell.

—(2000), 'Distributed properties: a new architecture for leadership', *Educational Management and Administration*, 28, (3), 371–38.

—(2003), *The New Work of Educational Leaders*. London: Sage.

Gunter, H. (1999), 'Researching and constructing histories of the field of education management', in T. Bush, L. Bell, R. Bolam, R. Glatter and P. Ribbins (eds), *Education Management, Redefining Theory, Policy and Practice*. London: Paul Chapman.

Hage, J. and Powers, C. (1992), *Post-industrial Lives: Roles and Relationships in the 21st Century*. Newbury Park, CA: Sage Publications.

Hallinger, P. (1995), 'Culture and leadership: developing an international perspective in educational demonstration', *UCEA Review*, Spring, 46, (2), 1–13.

Hargie, O. and Dickson, D. (2004), *Skilled Interpersonal Communication*. London, Routledge.

Hobson, A., Brown, E., Ashby, P., Keys, W., Sharp, C. and Benefield, P. (2002), *Issues for Early Headship — Problems and Support Strategies: A Review of the Literature*. London: NFER.

Hochschild, A. R. (1983), *The Managed Heart: Commercialization of Human Feeling*. Berkeley, CA: University of California Press.

Holligan, C., Menter, I., Hutchings, M. and Walker, M. (2006), 'Becoming a head teacher: the perspectives of new head teachers in 21st century England', *Journal of In-Service Education*, 32, (1), 103–22.

Kelchtermans, G. and Ballet, K. (2002), 'The micropolitics of teacher induction: a narrative-biographical study on teacher socialization', *Teaching and Teacher Education*, 19, (1), 105–20.

Lave, J. and Wenger, E. (1991), *Situated Learning: Legitimate Peripheral Participation*. Cambridge: Cambridge University Press.

Lumby, J. and Foskett, N. (2008), 'Leadership and culture', in J. Lumby, G. Crow and P. Pashiardis (eds), *International Handbook on the Preparation and Development of School Leaders*. London: Routledge.

Lumby, J., Crow, G. and Pashiardis, P. (eds) (2008), *International Handbook on the Preparation and Development of School Leaders*. London: Routledge.

Ozga, J. (2000), 'Leadership in education: the problem, not the solution?' review essay, *Discourse: Studies in the Cultural Politics of Education*, 21, (3), 355–361.

Quong, T. (2006), 'Asking the hard questions: being a beginning principal in Australia', *Journal of Educational Administration*, 44, (4), 376–88.

Rhodes, C., Brundrett, M. and Neville, A. (2009), 'Just the ticket? The National Professional Qualification and the transition to headship in the East Midlands of England', *Educational Review*, 61, (4), 449– 68.

Simkins, T., Close, P. and Smith, R. (2009), 'Work shadowing as a process for facilitating leadership succession in primary schools', *School Leadership and Management*, 29, (3), 239–52.

Spillane, J. P., Halverson, R. and Diamond, J. (2004), 'Towards a theory of leadership practice: a distributed perspective', *Journal of Curriculum Studies*, 36, (1), 3–34.

Stronach, I., Corbin, B., McNamara, O., Stark, S. and Warne, T. (2002), 'Towards an uncertain politics of professionalism: teacher and nurse identities in flux', *Journal of Education Policy*, 17, (1), 109–38.

Weindling, D. (1999), 'Stages of headship', in T. Bush, L. Bell, R. Bolam, R. Glatter and P. Ribbins (eds), *Educational Management: Redefining Theory, Policy and Practice*. London: Paul Chapman.

Whitaker, P. (1997), *Primary Schools and the Future*. Buckingham: Open University Press.

Wildy, H., and Clarke, S. (2008), 'Principals on L-plates: rear view mirror reflections', *Journal of Educational Administration*, 46, (6), 727–38.

Wildy, H. and Louden, W. (2000), 'School restructuring and the dilemmas of principals' work', *Educational Management and Administration*, 28, (3), 173–84.

Woods, P. A. (2004), 'Democratic leadership: drawing distinctions with distributed leadership', *International Journal of Leadership in Education: Theory and Practice*, 7, (1), 3–26.

Woods, P. A., Bennet, N., Wise, C. and Harvey, J. A. (2004), 'Variabilities and dualities in distributed leadership: findings from a systematic literature review', *Educational Management, Administration and Leadership*, 32, (4), 439–57.

Index